Economic and Financial Law & Policy – Shifting Insights & Values

Volume 5

This book series focuses on presenting critical legal and interdisciplinary research regarding the tools and instruments of free-market-driven societies and their economies.

For the last few decades, the world markets have been in turmoil, to a large extent is a result of value and policy choices which have been made since the late middle ages. As a result, on a global scale, economies and the legal systems giving form to them, have mainly if not exclusively become based on selfishness and greed, a reality which is moreover explicitly propagated by the theories of economic neo-liberalism.

It has nevertheless become clear in the recent past that said free market tools and mechanisms – such as private money creation by banks, next to the way huge corporations in general function and determine the outcome of economic processes – result in disastrous consequences, especially when remaining uncorrected by law and when not being submitted to clear public policy intervention measures.

Despite the evidence and growing understanding of the causes and consequences of neoliberal policy, few alternatives for the capitalist model as currently implemented, have so far been proposed.

In order to meet these concerns, this book series aims at offering an outlet for various forms of scientific research output, both monographs and edited collections.

The objective of every book of the series will hereby be to look critically at the legal methods and mechanisms shaping the free markets, and even to suggest alternatives for these.

Although the book series is initiated by legal scholars, it nevertheless aims to be truly multi- and interdisciplinary. The books series therefor welcomes and will incorporate all relevant disciplines, including law, economics, philosophy, ethics, religion, psychology, sociology, anthropology etc.

More information about this series at http://www.springer.com/series/15643

Saisai Wang

Market Access of Traditional Chinese Medicinal Product in the EU under WTO Legal Framework

Springer

Saisai Wang
Jinan, China

ISSN 2522-5243 ISSN 2522-5251 (electronic)
Economic and Financial Law & Policy – Shifting Insights & Values
ISBN 978-3-030-52847-8 ISBN 978-3-030-52848-5 (eBook)
https://doi.org/10.1007/978-3-030-52848-5

This Springer imprint is published by the registered company Springer Nature Switzerland AG.
The registered company address is: Gewerbestrasse 11, 6330 Cham, Switzerland

For my families, for their support,
understanding and love
For Peace of the world

Preface

This book is finished in a time that international laws are doubted and weak. The book is finished during a time of the global outbreak of pandemic—COVID-19. The author of this book wishes to inherit the rational principles of international law for better development of regional and domestic law. And she wishes to pursue advanced scientific knowledge for better development of medicine and medicinal product. The legal study in this book has been conducted deriving from combining these two thoughts.

Research and writing background: Traditional Chinese medicine (TCM) as a typical example of holistic and natural treatment is deemed to be one of the complementary and alternative medicines (CAM) in the European Union (EU). It has significant scientific research value based on a vast amount of references and empirical data. However, safety issues have been raised due to cases relating to the side effects of traditional Chinese medicinal products (TCMP) in the EU. The scientificity of TCMP is widely doubted based on the risk assessment system that the EU established. Directive 2004/24/EC strengthens the authorisation conditions on traditional use herbal medicinal products which seriously influences the export of TCMP. Since then, very rarely has TCMP been approved by EU competent authorities since the Directive went into effect. The study in this book discusses the hardship of market access of TCMP in EU practice, analyses the necessity to rethink of the rationality of EU pharmaceutical regulations as applied to CAM and seeks solutions for fostering traditional medicine (TM) to complement conventional medicine in the EU.

Market access of TCMP in the EU was a core issue discussed in the author's PhD research, and this book was written via collecting some essential parts of the author's PhD dissertation. The author expects to bridge a way for a common understanding of TCM between China and the West via acceptable legal languages of both sides. The book also describes a process of research logic and shows the link between law and science regarding TCM.

Practical problems, research question and the logic of study in the book: Very rare TCMPs have been authorised for market access of the EU. The situation reflects practical problems of TCMPs entering the EU market. The authorisation system that is designed for Western conventional medicine is rarely challenged within national or regional legal frameworks because of the preconceived opinion of medicine. Therefore, the practical problems are hardly ever carefully screened within the EU. By learning World Trade Organization (WTO) rules to seek solutions for domestic problem, the study of this book refines a core research question as whether EU pharmaceutical law applied to TCMP complies with WTO law on the issue of market access. In the course of answering this legal question, the legal issue of market access of TCMP in the EU is reviewed and the insufficiency of EU pharmaceutical law for the development of CAM, taking TCMP as a typical example, is tackled. The exploration of the main legal question aims at encouraging scientific research on TM in the EU and to subsequently better protect the public's health as well as facilitate the international trade of TCMP.

Structure of the book: Chapter 1 introduces the background, sense and novelty of the study in this book. It indicates the hypothesis that the technical standards and regulations in EU law have formed obstacles for TCMP to enter the EU market in practice. It introduces the main question relevant to market access of TCMP in the EU under the WTO legal framework for overcoming the practical problem. Chapter 2 states the theoretical framework of the study and explores relevant jurisprudential issues for establishing the logic of the study as a whole. Subsequently, Chap. 3 conceptualises TCMP in law. Chapter 4 assesses EU pharmaceutical law on the issue of market access of TCMP. Chapter 5 analyses Agreement on the Application of Sanitary and Phytosanitary Measures (SPS) and Agreement on Technical Barriers to Trade (TBT) for comparison between traditional Chinese herbal medicinal product and EU traditional herbal medicinal product (THMP). Chapter 6 reviews the risk assessment system of the EU and employs the tool of risk assessment as the basis of precautionary principle and seeks a way to control the safety, efficacy and quality of TCMP on a case-by-case basis authorisation. Based on the above analysis, Chap. 7 offers recommendations for the EU to address the practical problem.

Main findings in the study of this book: Practically, TCMP hardly meets the authorisation request of Western conventional medicinal product for market access. The study of this book notes that the traditional Chinese herbal medicinal product and EU THMP can be deemed similar products due to their chemical property and long-standing use records, but TCMP also have some unique characters, including consumers' bias to use TCMP and unique production process and methods. In addition, proper approaches are expected to be further developed for ascertaining active substances of herbal medicinal products, clarifying synergetic mechanism between different components in a herbal medicinal product and conducting toxicity experiment. Correspondently, it is hard to confirm the scientific certainty of TCMP without referencing to the holistic and systematic mechanism—TCM. Noticeably, scientific uncertainty also exists in EU THMP. Therefore, the EU has designed the simplified registration procedure to facilitate market access of THMP. However, the provision on 15 years use record within the EU as the prerequisite to apply to the simplified registration procedure provides less favourable treatment to market access of TCMP. The study in this book doubts the appropriateness of this provision. In practice, when considering market access of TCMP, the EU is generally concerned with the historical development of TCM in the EU and safety, efficacy and quality control. Thus, it is reasonable for the competent authority to conduct the evaluation for authorisation on a case-by-case basis. In this situation, applicants for authorisation bear the responsibility to provide sufficient evidence as required by the risk assessment system. As a consequence of this process, the development of TCM in the EU relies ultimately on the open-mindedness of policymakers who decide whether and how to develop TCM or any CAM at all.

Accessibility of the book: This book is readable for non-expert audiences. On the one hand, the study in the book aims at making the legislative status understandable by medical scientists and raising their attention to the current pharmaceutical legislation relevant to TM. On the other hand, it takes care to use explicit words to explain the scientific development and knowledge of TCMP to give policymakers and lawmakers a better understanding of the regulatory status of CAM in the EU. The book also aims at providing researchers a methodology for conducting the legal study relevant to science and technology.

Data is current through March 2020.

Jinan, China Saisai Wang
31 March 2020

Acknowledgements

I would like to give special appreciation to Professor Dr. Kim Van der Borght, for providing me this great opportunity to do my PhD research in Vrije Universities Brussel. Prof. Van der Borght encouraged my initial intention of researching this topic when I was doing my Master degree in Hull University, UK in 2005. And now, the book is finished, based on the essential parts of my dissertation which lead to a degree of Doctor in Law.

Many thanks to Prof. Dr. Jiaxiang Hu (Shanghai Jiao Tong University, China) and Prof. Dr. Xiaoting Song (Tong Ji University, China), for their support in conducting the research. Many thanks to Prof. Dr. Koen Byttebier (Vrije Universiteit Brussel, Belgium), Dr. Duncan Freeman (Research Fellow, EU-China Research Centre, EU International Relations and Diplomacy Studies Department, College of Europe, Belgium), Dr. Martin Mervyn (Teesside University, UK) and Prof. Dr. Katazyna Gromek-Broc (University of Pavia, UK) for their comments and advices on improving the author's PhD draft. Many thanks to Leigh Haynes, for proofreading and providing opinions as the first reader of the manuscript.

There are also many other professors, staff and friends who have supported this research both in China and in the EU. And in return for such substantial contributions to my research, I wish to share my opinions with the world. I welcome any amicable criticisms and discussion on relevant issues in the future.

The PhD study had been supported by the project—China and Europe Taking Care of Healthcare Solutions (Jan 2014–Dec 2017) funded by the European Union under the Marie Curie Actions—IRSES (GA no. 612589).

Contents

About the Author

Saisai Wang is a lecturer in the Law School of Shandong University of Finance and Economics, research fellow of Rural Development Research Institute of Shandong University of Finance and Economics and a lawyer of Jointide Law Firm, Jinan Office, China. She holds a PhD in Law from Vrije Universiteit Brussel (Belgium), an LLM from Hull University (England), a postgraduate diploma of management from Greenwich School of Management (England) and an LLB in international economic law and a dual degree of trade and economics from Zhongnan University of Economics and Law (China).

Abbreviations

AA	aristolochic acid
AB	Appellate Body
ARWG	Acupuncture Regulatory Working Group
ATCM	Association of Traditional Chinese Medicine
BAcC	British Acupuncture Council
BSCM	British Society of Chinese Medicine
CAM	complementary and alternative medicine(s)
CAMP	complementary and alternative medicinal product
CBD	Convention on Biological Diversity
CDE	Center for Drug Evaluation
CFDA	China Food and Drug Administration
CHMP	Committee for Medicinal Products for Human Use
CPC	Central Product Classification
CSM	Committee on Safety of Medicines
DG	Directorates-General
DH	Department of Health
DSB	Dispute Settlement Body
EBM	evidence-based medicine
EC	European Community
ECJ	European Court of Justice
EFSA	European Food Standards Agency
EHPA	European Herbal Medicine Practitioners Association
EHTPA	European Herbal and Traditional Medicine Practitioners Association
EMA	European Medicines Agency
ENCePP	European Network of Centres for Pharmacoepidemiology and Pharmacovigilance
EP	European Parliament
EU	European Union
FDA	Food and Drug Administration
GAP	Good Agricultural Practice

GATS	General Agreement on Trade in Services
GCP	Good Clinical Practice
GLP	Good Laboratory Practice
GMP	Good Manufacturing Practice
GP	general practitioners
GVP	Good Pharmacovigilance Practices
HKCMO	Hong Kong Chinese Medicine Ordinance
HMPC	Committee on Herbal Medicinal Products
HMRWG	Herbal Medicine Regulatory Working Group
HPC	Health Professions Council
HS	Harmonised Commodity Description and Coding System
IMF	International Monetary Fund
IPR	intellectual property rights
MCA	Medicines Control Agency
MEB	Medicines Evaluation Board
MFN	most favoured nation treatment
MHRA	Medicines and Healthcare products Regulatory Agency
NATCM	National Administration of Traditional Chinese Medicine
NCCIH	National Center for Complementary and Integrative Health
NDRC	National Development and Reform Commission
NHP	Natural Health Product
NHS	National Health Service
NHSA	National Healthcare Security Administration
NIH	National Institutes of Health
NMPA	National Medical Products Administration
NPC	National People's Congress
NT	national treatment principle
OTC	over the counter
Ph. Eur.	European Pharmacopoeia
PRC	People's Republic of China
RCHM	register of Chinese herbal medicine
RCTs	randomised clinical trials
REMS	risk evaluation and mitigation strategies
RMP	risk management plan
SAIC	State Administration for Industry and Commerce
SAMR	State Administration for Market Regulation
SDA	State Drug Administration
SFDA	State Food and Drug Administration
SmPC	summary of product characteristics
SPS	Agreement on the Application of Sanitary and Phytosanitary Measures
SR	statutory regulation
ST	science & technology
TBT	Agreement on Technical Barriers to Trade

TCM	traditional Chinese medicine
TEC	Treaty Establishing the European Community (Nice consolidated version)
TFEU	Treaty on European Union and the Treaty on the Functioning of the European Union (Lisbon consolidated version)
THMP	traditional herbal medicinal product
TM	traditional medicine
TUR	traditional use registration
U.S./US	United States of America
UK	United Kingdom
UN	United Nations
UNESCO	United Nations Educational, Scientific and Cultural Organisation
WB	World Bank
WCO	World Customs Organisation
WEU MA	well-established use marketing authorisation
WHO GPCL	WHO Good Practices for Pharmaceutical Quality Control Laboratories
WHO	World Health Organisation
WIPO	World Intellectual Property Organisation
WTO	World Trade Organisation

List of Figures

List of Tables

Chapter 1
Introduction

In Chinese, *Zhong Cheng Yao* refers to ready-to-use traditional Chinese medicinal product (TCMP) composed of one or more active ingredient(s), derived from herbal products, animal products or mineral substances, in their formulas. To further define the term, in the Hanyu Pinyin system Chinese *Zhong Cheng Yao* is written 中成药, 中 (*Zhong*) means Chinese; 成 (*Cheng*) means completed formula; 药 (*Yao*) means medicinal product. The term Zhong Cheng Yao is used by Chinese doctors and in Chinese law. However, it is rarely used in Europe.

Zhong Cheng Yao is one type of TCMP regulated under current EU pharmaceutical law and is the key object observed in the study of this book. With the approval of the competent EU authority, a *Zhong Cheng Yao* may become a medicinal product regulated for legal use under EU pharmaceutical law. However, in practice, TCMP may be in the form of either medicinal products or food products. As a medicinal product, it may be made of herbs, animal products, mineral substances or a combination of any of these. As a food product, it may be agriculture product, supplementary food or other type of processed food product. This book will focus particularly on *Zhong Cheng Yao* made of herbs compared to EU traditional herbal medicinal product (THMP), nevertheless other types are also discussed when necessary.

1.1 The Status of TCMP in the West

Traditional Chinese medicine (TCM) is treated as a complementary and alternative (CAM) medicine in the EU. It has unique theoretical system for curing disease, which differentiate it from other medicines. It includes diagnosis and therapy, where TCMP belongs to the later. Therefore, TCMP is often discussed in CAM, traditional medicine (TM) or herbal medicine in the West.

S. Wang, *Market Access of Traditional Chinese Medicinal Product in the EU under WTO Legal Framework*, Economic and Financial Law & Policy – Shifting Insights & Values 5, https://doi.org/10.1007/978-3-030-52848-5_1

1.1.1 Traditional Medicine in Western Thought

Many authors and scholars have compared TM and Western conventional medicine, where TCM is often taken as a particular example. Analysis on TM has been conducted from philosophy, medical ethics, historical development to scientific aspects and so on (Unschuld 1975, 2001; Kleinman 1978; Kunstadter 1980; Leslie 1980; Elling 1981; Teahan 1981; Zhou et al. 2013; Wu et al. 2013). An edited eBook—*Herbal Medicine: Biomolecular and Clinical Aspects*—summarises some important issues relevant to this book's subject matter (Iris and Sissi 2011). As a whole, it has taken a view of the West. It discusses many aspects of herbal medicine, for instance education, disease analyses and regulations relating to herbal medicines. A review on three chapters that closely relate to this book follows.

The book begins, in Part 1, by providing the legislative status of TM, globally, through 2010. It identifies TCM as a typical example of TM with a history of more than 3000 years. Indeed, the book *The Devine Farmer's Classic of Herbalism* was compiled about 2000 years ago in China and is treated as the oldest known herbal text in the world (Zhang et al. 2011). World Health Organisation (WHO) has recognised the important contribution of TM, including TCM to provide essential care, and many high-income countries began to set up a regulatory system for these products in the 1990s. For instance, the United States (U.S.) Congress established the Office of Alternative Medicine within the National Institutes of Health at the beginning of 1990s (see NCCIH n.d.), while the EU found the European Scientific Cooperative on Phytotherapy in 1989 (see ESCOP n.d.). Both of these entities aim at encouraging scientific research and harmonising phytomedicines. In the U.S., herbal medicinal products in the form of botanical and natural concentrate/metabolite are classified as a dietary supplement under the Dietary Supplement Health and Education Act (DSHEA) of 1994. Per the DSHEA, for products entering the market after October 1994, a dietary supplement manufacturer or distributor of a supplement with a 'new dietary ingredient' may be required to provide safety data and go through premarket review. In addition, the manufacture must follow the Good Manufacture Practice (GMP) regulations and cannot suggest on the label or any of the packaging that the product can diagnose, treat, prevent, or cure a specific disease or condition without specific approval of the FDA (U.S. FDA, Dietary Supplements n.d.). In Canada, herbal remedies must comply with the Natural Health Products Regulations 2003 legislation for achieving a license before they can be sold on the market (Canada Natural Health Products Regulations 2004). In the EU, Directive 2004/24/EC requires at least 30 years of in-use evidence and at least 15 years in the EU to register a product as a traditional use medicinal product.

The book also discusses, in Part 21, the ethics applying to the use of natural health products (NHP), and herbal medicine is included here. Beneficence, non-malfeasance, and patient autonomy are essential in the use of herbal medicine. Beneficence is a bioethical principle that requires the clinician to promote the well-being of patients. Evidence-based information is the prerequisite for physician and NHP practitioners alike to advise a patient on the safety and efficacy of a product. Nonmalfeasance emphasises the responsibility to do no harm. 'Natural' does not necessarily mean safe, so practitioners should be cognisant of the potential risks as well as the potential benefits before recommending the herbal medicines. Patient autonomy is a significant ethical principle for the use of NHPs. Medical law should provide reputable sources for patients to realise their right to autonomy, and not be left to less reputable sources, such as relatives, friends, magazines or the internet (Girard and Vohra 2011).

Concentration on the integration of herbal medicine into evidence-based clinical practice, the book goes on to suggest three ways to integrate TM and Western conventional medicine in Part 22. The first requires recognition of both as legitimate forms of medicine and integral parts of a country's formal healthcare system. Second suggests that individual health care practitioners integrate TM into their modern medicine practices. And, finally, the third modality is to recognise traditional and modern practices as two branches of medical science (WHO 1999). The Chapter explains that the first way of integrating TM and Western conventional medicine has been demonstrated to be practicable in many countries, particularly in Asian countries such as China, Japan, Korea, and India (WHO 1998), however it is more difficult to apply the other two suggested methods of healthcare integration for reasons such as scientific, cultural, educational, and legal concerns. The Chapter notes that even in clinical practice in China there is lack of integration of TCM and evidence-based medicine (EBM). Nevertheless, for many decades, the People's Republic of China (PRC) has set up a system of medical education 'in which its modern medicine practitioners have been required to receive some formal training' in TCM 'so that they are aware of suitable approaches in TCM during their practice of Western medicines' (Zhang et al. 2011). The Chapter stresses that proof of efficacy or safety has not been established through an evidence-based approach on TM. Only a few thousand TCMPs have been subjected to randomised clinical trials (RCTs) under the International Conference on Harmonisation (ICH) Good Clinical Practice Guidelines to determine their efficacy and/or safety. As of June 2009, most studies on the Cochrane Controlled Trials Registers concern single-plant herbs or phytomedicine as of June 2009. Even though the number of cases of multicomponent herbal medicines in RCTs is increasing, the quality of the majority of the clinical studies of herbal medicines was thought to have rendered the data of dubious value in the Chapter. The Chapter highlights that '[i]n a review of 206 RCTs, which was published in Medline from 1966 to 2003, important methodological components of RCTs, particularly allocation concealment, generation of the allocation sequences, and intention-to-treat analyses were incompletely reported'.

1.1.2 Cases Raising Concern for Legislation

There have been positive and negative cases related to use of TCMP in practice. Negative cases include those in which complaints regarding the safety TCMP have been brought by victims, and positive cases include those in which TCMP have been approved by the competent authorities in the EU or where diseases have been successfully cured by TCMP. Such cases raised awareness around the issue of market access of TCMP in the EU and impacted the legislative attitude towards TCMP. Herein, negative cases that have drawn broad public attention to TCMP in the EU is reviewed for initiating following discussions on legislation.

Two similar cases of rapidly progressive fibrosing interstitial nephritis in young women who followed the same weight-loss regimen led to an epidemiological survey of nephrology centres of Brussels in 1992–1993. Seven other women under the age of 50 in terminal or preterminal renal failure were admitted for dialysis in 1991 and 1992 who had all followed a weight-loss regimen in the same medical clinic. Renal biopsy samples in eight of the nine cases showed extensive interstitial fibrosis without glomerular lesions. Two of the patients were seen for the first time in terminal renal failure and were started immediately on dialysis. For the seven other women, the nephropathy was characterised by a rapid deterioration in renal function, with initial serum creatinine doubling within about 3 months. The clinic in question had specialised in weight-loss treatments for the previous 15 years without any problems. However, in May 1990 the clinic added two Chinese herbs to its weight-loss treatments. In June 1992, testing of twenty-five randomly selected women who had followed the same weight-loss regimen for at least 3 months in 1990 resulted in three having impaired renal function. Chemical analysis of some brands of the Chinese herbs the clinic used did not show nephrotoxic contaminants of fungal or plant origin (ochratoxin or aristolochic acid) or adulteration by diuretics or antiinflammatory drugs. However, the medicinal preparation of the capsules patients took had different alkaloid profiles from those expected Chinese plants. The striking relationship between a specific type of fibrosing interstitial nephritis in young women and a weight-loss treatment involving Chinese herbs led to more arguments against uncontrolled therapy with herbal preparations (Vanherweghem et al. 1993).

Herb Nephropathy, specifically caused by aristolochic acid (AA), garnered wide attention from then on. The above cases highlighted the problem of oversight of herbal medicinal product, undermining the longstanding impression that TCM is pure, natural and has no side effects. Emergency measures were taken by different countries to counter any side effects of herbal medicinal product (WHO 2003). Australia, Canada, France, Oman, and the U.S. all took actions in 2001 against AA. For instance, the Food and Drug Administration (FDA) of the U.S. issued clear warnings and an alert that herbal products were unsafe if they contained or were suspected to contain AA (U.S. FDA 2001). In the UK, Aristolochia was banned even earlier in 1999 (Inpharma Weekly 1999).

An article published by WHO pointedly stated that 'Herbal medicines, however natural, can cause serious illnesses, from allergy to liver or kidney malfunction, to cancer, and even death' (Aschwanden 2001). Taken together, these negative cases, as well as articles and reports criticising the safety of TM, made people in the West feel frustrated with the use of TM.

1.1.3 The EU Regulation for an Intention to Regulate and Develop CAM in the EU

While TCM raises certain concerns, Western conventional medicine has its own drawbacks, such as serious side effects (Xiong et al. 2011), high cost and inefficacy for some diseases. Especially with regard to chronic diseases, serious side effects may easily damage organ functioning through drug metabolism and excretion (Universite de Lausanne n.d.). For instance, to treat high blood pressure, a patient might use a hypotensor every day, and in the course of drug metabolism the liver is often affected, while in the course of excretion the kidneys are often affected. In addition to this, pharmaceutical dependence often occurs when treating chronic diseases. For instance, in cases of patients with hyperglycemia, symptoms quickly become worse once the patient stops injecting insulin if the patient does not pay attention to their daily diet; this is especially the case when the injection dose is not properly controlled.

By recognising the insufficiency of Western conventional medicine, the EU perceives the sense of developing CAMs. TCM as a type of CAM in Europe is generally discussed in terms of its natural and holistic nature stemming from its diagnostic and therapeutic philosophy. Its diagnostic theories and therapeutic formulas are based on addressing an entire syndrome instead of eliminating a single symptom, while also making an effort to decreasing the side effect of the medicinal product and predicting the disease complication. However, the clinical side effect reports raised much anxiety on the safety and efficacy of TCMP.

The EU enacted Directive 2004/24/EC (2004), to regulate the authorisation process of THMP as an amendment of Directive 2001/83/EC. Directive 2001/83/EC provides three registration pathways for a new herbal medicinal product to access the market. The three pathways are traditional use registration (TUR), well-established use marketing authorisation (WEU MA) and full application (Directive 2001/83/EC 2001, art 16(1), 10a, 8(3)). Theoretically, herbal medicinal products can go through any of them. However, currently it is not easy for herbal medicinal products—especially, compound product—to meet the requirements of the full application, which is usually applied to Western conventional medicinal products, or be included in the scope of products that can apply to WEU MA. EU pharmaceutical law provides TUR that is a simplified registration procedure for THMP in Directive 2004/24/EC. As of 31 December 2012, 1017 EU THMP have been successfully registered in the EU (EMA/322570/2011 2017, p. 4). However, TUR does not favour of TCMP. By the end of 2012, only one TCMP, Diao Xin Xue Kang, had been successfully approved. A little movement was seen on 18 February 2015 in Europe. The Medicines and Healthcare Products Regulatory Agency (MHRA) of the UK granted Phynova Group Ltd. a Traditional Herbal Registration Certificate for Phynova Joint and Muscle Relief Tablets (UK MHRA 2015).

1.2 State of Art of the Scientific Development of Traditional Medicine

Almost every culture has its distinct herbal traditions. Some have tried to find one premise to unite all of these traditions (Fan et al. 2014b, p. S4), which is a challenging task as well as a hypothesis still needing for scientific evidence. The effort of finding one premise for all herbs brings chaos to the academic research and regulation on TM. Understanding the chaos is the pre-requisite of dispelling chaos, and knowing each distinct herbal tradition well is key to understanding the chaos.

The Art and Science of Traditional Medicine is a publication with a series of articles discussing how to integrate TM into modern medical practice (Fan et al. 2014a), in which TCM has been taken as a typical example of TM and discussed in may articles. These articles represent the current medical scientific development status of TCMP. Some sections relevant to the study of this book are reviewed as below.

1.2.1 Chances and Difficulties for Integration

The editorial team write a summary part for reviewing issues of integrating TM into modern health care (Fan et al. 2014b, p. S4). First, the team reviews some historical traces of TM as well as TCM in Europe. In Britain, the rich history of the use of TM was given credence in the early 1500s by the Herbalists Charter of Henry the VIII (1491–1547). Contemporarily in China, Li Shizhen (1518–1593) was spearheading a 40-year research project that led to the publication of *Ben Cao Gan Mu*, a Pharmacopoeia and treatise on botany, Zoology, mineralogy, and metallurgy. The editorial team then explains that it has chosen TCM to describe the art and science of ancient practice of holistic healing in their work. While it is usually not proper to use TCM to represent all TMs because of the concern that '[a]lmost every culture has its distinct herbal traditions, each with its indigenous plants and unique practice', these authors represent the art and science in a way that makes sense for understanding TCM and TCMP. The summary also explains the importance of developing biological techniques from plants. For instance, the therapeutic potential of herbal remedies has been found for influenza, cancer, diabetes, and cardiovascular diseases; the gut microbiota targeted dietarily has been explored for intervening against chronic inflammation; and the biological activities of complex polysaccharides presented in medicinal plants has been studied.

Ms Margaret Chan M.D. notices that TM 'needs rigorous, scientific data to demonstrate its efficacy' in the foreword written for *The Art and Science of Traditional Medicine* (Chan 2014). She notes that TM also needs 'evidence-based standards for quality and safety evaluation to support its appropriate regulations' in order 'to move into mainstream medicine on an equally trusted footing'. Chan believes that '[w]ithin the context of primary health care', traditional and Western medicine 'can blend together in beneficial harmony, taking advantage of the best feature of each system and compensating for certain weaknesses in each'. She points out merit of TM in the West as 'TM can contribute to addressing a number of global health challenges of the 21st Century, in particular in the area of chronic, noncommunicable diseases and population aging'. She also points out the demand for TM in the West as people in wealthy countries 'increasingly seek natural products' to 'protect against illness and diseases in a holistic, nonspecialised way'. She highlights that 'TM is thus a resource for primary health care, but also for innovation and discovery'.

Dr. Alan Leshner uses very simplified language to express the different philosophies of TM and Western conventional medicine in *A Middle Way for Traditional Medicine* (Leshner 2014). At the same time, he compares the emergence of biology in the West. Leshner explains that conventional medicine in the West 'often [takes] a reductionist approach to medicine, breaking down the body into ever-smaller parts in order to understand its inner workings' whereas, in TCM 'medical practitioners are seen to take a more holistic view, regarding the body as a complex, integrated system and treating it as such'. Thus, researchers of biology are noticing that they can 'learn much from understanding the finest detail at a molecular level, particularly when it comes to treating disease', and they are noticing that it is essential to have a deeper knowledge of the interactions between systems and network. Leshner also assumed that philosophy in TM might have been affected by the religious thinking of Buddhism. He explains that in Buddhism, the Middle Way is illustrated as 'the route to enlightenment—a path found by balancing opposing views, accepting neither extreme, but rather investigating both sides and finding a middle ground' (Leshner 2014). This explanation is a highly refined depiction of the philosophy of TCM.

Josephine P. Briggs (2014) delivers a view of herbal medicinal product from a global scientific challenge perspective. She calls for learning lessons from ancient healing practices. She mentions that 'many modern therapeutics exploit the ability of plants to synthesise a wide range of small molecules of great variety and complexity' (Briggs 2014, p. S7). To demonstrate this, Briggs uses the work of Project 523, which was funded by the Chinese government. Project 523, tested thousands of herbs and hundreds of extractions 'recipes' on a mouse model of malaria using a labor-intensive methodology. Finally, a gentle extraction method that maintained activity of the active principle was developed by a Chinese scientist, Tu Youyou (Tu 2011) and her research team to conquer the difficulties of persistence of the isolated bioactive compound.

Six coauthors worked together on an article to discuss the possibility of merger between Western medicine and the Eastern medicine (Schroen et al. 2014). They point out that Western biomedical sciences rely more on the 'reductionistic approach' of Western biomedical sciences and generate knowledge of anatomy, physiology, histology, genetics and biochemistry. On the other hand, TCM is based on a phenomenological, descriptive and systems-based approach and has produced a more holistic understanding of biology. Nevertheless, TCM and Western medicine are perceived as wholly distinct paradigms in the rheumatoid arthritis case study as the article explains. The article concluded that the merger between Chinese and Western medicine fit the personalised systems medicine, wherein patients can take a greater role in managing their own health and wellness.

Another impressive article in this issue is about Zheng which is translated as syndrome in English. However, the English translation is not exact. Zheng is a very important concept in TCM and discloses the essential difficulty researching TCM using molecular theory. The article reads that:

> Zheng (meaning syndrome or pattern) is the overall physiological and/or pathological pattern of the human body in response to a given internal and external condition, which usually is an abstraction of internal disharmony defined by a comprehensive analysis of clinical symptoms and signs gathered by a practitioner using inspection, auscultation, olfaction, interrogation, and palpation of pulses (Wang and Xu 2014).

The article notes the lack of research on Zheng, which suggests that Zheng-guided treatments are still scarce people due to the lack of evidence-based interpretations of syndromes and treatment efficacies. Because of the highly interconnected nature of the human interactome, it is difficult to study different diseases at the molecular level completely independent of one another. A description of a group of Zhengs may reflect the appearance of different diseases on one body but does not explain the problems at the molecular level. Western medicine construes medical conditions as associated with specific symptoms, while Zheng gives a very different definition of a disease and encompasses all of the symptoms a patient presents. A group of Zhengs are dynamic with changing boundaries, overlapping symptoms and a multiscale nature. Moreover, to provide treatment based on the clarification of Zhengs has been historically applied as the key pathological principle guiding the prescription of herbal formulas. The article suggests creating the 'Zhengome' as a new 'omics field in which a network is the basic research unit for investigating the hierarchy in the human body, from the molecular to the systems level.

To a certain extent, the difficulty in understanding Zheng lies in the expression of Chinese. In China, people use concepts such as *Yin-Yang*, exterior-interior, cold-heat, and deficiency-excess to describe patients' conditions. These concepts are highly generalised and mainly based on empirical study and written records of practitioners. Modern 'omics techniques combine bioinformatics and bionetwork models by using a systems biology approach and can help with understanding Zhengs. They have been applied to investigate the differences between Zhengs and to identify novel biomarkers. Rheumatoid arthritis patients have been given as an example to illustrate the 'hot' and 'cold' Zhengs with different underlying genomic and metabolomic profiles. However, Wang and Xu (2014) observe that 'most of the current studies have relied on only one or two approaches for molecular profiling', and they lack an efficient method to integrate data obtained at different 'omic levels. Therefore, the empirical study of Zhengs in China has gathered much more data than is currently possible from laboratory results using a modern scientific approach.

In another article of this publication, Leung et al. (2014, p. S16) deliver the same message on the significance of studying TCM by using networks. They aim to find the relationships between internal physiological networks and external environmental networks, pointing out that '[r]eductionist approaches to medicine, such as phenotype-based and target-based biomedicine (TBBM), are limited by their failure to consider the interactive nature of the human body and its environment'. It also points to the deleterious effects on the body's overall system because of focusing on a single target. A Western conventional medicinal product, Indomethacin, is used as an example since 'it exerts an anti-inflammatory effect by inhibiting prostaglandin E2 (PGE2) synthesis, but this suppression of PGE2 also affects a receptor for mucus secretion, leading to gastric mucosa damage'. A holistic view of the body's network is expected to balance such positive and negative impacts of medical treatments. Ultimatey the authors call for integrated network-based medicine (INBM) which takes a systems approach.

TCM has many principles and resources to help achieve INBM, including 'pattern differentiation in diagnosis and treatment of diseases'. (Leung et al. 2014, p. 16) The authors recognize 'multi-chemical components', 'multi-pharmacological effects', and 'multi-action targets and pathways', called the 'three m's', as the key characteristics of complex herbal formulas of TCMP.[1] The 'three m's' have been seen to be useful to 'holistically modulate a person's physiological/pathological networks' and 'in developing new drug combinations'. The article estimates that one major step to move from TBBM to INBM 'would be the systematic quantitative and qualitative analysis of individual CHM (Chinese herbal medicine) components' combining with "'digitalised medicine advances such as systems biology techniques, computational technologies and translational research to provide the foundation for a 'personalised' INBM strategy'. While the authors again mention 'omics technologies as an approach to optimise the synergistic effect of the herbal remedies, they treat INBM as a tool for enhancing the medical and health care system. Nevertheless, there are still obstacles in the route from TBBM to INBM, from illustrating the 'crosstalk' of multiple molecular pathways to understanding the

[1]TCMPs have unique formulating methods and principles called '*Jun, Chen, Zuo* and *Shi*' for formulating the medicinal products, which is quite close to the 'three m's'. One single herb may not cure the patient efficiently, for instance, it has toxicity which may raise serious side effects. Therefore, TCM uses '*Jun, Chen, Zuo* and *Shi*' to harmonise the different herbs in one formula. *Jun, Chen, Zuo* and *Shi* can be explained in four ingredients. *Jun* as the main ingredient is 'a substance that provides the main therapeutic thrust'; the Chen ingredient 'enhances or assists the therapeutic actions of *Jun*; the *Zuo* ingredient may work on some reactions accompanying symptoms; while the Shi ingredient 'enhances or assists the therapeutic actions of the *Jun*'. However, in one formula, two biologically active substances may have the effect of 'mutual accentuation, mutual enhancement, mutual counteraction, mutual suppression, mutual antagonism and mutual incompatibility' (Yuan and Lin 2000). In addition, ideally, different ingredients in a TCMP formula are selected as for better functioning together. However, the chemical changes between any two ingredients or more are difficult to be measured by using current scientific techniques. Any change of a small amount of each ingredient also may bring different effects to the body. What is even worse is that the way of extracting the effective part of the herbs is rough in TCM, and the effective part may contain many other substances besides the active ingredient. Therefore, the use of '*Jun, Chen, Zuo* and *Shi*' brings difficulties for evaluating the safety of compound herbal medicinal products. Currently, developing scientific tools for capturing and accurately recording the

network effects of TCM, to digitalising the large amounts of data. The authors conclude that 'TCM offers a blueprint for establishing and implementing an INBM system for the betterment of humankind'.

1.2.2 Interdisciplinary Approaches to Study Traditional Medicine

Two tasks must be undertaken in the scientific research of TCMP. One is to keep searching the scientific evidence for safety, efficacy and consistent quality control of the product; the other is to research and develop new products via inheriting the traditional way of producing TCMP. As required by law, the ingredients must be clarified in the specifications of medicinal products. In addition, any side effects need to be clearly stated when labelling. These requirements can only be fulfilled when there are sufficient scientific data collection and evidence. Records on TCM and TCMP are abundant. For example, *Ben Cao Gang Mu* is a collection of empirical achievements and summary of the long historical development and can serve as a resource in working on the two tasks mentioned above. TCM has accumulated unique diagnostics and therapies on curing diseases, and in particular, the compound TCMP, formulas and processing procedures distinguishes TCMP from Western conventional medicine. The first task must be completed before the second task may be fully achieved. Otherwise, TCMP may become exactly the same as Western conventional medicine and lose its unique identification. The difficulties in proving the safety and efficacy of TCMP lie in the complexity of its constituents and the chemical changes between these constituents under certain conditions.

Scientists have developed some approaches to identify the crude drug materials in TCMP, assess their toxicity, and test their efficacy. Hereinafter, three references are reviewed for stating the art of the science of identifying ingredients as well as assessing the safety and efficacy of TCMP. The development of the interdisciplinary technologies including medical science, biological science, computer science, chemical and physical science, pushed the innovation of these approaches. Herbal genomics and pharmacokinetics made a substantial contribution to the research of TCMP.

The first reference hereinto reviewed is an online book—*Systems Biology for Traditional Chinese Medicine* (Luo et al. 2012). The book begins by identifying methods on crude drug materials, including sources, characteristics, microscopic and physiochemical techniques. These methods are usually conducted according to the morphological classification and anatomic characteristics. The benefits to use these methods are comprehensive, clear, simple and easy to use. However, they are not suitable for identifying some ingredients in formulas, such as the 'multichannel-processed herb' or animal medicines, because they lack morphological structures,

---

interactions between ingredients or/and developing other valid tools for illustrating the risks is essential for proving the safety of TCMP.

making it is difficult to identify them with traditional techniques. To overcome these obstacles, a convenient and accurate molecular identification methodology has been developed by using genetic engineering analysis in order to obtain the DNA characteristic spectrums of herbal medicines. A research group at Tsinghua University of China explained:

> The principle of this method is that NDA of each individual organism is separated by electrophoresis after restriction enzyme cutting. The distribution of electrophoretic bands formed after hybridized with labeled DNA probes and authoradiograph should be different, that is, individual-specific, population-specific, and species-specific (Luo et al. 2012, p. 44).

When it is possible to identify the genes of compound TCMP by using 'omics, herbal genomics can be further used on the research of TCMP for capturing the active compound substances.

The article, *Herbal Genomics: Examining the Biology of Traditional Medicines*, summarises well the recent development on herbal genomics based on the multidisciplinary techniques (Chen et al. 2014). Herbal genomics is used to examine the biology of TM, and it provides a platform to support the chemical and biological analyses of the materials in compound herbal products. It can be used to explain the Chinese concept of geoherbalism which encompasses the use of 'authentic' or 'superior' herbs that are produced in a specific region or environment. Along with the application of the 'omics technologies to geoherbalism, the optimal growth conditions of the raw materials and specific herb genotypes can be explored in order to target the reproducing of raw materials. Currently, herbal genomics is being applied to many areas of herbal-related biological research to help understand the quality of TM as well as to help molecular herb identification through establishment of the herbal gene bank. In this article, Chen et al. (2014) found that the primary coding genes or even regulatory genes in the biosynthetic pathways are not sufficient for observing efficacy, and 'compartmentalization, transport, storage, and co-factor availability' may also be the important rate limiting factors. Therefore, 'a better understanding of pathways involved would build a foundation for a more comprehensive approach to metabolic engineering'. The authors note that several herb-related databases have already been developed to categorise current resources. However, 'these distributed resources are not subjected to a long-term maintenance and require bioinformatics skills to use'. Therefore, they call for a comprehensive and easily accessible database 'that stores molecular and biological data for herbal medicines' and possibly covers the DNA/protein sequences and metabolomes of herbs.

The final article of these three, *Evaluating the Safety of Herbal Medicines: Integrated Toxicological Approaches* explores the reasons that lead to the problems of the safety and the quality control of TCMP (Williamson et al. 2014). The authors stress that intrinsic herbal toxicity and malpractice should be distinguished from each other and summarise several reasons that may cause the safety problem of herbal products for clinical use, including incorrect botanical identification, errors in processing, adulteration, lack of standardisation to active compounds, clinical conditions and contaminants. While most of the reasons may be explained by pharmacovigilance systems, the botanical identification, standardisation to active compounds and toxicity assessment are safety issues in the preclinical trial phase. The authors note that 'preclinical and clinical toxicology research on herbal medicines is in most cases inadequate or insufficient to fulfill official medicine registration requirements'. It may take months or even years for any adverse events to manifest in the event of inadequate evaluation of complex mixtures of which the composition is not fully known, however the principles of formulating a prescription are designed to address one of these issues—decreasing the side effect, in the other words harmonising the toxicity in TCM. The variable potencies and relations found in a large number of components in complex herbal medicines targeting various symptoms increase the difficulty of safety assessments. Toxicity and efficacy are often the result of the mixture of active compounds rather than a single chemical entity. In addition, insidious toxicities 'which are not easily detected by pharmacovigilance, including genotoxicity, carcinogencity, and development toxicity' must be given attention. The authors warn that 'toxicological and pharmacokinetic studies of individual constituents of herbal materials must be compared with qualitative and quantitative profiling data for the total extract using appropriate analytical tools'. Therefore, different tools for testing the risk of the active compounds are imperative. The article compares the pros and cons of the in vitro method, in silico method and modern screening techniques applied in the risk assessment. They also stress that at all stages the multicomponent nature and variability of herbal remedies must be remembered and that studies using incorrectly identified, processed, contaminated, or adulterated preparations will lead to an invalid result as well as an incorrect toxicological evaluation. Scientific approaches to better test the safety and efficacy of TCMP have been developed, but they are still not good enough to ascertain the safety and efficacy of TCMP for meeting the standards set up by the current risk assessment system for the authorisation of chemical pharmaceutical products. Therefore, the authors emphasise empirical clinical assessment must be carried out through pharmacovigilance to compensate the lack of safety evaluations of herbal drugs; the systems-based approaches should be used due to the complex chemical interactions taking place in herbal mixtures. The article concludes that 'omics and bioinformatics as well as the emerging systems-based technologies with conventional means techniques have made it possible to investigate TCMP's efficacy and toxicity at the organism level and in an individual manner. However, further toxicological investigation is urged for novel methods that are able to rapidly pinpoint indicators of major mid-term and long-term toxicities, yield warning signals, and identify those herbal drugs and formulas.

To sum up the current literature has noticed the merit of developing a systematic or holistic treating methodology for TCMP, and multidisciplinary research has contributed to finding more scientific evidence of the safety and efficacy of TCMP. However, these successes have only been achieved in limited cases and specific sample tests. In the future, more approaches are expected to prove the scientificity of TCMP with respect to the characteristics of TCM.

1.3 The Inspiration for Writing This Book

1.3.1 The Author's Concerns for Writing This Book

The book is based on the PhD study conducted by the author. The author choses market access as a core issue, discussed from the beginning to the end of this book. Because the current problem in the international trade of TCMP rests in the phase of market access in Europe. The book regards the common understanding between the EU and China on protection of public health as well as the development of medical science. While, it also notices the culture differences between the EU and China as well as different beliefs on TM. Therefore, it tries to eliminate the different recognitions of TCMP in EU and Chinese law through analysing the issue within WTO legal framework—which is a legal framework both the EU and China have committed to. In addition, the study in this book respects the most up to date development knowledge of medical science. It intends to explore the relationship between science and law and intends to draw a line between these two. The impact of science upon law is supposed to ride on the line, which shows what is the issue of scientific research and what is the issue of legal research, as well as their interaction.

1.3.2 Problem, Hypothesis and Main Questions of the Study Developed in This Book

As previously mentioned, the cases caused damages because of herbal remedy containing AA brought much anxiety about the risk of using TCMP. Later on, EU pharmaceutical law was revised by Directive 2004/24/EC on herbal medicinal products of human use. From then on, rarely TCMPs enter the market of the EU. Therefore, this book begins from the current practical problem, the hardship TCMP has in the EU, and sets up a legal hypothesis that the current EU pharmaceutical law has formed legal obstacle in the way of TCMP access the EU market.

The study notes that the forms of obstacles in EU pharmaceutical law are technical standards and regulations. The problem has spilt over into the sustainable development of medical science of CAM and influenced the patients' right on the free choice of medicine in the EU. However, the authorisation system that is designed for Western conventional medicine and THMP is rarely challenged within the national or regional legal framework because of the preconceived opinion on medicine. Therefore, the practical problems are hardly exposed.

The EU technical standards and regulations relating to market access of TCMPs compose a closed loop based on beliefs about Western conventional medicine within the EU. Therefore, they are rarely challengeable on issues of TCM. However, the incompatible understandings of TCM between China and the EU come to a head in the international trade of TCMPs where the commitments of the Members of the World Trade Organisation (WTO) compose the restriction to the national and regional legislations in international trade. Therefore, the study refines a core legal question, whether EU pharmaceutical law as applied to TCMP would comply with WTO law on the issue of market access. In the course of answering this legal question, the legal issue of market access of TCMP in the EU is reviewed, and the rationality and insufficiency of EU pharmaceutical law for the development of CAM, using TCMP as a typical example, is tackled. Regarding public health and free trade, which have been set forth as legislative goals of both EU pharmaceutical law and WTO law, the exploration of the main question aims at encouraging the scientific research on TM in the EU to better protect the public health as well as facilitate the international trade of TCMP.

1.3.3 Designing the Study in This Book

For this author, methodology is the general research strategy that drives the way in which the research is to be undertaken and how the proposition is to be proven. It embodies the process to achieve the findings and to solve the problem(s). It serves as evidence that the researcher has done either a convincing research or one that is more susceptible to challenge. In the course of designing the study as a whole, specific research tools are applied for analysing certain issues.

Methodology can be categorized into concepts of paradigm, theoretical model, phases, quantitative and qualitative techniques and other concepts (Berg 2009). These concepts can be used either to complete an entire study or just for solving partial problems. However, Feyeralxend (1993) in his *Against Method* put forth a critical view stating that '[t]he consistency condition which demands that new hypotheses agree with accepted theories is unreasonable because it preserves the older theory, and not the better theory'. Indeed, it is arguable if unchangeable theories exist or should exist. On one hand, the use of methodology supplements a researcher's lack of experience; on the other hand, it restricts the thought of exploring new things as 'all methodologies, even the most obvious ones, have their limits' (Feyeralxend 1993, p. 23). In legal research, when the applicable law (s) is/are well defined, rules in the applicable law(s) will be applied to prove the hypothesis and question(s). However, what law is and what law ought to be are two questions. Therefore, the solution for solving the practical problem(s) lies not only in the current applicable rules but also in what the law ought to be. Usually, legislative aims and principles are expected to adhere to what the law ought to be, but there is always a question first as to how to define what the law ought to be. In such case, jurisprudence provides some clues for exploring the question.

Broadly speaking, methodology is the systematic and theoretical analysis of the methods applied to a field of study. Some conclude that a completed study circle includes activities of properly finding, describing, defining, and measuring problems, designing research, investigating practice, collecting and analysing data, reporting findings and verifying solutions for solving problems (Leuven Statistics research Center 2017). Specifically, in a legal research, the practical problem needs

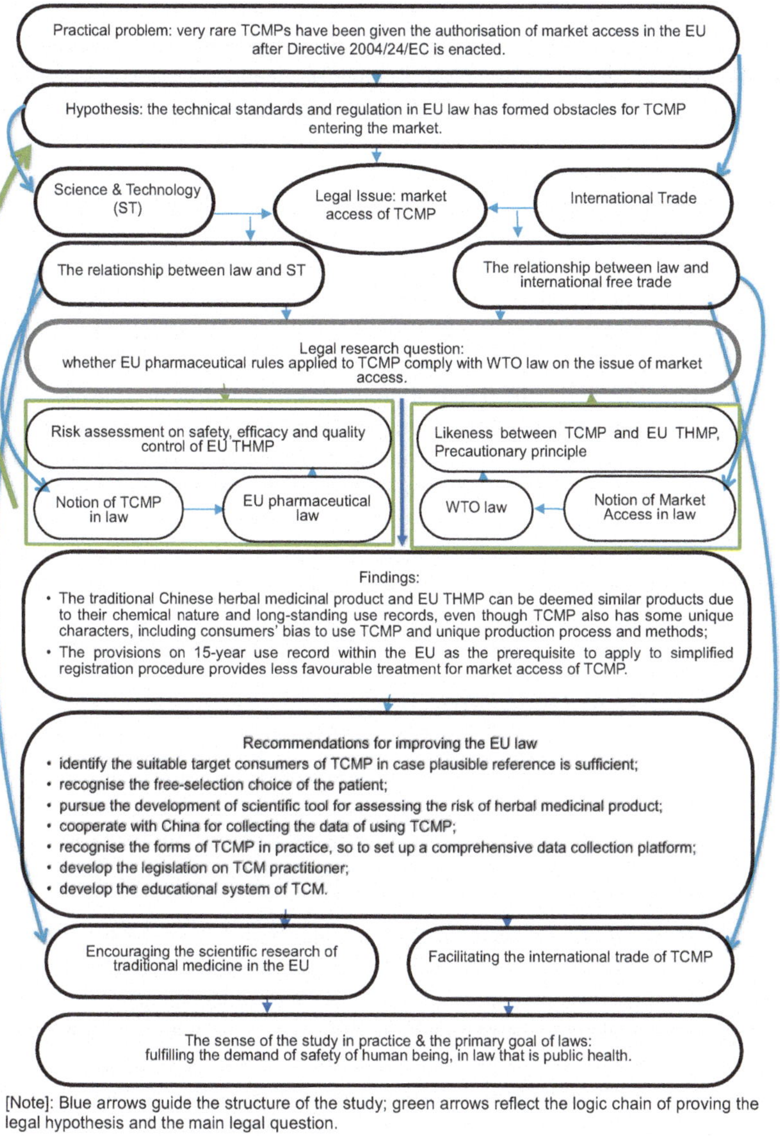

Fig. 1.1 Flowchart of the study structure

to first be refined or transformed into a legal question. Subsequently, the problem can be discussed based on legal factors which can be used to describe, define and measure the problem for a legal solution. A flowchart of the study structure is illustrated in Fig. 1.1.

To read Fig. 1.1, this research started from a practical problem—very rare TCMPs entering the EU market after the enforcement of Directive 2004/24/EC—which initiated the rest of the study. To describe, defend, measure and solve the practical problem, a legal hypothesis is set forth: technical standards and regulations in EU law have formed obstacles for TCMP to enter the market. The main legal issue is deduced from this hypothesis, and two relevant domains appear, science & technology (ST) and international trade. Therefore, the study investigates the relationships between law and ST and law and international trade. Based on these relationships, the study further highlights two essential concepts, one is TCMP in pharmaceutical law and the other is market access in international trade law. Subsequently, the two concepts are described, defined, and measured based on the applicable rules, but with a critical analysis. Based on the exploration on those two relationships, the main question—whether EU pharmaceutical law as applied to TCMP would comply with WTO law on the issue of market access—is searched. Through analysing the main question, clues on solving the practical problem are provided. In addition, philosophy provides general methodology to reveal the relations for finding intrinsic laws between phenomena. At the same time, incidental interventions need to be discussed since law also functions directly on predicting the result or consequence for incidental affairs via providing regular rules. Therefore, the theoretical and conceptual framework, including main philosophical theories which significantly affect the research, are introduced prior to the specific issues of market access of TCMP.

1.3.4 The Use of Qualitative Study

The study in the book uses qualitative study methodology as a whole (Kumar 1999; Packer 2010; Weston 2000). Legislation, cases, official reports and documents are chosen as the main resources instead of collecting data from samples. Some specific research tools, included but not exhausted in the study, are listed as below (Kumar 1999, pp. 57, 88, 126–130).

The legal interpretation methodology is conducted throughout the study. This methodology should be applied when the linguistic meaning of the legal texts and the content of law should be distinguished. Through understanding the linguistic meaning of the legal texts, the main goal of the research is to find the content of the law which is based on legal principles affected by jurisprudential theories (Greenberg 2017). The classical methods of interpretation include literal interpretation, contextual interpretation and teleological interpretation as recognised by 1969 Vienna Convention on the Law of Treaties.[2] Literal interpretation (or textualism) explains 'what a normative text conveys by looking at the usual meaning of the

[2]See UN, Vienna Convention on the Law of Treaties, 1155 (1980). Art. 31 of the Convention states that, in accordance with a general rule of interpretation, '[a] treaty shall be interpreted in good faith in accordance with the ordinary meaning to be given to the terms of the treaty [literal interpretation] in their context [contextual interpretation] and in the light of its object and purpose [teleological interpretation]'. Art. 32 explains the supplementary means of interpretation as 'the preparatory work of the treaty and the circumstances of its conclusion'.

words contained therein' (UN Vienna Convention on the Law of Treaties 1980). It guarantees a high degree of predictability in the judgement (Lenaerts and Gutierrez-Fons 2013). Practically and lawyerly speaking, answers are expected to be found in law, so to avoid abstract and theoretical complexities. When neither the literal interpretation nor the context is clear, either within a legal text or affiliated documents, the purpose of signing an agreement must be interpreted according to 1969 Vienna Convention. In this research, aside from legislation and selected precedents, many official documents, guidelines, standards and scientific advisory papers are read as well. In addition, to break though the limitation of the current statutory regulation (SR), the law must be interpreted more comprehensively via pertinent jurisprudential theories. The legal interpretation methodology helps the researcher clarify the current regulative status of EU pharmaceutical law on the issue of market access of TCMP and refine relevant legal principles that can be applied to the case. It provides feasibility for the researcher to access scientific evidence for further legal analysis, because the law transmits the technical standards into understandable legal languages so as to make the rule transparent, non-discriminate and implementable. Moreover, this methodology helps find effective data for the research, since EU legislations and legal documents already include detailed risk assessment methodologies, as well as sophisticated administrative procedures on regulating comparably similar pharmaceutical products of TCMP.

Care has been taken when adapting the legal interpretation methodology to the research key issue. Which legislation should be analysed for answering the main question and solving the practical problem? Law is often defined as the instrument to adjust the relationships of people. But noticeably, the problem that initiated the study is an issue directly relating to the market access of TCMP. In this case, the study notices that the subjects of the legal relationship also execute the rules set out by law. They investigate whether the rule is rational for market access is essential and fundamental rather than focusing on the rights and obligations of the subjects for analysing the practical problem. Nevertheless, it is necessary to explore the relationship between the rule of market access and the rights/obligations set out by law. Rights and obligations are obtained through the ratification or enactment of law, or they are embodied by precedents, or judge-made law. In addition, the relationships between law and policy, culture or other matters puts weight on law making. However, the decision making on market access of TCMP should be based more on objective standards of pharmaceutical techniques. Therefore, the study argues for the significance of recognising the relationship between law and science; it claims to limit the influence of political and social matters when making and implementing law on market access of TCMP. Consequently, it pays more attention to the Technical Regulations and standards.

Critical analysis is often used to evaluate a work, such as a book, an essay, reports or decisions of cases, so as to increase the reader's understanding of it. The strategy of the critical analysis includes identifying the author's thesis, purpose, main ideas, consulting a dictionary, encyclopedia or other extended reading materials to understand material that is unfamiliar to the researcher; writing a summary of the work (Southeastern Louisiana University n.d.);[3] and critically reading and highlighting the points in the reading material. By employing this method, the study develops knowledge, achieves its inspirations and may develop theories of law. In addition, critical analysis is used to find supporting views for the points the study holds. It also helps find comparable points of view for more sufficiently explaining the holding point(s).

Retrospective-prospective study focuses on past trends in the phenomenon of market access of TCMP and studies it into the future (Kumar 1999). The history of legislation relevant to TCMP in the EU and China are reviewed. Other impact factors such as the cultural, social and economic factors are concerned as well. Based on this, recommendations are given for improving the legislations.

Case study is an approach to study a social phenomenon through a thorough analysis of an individual case. It can be used in different purposes, for instance, to illustrate an event, to collect data or to argue for a point based on the similarities between the chosen cases. In different parts of the book, proper cases are chosen for analysing and indicating certain points. For instance, in Chap. 4 the first authorisation case of TCMP in the EU is selected for illustrating the process of applying for registration through the simplified pathway. In Chap. 5 WTO cases regarding the application of precautionary principle are selected and explicitly analysed for evaluating the rationality of EU pharmaceutical law.

Open questions are designed in questionnaires and asked in interviews. This methodology is used for exploring problems and collecting information from the people who represent the most relevant stakeholders including the national competent authority in the EU and Chinese manufacturers of TCMP. Two surveys were processed for the study in this book, one was an interview to the Head Botanical & Novel Foods, Medicines Evaluation Board Netherland (MEB 2020), and the other for investigating TCMP pharmaceutical industries in China.

Comparative research is a research methodology in social science, and it aims to make comparisons across different regions or cultures, or between different developing phases. An effective comparative research is based on the analysis of comparability. It is fundamental to identify the object and clarify the comparative factors in the comparative study. After properly defining the object, it is possible to process further comparison study surrounding impact factors. The comparative research broadens the thinking of a closed system and brings innovative ideas for the development of a study. The study in this book has applied comparative research in many situations. For instance, it compares TCMP and EU herbal medicinal products, and it illustrates the EU institutional system on the authorisation of market access of TCMP through comparing with the Chinese system.

[3]Critical reading guided by Southeastern Louisianan University points to '[e]valuate the means by which the author has accomplished his purpose'. In details, '[i]f the purpose is to inform, has the material been presented clearly, accurately, with order and coherence'; '[i]f the purpose is to persuade, look for evidence, logical reasoning, contrary evidence'; '[i]f the purpose was to entertain, determine how emotions are affected: does it make you laugh, cry, angry? Why did it affect you?'.

To sum up, the above is a general introduction of the study that the book is based on. The next Chapter begins the analysis of the theoretical framework for understanding market access of TCMP in the EU under the WTO legal framework.

References

Aschwanden C (2001) Herbs for health, but how safe are they? Bull World Health Organ 79

Berg B (2009) Qualitative research methods for the social sciences, 7rd edn. Pearson Education Inc, Boston

Briggs J (2014) A global scientific challenge: learning the right lessons from ancient healing practices. In: Fan T-P et al (eds) The art and science of traditional medicine, Part 1: TCM today—a case for integration. The Science/AAAS Custom Publishing Office, pp S7–S9

Canada Natural Health Products Regulations, Food and Drugs Act (2004) SOR/2003-196. http://laws-lois.justice.gc.ca/eng/regulations/SOR-2003-196/

Chan M (2014) Supporting the integration and modernisation of traditional medicine. In: Fan T-P et al (eds) The art and science of traditional medicine, Part 1: TCM today—a case for integration. The Science/AAAS Custom Publishing Office, p S2

Chen S et al (2014) Herbal genomics: examining the biology of traditional medicines. In: Fan T et al (eds) The art and science of traditional medicine, Part 2—multidisciplinary approaches for studying traditional medicine. The Science/AAAS Custom Publishing Office, pp S28–S29

Directive 2001/83/EC (2001) Directive 2001/83/EC of the European Parliament and of the Council of 6 November 2001 on the Community Code Relating to Medicinal Products for Human Use. OJ L 311: 67-128, Art 16a(1), Art 10a, Art 8(3)

Directive 2004/24/EC (2004) Directive 2004/24/EC of the European Parliament and of the Council of 31 March 2004 Amending, as Regards Traditional Herbal Medicinal Product, 2001/83/EC on the Community Code Relating to Medicinal Products for Human Use. OJ L 136:85–90

Elling R (1981) Political economy, cultural hegemony, and mixes of traditional and modern medicine. Soc Sci Med 16A(2):89–99

EMA/322570/2011 (2017) Uptake of the Traditional Use Registration Scheme and Implementation of the Provisions of Directive 2004/24/EC in EU Member States, Rev. 7

European Scientific Cooperative on Phytotherapy (ESCOP) (n.d.). http://escop.com

Fan T et al (eds) (2014a) The art and science of traditional medicine, Part 1: TCM today—a case for integration. The Science/AAAS Custom Publishing Office

Fan T et al (2014b) Integrating traditional medicine into modern health care. In: Fan T et al (eds) The art and science of traditional medicine, Part 1: TCM today—a case for integration. The Science/AAAS Custom Publishing Office, p S4

Feyeralxend P (1993) Against method, 3rd edn. Verso, London

Girard L, Vohra S (2011) Ethics of using herbal medicine as primary or adjunct treatment and issues of drug-herb interaction. In: Iris FFB, Sissi W (eds) Herbal medicine: biomolecular and clinical aspects, 2nd edn. CRC Press/Taylor & Francis eBook, Boca Raton. https://www.ncbi.nlm.nih.gov/books/NBK92771/. Chap. 21

Greenberg M (2017) What makes a method of legal interpretation correct? Legal standards vs. fundamental determinants. UCLA School of Law, Public Law Research Paper No. 17-06

Inpharma Weekly (1999) Aristolochia Banned in the UK. 1199(1):21

Iris FFB, Sissi W (2011) Herbal medicine: biomolecular and clinical aspects, 2nd edn. CRC Press/Taylor & Francis eBook, Boca Raton. https://www.ncbi.nlm.nih.gov/books/NBK92771/

Kleinman A (1978) Concepts and a model for the comparison of medical systems as cultural systems. Soc Sci Med 12B:85–93

Kumar R (1999) Research methodology a step-by-step guide for beginners, 3rd edn. SAGE, London
Kunstadter P (1980) Medical ethics in cross-cultural and multi-cultural perspectives. Soc Sci Med 14B(4):289–296
Lenaerts K, Gutierrez-Fons J (2013) To say what the law of the EU is: methods of interpretation and the European Court of Justice. Working Papers of European University Institute Academy of European Law
Leshner A (2014) AAAS a middle way for traditional medicine. In: Fan T et al (eds) The art and science of traditional medicine, Part 1: TCM today—a case for integration. The Science/AAAS Custom Publishing Office, p S3
Leslie C (1980) Medical pluralism in world perspective. Soc Sci Med 14B(4):191–195
Leung E et al (2014) Integrated network-based medicine: the role of traditional Chinese medicine in developing a new generation of medicine. In: Fan T et al (eds) The art and science of traditional medicine, Part 1: TCM today—a case for integration. The Science/AAAS Custom Publishing Office, pp S16–S18
Leuven Statistics research Center (2017) Doctoral Courses in Flanders Training Network for Methodology and Statistics (FLAMES)
Luo G et al (2012) Systems biology for traditional Chinese medicine. A John Wiley & Sons, Inc., Chichester
MEB (2020) Medicines Evaluation Board. https://english.cbg-meb.nl
National Center for Complementary and Integrative Health (NCCIH) (n.d.). https://nccih.nih.gov
Packer M (2010) Science of qualitative research. Cambridge University Press, London
Schroen Y et al (2014) East is East and West is West, and never the twain shall meet?. In: Fan T et al (eds) The art and science of traditional medicine, Part 1: TCM today—a case for integration. The Science/AAAS Custom Publishing Office, p S10
Southeastern Louisiana University (n.d.) Critical Analysis. https://www2.southeastern.edu/Academics/Faculty/elejeune/critique.htm
Teahan J (1981) Mystical ontology, health and healing: a cross-cultural exploration. Religion 11:321–351
Tu Y (2011) Nat Med 17:1217
U.S. FDA (2001) Aristolochic Acid: Letter to Industry Associations Regarding Safety Concerns Related to the Use of Botanical Products Containing Aristolochic Acid
U.S. FDA, Dietary Supplements (n.d.). https://www.fda.gov/food/dietarysupplements
UK MHRA (2015) Phynova Joint and Muscle Relief Tablets. THR 41783/0001
UN (1980) Vienna Convention on the Law of Treaties. 1155, Art 31, 32
Universite de Lausanne (n.d.) Faculte de biologie et de medecine, Pharmacokinetics, Metabolism, Pharmacokinetics, Excretion. https://sepia.unil.ch/pharmacology/index.php?id=55&L=-1%27, https://sepia.unil.ch/pharmacology/index.php?id=56
Unschuld P (1975) Medico-cultural conflicts in Asian settings: an explanatory theory. Soc Sci Med 9(6):303–312
Unschuld P (2001) What is medicine? Western and eastern approaches to healing (trans: Reimers K). University of California Press, London
Vanherweghem J et al (1993) Rapidly progressive interstitial renal fibrosis in young women: association with slimming regimen including Chinese herbs. Lancet 341(8842):387–391
Wang Y, Xu A (2014) Zheng: a systems biology approach to diagnosis and treatments. In: Fan T et al (eds) The art and science of traditional medicine, Part 1: TCM today—a case for integration. The Science/AAAS Custom Publishing Office, p S13
Weston A (2000) A rulebook for argument, 3rd edn. Hackett Publishing Company
WHO (1998) Regulatory Situation of Herbal Medicines. A Worldwide Review
WHO (1999) Traditional and Modern Medicine: Harmonizing the Two Approaches
WHO (2003) Medicines Policy, Pharmaceuticals: Restrictions in Use and Availability, Essential Drugs and Medicines Policy

Williamson E et al (2014) Evaluating the safety of herbal medicines: integrated toxicological approaches. In: Fan T et al (eds) The art and science of traditional medicine. The Science/AAAS Custom Publishing Office, Part 2, p S47

Wu H et al (2013) Recent developments in qualitative and quantitative analysis of phytochemical constituents and their metabolites using liquid chromatography—mass spectrometry. J Pharm Biomed Anal 72:267–291

Xiong X et al (2011) Clinical application of the TCM classic formulae for treating chronic bronchitis. J Tradit Chin Med 31(1):69–72

Yuan R, Lin Y (2000) Traditional Chinese medicine: an approach to scientific proof and clinical validation. Pharmacol Ther 86(2):191–198

Zhang L, Xue C, Fong H (2011) Integration of herbal medicine into evidence-based clinical practice. In: Iris FFB, Sissi W (eds) Herbal medicine: biomolecular and clinical aspects, 2nd edn. CRC Press/Taylor & Francis eBook, Boca Raton, https://www.ncbi.nlm.nih.gov/books/NBK92771/. Chap. 22

Zhou J et al (2013) Logical thinking in pattern differentiation of traditional Chinese medicine. J Tradit Chin Med 33(1):137–140

Chapter 2
The Legal Theoretical Framework for Market Access of TCMP

The Oxford Living Dictionaries defines theory as '[a] supposition or a system of ideas intended to explain something, especially one based on general principles independent of the thing to be explained.' It can be '[a] set of principles on which the practice of an activity is based'; or '[a]n idea used to account for a situation or justify a course of action'; or '[a] collection of propositions to illustrate the principles of a subject' (Oxford Living Dictionaries).

Theories that have inspired the study in this book are set out hereinto, including the philosophical theories that have guided the research, the schools of law and their rational components to which the research adheres. While the conceptual framework covers the specific legal notions relating to the research topic, not all of the theories and concepts included in the research are discussed in this Chapter. Some theories and concepts are mentioned in later chapters if they serve as the core point(s) of those chapters. The theoretical framework consists of the theories or issues in which the study is embedded, the fundamental issue(s) of the study, whereas the conceptual framework describes the details of the specific aspects deduced from the theoretical framework (Packer 2010, p. 39). Both the theoretical framework and conceptual framework are the basis of the study and include the assumptions on which the research is based.

2.1 Philosophical Theories That Influenced the Study

Philosophy is a methodology as well as a world view. As a methodology, it guides people to raise and analyse meaningful questions through observing practical problem(s) and finding the relations between various natural and/or social phenomena surrounding the questions. As a world view, it decides how far a researcher can go to find answers to those question(s). As a mechanism to explore and solve a problem,

S. Wang, *Market Access of Traditional Chinese Medicinal Product in the EU under WTO Legal Framework*, Economic and Financial Law & Policy – Shifting Insights & Values 5, https://doi.org/10.1007/978-3-030-52848-5_2

philosophical thinking is a part of the theoretical system for analysing a particular issue.

2.1.1 Dialectics and Contradiction Theory

Dialectics and contradiction theory is the philosophical thinking running through the research. Trotsky noted that Hegel (1770–1831) wrote in detail about Dialectics before Darwin and before Marx (1818–1883). Inspirited by the French Revolution, Hegel 'anticipated the general movement of science' (Trotsky 1942, cited in Woods and Grant 1995, p. 8). After Hegel, the laws of dialectics were developed by the philosophers and ideologists who followed.

Marxists treat dialectics as a method of 'thinking and interpreting the world of both nature and society'. Universally, dialectics 'sets out from the axiom that everything is in a constant state of change and flux'. More meaningfully stated, '[d]ialectics explains that change and motion involve contradiction and can only take place through contradictions' (Woods and Grant 1995, p. 8).

The fundamental proposition of dialectics is that everything is in a constant process of change, motion and development. Even when it appears to us that nothing is happening, in reality matter is always changing. Molecules, atoms and subatomic particles are constantly changing places, always on the move. Dialectics is thus an essentially dynamic interpretation of the phenomena and processes which occur at all levels of both organic and inorganic matter. 'To our eyes, our crude eyes, nothing is changing', notes the American physicist Richard P. Feynman, 'but if we could see it a billion times magnified, we would see that from its own point of view it is always changing: molecules are leaving the surface, molecules are coming back' (Feynman 1963).

Engels (1820–1895) defines dialectics as 'the science of the general laws of motion and development of nature, human society and thought'. In *Dialectics of Nature*, Engels gives an account of the laws of dialectics, beginning with the three most fundamental ones: (1) the law of the transformation of quantity into quality and *vice versa;* (2) the law of the interpenetration of opposites; and (3) the law of the negation of the negation (Feynman 1963).

The essential point of dialectical thought is that motion and change are viewed based upon contradiction, and '[c]ontradiction is an essential feature of all being. It lies at the heart of matter itself. It is the source of all motion, change, life and development'. Contradiction raises the transformation of quantity into quality and *vice versa*. The law of transformation of quantity into quality and *vice versa* discloses that there is 'a line which is interrupted by sudden and explosive periods in which slow, accumulated changes (quantitative change) undergo a rapid acceleration, in which quantity is transformed into quality'. The process is not smooth and uninterrupted; contradiction is always present where dialectics is the logic. Contradiction is the reflection of the law of the unity and interpenetration of opposites, and the unity and interpenetration of opposites composes the relations between things.

The law of the negation of negation expresses that processes continually repeat themselves. It forms the development led by successive contradictions, from simple to complex, from lower to higher (Woods and Grant 1995, p. 26).

Contradiction can be divided into principal contradiction and secondary contradiction. Mao Tse-tung noticed that special attention needs to be paid to grasping the principal contradiction. This means that in any given contradiction, principal and secondary contradictory aspects should not be treated as equal, since '[i]n any contradiction the development of the contradictory aspects is uneven. Sometimes they seem to be in equilibrium, which is however only temporary and relative, while unevenness is basic'. The principal aspect leads the changing direction in the contradiction. The nature of a thing is determined primarily by the principal aspect of a contradiction, the aspect which has gained the dominant position (Mao 1937).

Dialectics and the contradiction theory run through the study in this book from the understanding of TCM to the legal analysis of the market access issue of TCMP. For instance, *Yin-Yang* is one of the most fundamental concepts in TCM, and its earliest reference is in the *I Ching* in approximately 700 BC. *Yin-Yang* is a concept invented by ancient Chinese people, but it comprehensively reflects dialectics and the contradiction theory. It experiences a long historical development. And It was 'systematically elaborated and written down by Tsou Yen of the *Yin-Yang* (Naturalist) School in the Warring States Period (476-221 BC)' (Sacred Lotus n.d.-a). It has been used to explain all the natural phenomena by Element Theory through describing the generating of Wood, Fire, Earth, Metal and Water respectively and the relationship in between these five elements. Traditional Chinese doctors contrasted wood to liver, fire to heart, earth to spleen, metal to lungs, and water to kidney through imagining the similar properties between each pair and also tried to find out the relations between different parts of the body (Sacred Lotus n.d.-b).

TCM treats the normal body without disease as a natural body, and different parts of the body function well in balance. However, syndromes and symptoms of disease reflect a change in the normal body and the destruction of balance. Through observing and comparing the balanced and unbalanced status of the human body, TCM doctors recognise the changes in a body, record the syndrome which is represented by a set of symptoms based on the changes, and identify various diseases in the body by applying diagnostic techniques. Diagnostic techniques in TCM include looking, listening, asking and pulse (palpation). Looking, listening, asking and pulse are the process to ascertain the disease. Among these four techniques, palpation can help the Chinese doctor reach the invisible parts inside of the body through feeling the throb of the pulse. It helps the Chinese doctor notice the changing of the viscera. Of course, it has taken a long time for Chinese doctors to develop these techniques, and subsequently, the newer doctors have to be educated and trained in these techniques. Focusing on the changing of the pulse and achieving the regulation of this changing are the basis to diagnosing a disease.

The changing of the body follows the law of transformation from quantity change into quality change and *vice versa* because of the contradiction between self-immunity of the body and disease. The goal of the TCM treatment is to consider the body as a whole and recover the sick body back to the natural and balanced one via using TCMP instead of deciding on and targeting a single point of the sick body. TCM diagnoses and cures by recording the relations between symptoms and summarising the syndrome that has appeared in the body. It is easier to recover the body back to its natural and balanced state when a changing which causes a disease is mini or small. However, when the quantitative change has accumulated and transforms into a qualitative change, it is difficult to find the re-balance. Therefore, TCM encourages people to protect themselves by carefully observing their natural and balanced body, noticing the changing of their body, and finding the reason for the change. If a change is something unexpected, factors known to bring about change should be avoided. While Western people did also recognise the importance of observing changes in the body (E.g.: WebMD n.d.), nevertheless, they did not develop a sophisticated diagnostic and therapeutic system like TCM.

Notably, it is not easy to ascertain the relationship between a syndrome and a disease, even though symptoms may raise signals of unbalanced body condition. The same symptom may be caused by different diseases or reasons. For instance, the symptoms of chills and fever are divided into wind cold and wind heat in TCM. Chills and fever caused by wind cold is accompanied by 'absence of sweating, headache, general aching, and a superficial tight pulse', while chills and fever caused by wind heat is accompanied by 'thirst, sweating and a superficial rapid pulse' (Sacred Lotus n.d.-c). Accordingly, therapies are different when facing these two types of cold. For treatment, TCM aims at eliminating all the symptoms by formulating drugs. When more than one disease coexist at the same time and appear to be a syndrome, the rule of principle contradiction and secondary contradiction can be applied again.

Principles of TCMP formulation are consistent with dialectics and contradiction theory. *Jun-Chen-Zuo-Shi* is the principle in formulating TCMP. *Jun, Chen, Zuo* and *Shi* can be explained as four ingredients. *Jun*, as the main ingredient, is 'a substance that provides the main therapeutic thrust'; the *Chen* ingredient 'enhances or assists the therapeutic actions of Jun'; the *Zuo* ingredient may work on some reactions' accompanying symptoms; while the *Shi* ingredient 'enhances or assists the therapeutic actions of the Jun'. In one formula, two biologically active substances may have the effect of 'mutual accentuation, mutual enhancement, mutual counteraction, mutual suppression, mutual antagonism and mutual incompatibility' (Yuan and Lin 2000). For instance, the principle of *Jun-Chen-Zuo-Shi* recognises that a side effect may rise from the *Jun* ingredient, so it aims to neutralise the *Jun* ingredient and decrease the toxicity by others. This is another application of contradiction theory. Hereinto, the study in this book neither involves any debate on the scientific basis of the five-element theory in TCM nor does it intend to explain the mechanism of TCM diagnosis and therapy. But it calls attention to the rational and logical thinking in the philosophy of TCM and TCMP by having situated some traditional principles of TCM into the philosophy of dialectic and contradiction theory.

Natural law theory, legal positivism, legal realism, critical legal studies, legal formalism, Marxist theory of law, etc. appeared in the course of the evolution of the Western philosophy of law. Some ancient Chinese philosophies, such as Ru Jia, Dao Jia, Fa Jia and Mo Jia, and contemporary Maoism have deeply affected the systematic idea of modern Chinese logic. The study does not intend to illustrate the whole picture of the history of philosophical development, but it observes the similarities of ideas which may affect the development of modern science and medicinal techniques between Europe and China. For instance, China has Feizi Han, a representative of Mo Jia, who subscribed to materialism, encouraged utilitarianism and considered his Dao, the core idea of his school, to be the law of the development of things (Liu 2002).

In addition, contradiction theory runs through the legal discussion in the study. For instance, national law and international law sometimes form a contradiction in international trade issues; the goal of public health and the goal of free trade may compose a contradiction in pharmaceutical law; beneficence & nonmalfeasance and the autonomy principle coexist in the process of lawmaking; the precautionary approach and the National Treatment (NT) rule form a contradiction in WTO law. Two sides of a contradiction are not always in conflict with each other. However, recognising and clarifying those contradictions are the process of finding, analysing, and solving the problem in law regarding the issue of market access of TCMP.

2.1.2 Schools of Law

Noticeably, the study in this book neither goes through all details of each school of law nor provides critical analysis on each of them. Instead, it highlights some points lying in some schools of law that have an effect on the research. The discussions relating to the school of natural law and the school of positivism are mainly referenced to the book *A Companion to Philosophy of Law and Legal Theory compiled* by Dennis Patterson (2010). The book is a collection of many essays, which offers a comprehensive survey of legal philosophy as a whole. Among the various schools discussed in part two of the book, natural law theory (Bix 2010, pp. 209–227) and legal positivism (Coleman and Leiter 2010, pp. 228–248) can be well-linked to some of the philosophical thinking on law in this book, either consistently or oppositely. In addition, sociological jurisprudence includes a rational methodology to study the law, where the evolution of sociological jurisprudence, which James A. Gardner (1961) reviewed in *The Sociological Jurisprudence of Roscoe Pound*, supports the focus of the study in this book and is also referenced hereinafter.

2.1.2.1 School of Natural Law: The Importance of the Relationship Between Law and Science & Technology

Natural law theory has a profound influence on contemporary jurisprudence with its long and distinguished history. Bix (2010) divided natural law into traditional natural law and modern natural law, describing the former as 'higher law'. For some, it is derived from divine revelation, religious texts, a careful study of human nature, or consideration of nature, while for others, it links to moral status of law. Cicero described 'natural law' as '[t]rue law is right reason in agreement with nature; it is of universal application, unchanging and everlasting'. However, Bix criticized Cicero's discussions of law and other related remarks of earlier Greek and Roman writers noting that they often mix up the nature and 'natural law'. Bix states that:

> [I]t was not always clear whether the standards were 'nature' because they derived from 'human nature' (our 'essence' or 'purpose'), because they were accessible by our natural faculties (that is, by human reason or conscience), because they derived from or were expressed in nature, that is, in the physical world about us, or some combination of all three (Bix 2010, p. 223).

Aquinas clarified natural law with mortality. "[A]ccording to Aquinas, positive laws which are just 'have the power of binding in conscience'" (Bix 2010). Aquinas asserted three criteria for making a law just: (1) the law should be 'ordered to the common good'; (2) 'the law-giver [should not exceed] its authority'; and (3) 'the law's burdens [should be] imposed on citizens fairly'. Modern natural law theory claims that moral evaluation is essential for properly understanding or describing the law.

The study in this book pays more attention to the aforementioned traditional natural law theory described by Cicero, since he pointed out the important relationship between rule of nature and rule of law. It is always arguable whether a human can really change nature, but indeed, humans never stop exploring nature. The study holds that the existence of the rule of nature is independent of human will, which opens the possibility for the rule of law.

Natural science aims at finding the rule of nature and using it for human's purpose through the development of technology. Law should recognise and respect the rule of nature. This discloses the essential relation between law and ST. Discussion of the relationship between law and ST not only follows the direction of science's impact upon law but also *vice versa* (Gibbons 1981–1982, p. 43). Laws are either in favour of the development of certain ST or inhibit it (Baldwin 1966); at the same time, the development of ST deeply influences the decision-making of policymakers. In practice, lawyers and scientists have difficulty communicating with each other (Gibbons 1981–1982). Lawyers think in terms of guilt and innocence, sanity and insanity, and right and wrong, while scientists think in probabilities, trends and tendencies, forces and parameters. Lawyers want the answers that scientists cannot give, for instance: is the drug safe (Gibbons 1981–1982, p. 47)? It is quite true that we do not know how to use law to control ST. We should never intend to use law to lead the development of ST, but '[w]hat is needed is research into the way that law controls behaviour and a measure of its effectiveness in doing so' (Gibbons 1981–1982, p. 51). Science is closely connected with the rule of nature and aims at finding the truth of the world; it tries to understand the dynamic mechanism of what it explores. Therefore, law should respect the findings and principles of ST in order to produce legislation that complies with the rule of nature.

Regarding the study, TCMP is used for humans' goal of curing disease. Law applied to TCMP should recognise and respect the level of development of the pharmaceutical ST of producing TCMP. Therefore, the state of the art of TCMP should be the basis for discussing the law of TCMP. However, ST has limitations in disclosing the entirety of the rule of nature. Empiricism also provides a philosophy for recognising the world, but it might present a false appearance. Therefore, lawmakers need proper procedures or legislative techniques to supplement the insufficiency or incapability of ST and empiricism.

2.1.2.2 School of Legal Positivism: The Current Law Should be Obeyed, But a Developmental Perspective Is Also Significant

Scholars of legal positivism share two central beliefs. First, what counts as law in any particular society is fundamentally a matter of social fact or convention ('the social thesis'); second, there is no necessary connection between law and morality ('the separability thesis'). The representatives of the school of legal positivism include John Austin, Jeremy Bentham, Hans Kelsen, H. L. A. Hart and Joseph Raz (Patterson 1996, 1999, p. 241).

Hart (1961) adopted his method of 'conceptual analysis' for questions in legal philosophy when others still followed 'linguistic' philosophy in the English-speaking world. Linguistic philosophy as a methodology claims that philosophical problems may be solved either by reforming language, or by understanding more about the language we presently use. But critics have noted that through adopting this method, '[p]roblems are solved by showing that they are wrongly formulated, and that there are no such problems.' Improving upon the linguistic philosophy Cornforth (1967) stated, 'a critical and analytic approach to the problems of human thinking requires, not metaphysics, but an investigation of the uses of language'. The approach of legal positivism differently holds that '[j]urisprudence aims to give a satisfactory analysis of the uses to which the concept of 'law' is put in various social practices (for example, legal arguments in court, in legislatures, in everyday settings)' (Patterson 1996, 1999, p. 241). Hart claimed that 'there is a difference between the way the law is and the way it ought to be' (Hart 1983, cited in Patterson 1996, 1999, p. 243). The former is considered to be the social criterion of legality, while the latter is concerned with the separability of the theses included in legality. Therefore, Hart claims first, that it is not necessary in all legal systems that for a norm to be a legal norm it must possess moral value; and second, 'that what norms count as legal norms in any particular society is fundamentally a matter of social conventions.' 'The latter can include a convention among relevant officials to make the moral value of a norm a condition of its legal validity' (Hart 1983, cited in Patterson 1996, 1999, p. 243). Therefore, even though positivism does not deny that 'there may be a great deal of overlap between a community's law and its morality', morality is only considered when it is the condition of legal validity but 'not about the extent to which moral and legal norms overlap in practice' (Patterson 1996, 1999, p. 241).

On one hand, the author of this book holds that society should give enough respect to 'the way the law is'. That leads to a consequence in which valid legislation should be obeyed and respected within its authority and jurisdiction. Indeed, it is important to well implement current legislation to keep an orderly and stable society, where interpreting the current SR becomes a way to understand the current social phenomena and judicial precedent analysis helps find the practical problems relating to the regulated phenomena. On the other hand, procedurally, the law should leave space for people to adjust the law and develop law based on 'the way the law ought to be' because the world is changing, and the social rules should be adjusted accordingly. By noticing the necessarily changing of social rules, contemporary law developed many legislative techniques to adapt to change, such as the affirmation of discretion of a judge, the use of the rule of recognition,[1] legal review mechanisms and so on. However, these legislative techniques only can function along with the substantive law. Therefore, how to guarantee the realisation of the way the law ought to be is a goal for the legislature to create good substantive laws. Thereinto pursuing and exploring a value of natural law, as mentioned in the above subsection, is necessary and significant, especially for affirming and finding the law that complies with nature.

The study in this book respects existing legislation within a jurisdiction, so the SR and precedents of the EU should be read and interpreted when analysing the legal issue of market access of TCMP in the EU. However, the study loyally supports the school of natural law rather than fully being a believer of legal positivism, even though it claims to strictly obey 'social convention'. Since the morals advocated by the valid legislation of a society is limited by the nature of that society, realising the limitation of the society is the way to solve the problem. From this point of view, Socrates's death is understood and celebrated (Olsen 1984; Weiss 1998, p. 157). Therefore, continuously exploring the way the law ought to be and tackling the loopholes of contemporary law are the permanent tasks of legal research. In the study in this book, the legal problem is derived from social phenomena, and the legal question is refined from a practical problem. Maintenance of the dignity of social convention is pursued, and, thus, all analyses are based on the understanding of EU law. The principle of *pacta sunt servanda* is an underlying assumption, which is somewhat of a deviation of social convention, so rules in the WTO—an international body dealing with trade issues—are undoubtedly obeyed.[2]

[1]Hart divides rules into two types, including 'primary rules that either limit or expand liberty; and secondary rules that are about the primary rules'. Hart also distinguishes three different kinds of secondary rules, including 'those that create a power to legislate; others that create a power to adjudicate; and finally, a 'rule of recognition'. The rule of recognition is 'not a power-conferring rule, instead, it sets out the conditions that must be satisfied in order for a norm to count as part of the community's law'. Cited by Patterson in Philosophy of Law and Legal Theory at p. 245.

[2]*Pacta sunt servanda* is Latin for 'agreements must be kept'. See, Garner (2004), p. 1217.

2.1.2.3 Sociological Jurisprudence: Disclosing the Relation Between Law and Society

James A. Gardner (1961) reviewed the evolution of Pound's theory of interests in the context of sociological jurisprudence in one article. Hereinafter, Gardner's article is reviewed to explain sociological jurisprudence.

Gardner explains that Montesquieu was treated as the forerunner of sociological jurisprudence, who assumed the fundamental principle of sociological jurisprudence. Montesquieu interrelated the living growth and development with the physical and societal environment.

Subsequently, Rudolph von Jhering stressed the social purpose of law and insisted that law should be brought into harmony with changing social conditions. Jhering's basic idea is called social utilitarianism, and claims that the 'individual's welfare is not an end in itself but is recognised only insofar as it aids in securing the welfare of society'. Gardner commented that Jhering's idea links Bentham's individual utilitarianism and two important movements of the twentieth century—the 'jurisprudence of interests' in Germany and the sociological jurisprudence of Roscoe Pound. Even though, Jhering recognised altruistic interests as well as egoistic, he gave the former little consideration. Nevertheless, his scheme has been criticised as lacking 'a reasonably objective criterion for selection and evaluation of interests', his idea heavily influenced the thought of Pound.

Rudolph Stammler focused on the relation of ethics and law rather than the administration of justice by legal rules. Stammler's greatest achievement is the 'functional sociological approach' and stated that the duty of the state is to study social phenomena and to use its findings for the attainment of just law. He regarded the universal element in every rule to be the adjustment between the individual purposes and the unitary purposes of society. Joseph Kohler held that 'law is relative to the civilisation of the time and place' and regarded the 'mission of law' as 'the advancement of civilisation through the forcible ordering of society'. Law should adapt itself to the tasks of 'the time and place to perform its proper function' since law has a two-fold purpose 'to maintain the existing values of civilisation and to carry forward human development'.

William James and his pragmatism specifically influenced Pound to derive the ethical and philosophical basis for his theory of interests. James noted that '[e]very end of desire that presents itself appears exclusive of some other end of desire'. It is difficult for the philosopher to objectively find the basis of selection, since '[i]f he is to keep his judicial position, he must never become a party to the fray' (James 1891, p. 344). 'The course of history', says James, 'is nothing but the story of men's struggles from generation to generation to find the more and more inclusive order.' For this reason, James finds, society has already made a better casuistic scale for the philosopher than he can ever make for himself (James 1891, p. 346). James tried to seek out an ethical philosophy, and he mentioned the metaphysical question as to the meaning of 'good' and the measure of the good which man recognises. He commented 'that the essence of good is to satisfy demand', 'to satisfy the most demands with the least friction and waste' (Gardner 1961).

Gardner explained that '[s]ociological jurisprudence is not, strictly speaking, a legal philosophy', but rather 'a method which attempts to use the various social sciences to study the role of the law as a living force in society and seeks to control this force for the social betterment'. He formulated seven practical objectives of sociological jurisprudence. One is to study the social effects of legal institutions, legal precepts and legal doctrines of the law in action. Two is to make a sociological study as the essential preliminary step in lawmaking. Three is to ascertain 'the means by which legal rules can be made more effective in the existing conditions of life'. Four is to try to understand the actual development of the law through studying the judicial methods and modes driven by the thought of the great judges and lawyers. Five is to study the evolution of the law. Six is to individualise the application of legal rules based on the concrete circumstances of particular cases. And seven is to establish a 'Ministry of Justice' of the state to participate in the program (Gardner 1961).

These practical objectives reflect the thinking of positivism. They emphasise social study of the implementation of law, law-making, effectiveness of law, legal practice, relations between law and social institutions, individualisation of the application of legal rules, etc. The study of these practical objectives composes a methodology to understand the history and the present state of law, in order to further develop the law. As Pound noted, law is 'experience developed by reason and reason tested by experience' (Pound 1950, cited in Gardner 1961). He mentioned that '[l]aw as an instrument of progress toward civilisation cannot stand still, yet it must be stable, and [a] task of the law is the reconciliation of the need for stability with the need for change' (Pound 1923, cited in Gardner 1961). This expression reflects the philosophy of dialectics. What has pushed the law to progress is the quantitive and qualitative change of civilisation in a society.

The study in this book agrees that sociological jurisprudence is rather a methodology than a philosophy. To a certain extent, it applies the method for analyzing of market access of TCMP. Specifically, it pays attention to research evolution of the current legal framework as well as the importance of the development of law along with the understanding on EU culture and politics which are a reflection of EU society. For instance, this study adopts systematology. By using that methodology, the legal issue of the market access of TCMP in the EU comes into focus. Other closely related social issues, including the administrative institutional structure, the administrative organisational system and the external environments around the core legal issue are also discussed.

In addition, inspired by Jhering and Stammler, the study in this book notes the conflict between individual interest and social interest, where society can be treated as a collection of individuals. It questions: When altruism meets egoism, does the enthusiast of altruism have a future? When socialism meets utilitarianism, which follower can access a better life more easily? Democracy, initiating from the West, is designed in the form of decision-making by majority vote. When a system carries out criteria on equality and fairness, pursuing a value of egoism and utilitarianism, can the supporter and executor of altruism and socialism still live happily? Possibly, if they just keep silent! Therefore, the study here makes a point to base the criteria of justice and fairness of law on objective factors instead of relevant social elements, even though it recognises that observing the social and political element is significant for disclosing the problem. It notices the conflict of interest between the public and the individual producer of pharmaceutical products. So, it discusses the demand of the public, and holds that pursuing or deferring to the natural demand of the human being is a reflection of natural law. Setting such demands as the goal of law is most in line with the common welfare of a society in nature. This point of view also spontaneously coincides with James's thought on the essence of good law.

2.1.2.4 Some Thoughts on Fundamental Law

How to tell whether a law is good or bad is a basic question in legal philosophy. To find an answer to the question, law should first be illustrated. Hereinto, we talk about the law within the discipline of law instead of the general rules of the world.

The definition of law can be given through an expression of legal sources or its class nature. In terms of the former, a law can be a sum of regulations which adjust certain social relations between people—or taking a more challenging opinion between a person and a thing (Kocourek); and in terms of the latter, it can be a tool which embodies and safeguards the interests of certain groups of people. The social relations can be transformed into the concept of jural relations for legal analysis. Some split the jural relation into factors including subject(s), object (s) and the content. They observe the relation between subjects and focus on the rights and obligations surrounding the object(s), which reflects the modern concept of jural relations (Kocourek 1920). Subjects can be natural persons, legal persons, states or organisations. They hold the right and undertake the obligation. The object of the jural relation varies in different laws and is pointed by the right and obligation. For instance, in criminal law it stands for a certain public social relation that both the prosecutor and accused are obliged to protect; in other areas of law, it may point to a material object, mental object or behaviour (Zhang 2007, p. 99). In law, the relation lies in between the legal subjects with the position of either equal or unequal. For instance, civil law often deals with the legal relation between persons with equal position, while administrative law adjusts the relations between the administrative organisation and its counterpart, who has an unequal position which is embodied as managing and being managed.

SRs and precedents are the forms of Law by which people obey, understand and access law. But can the forms of law reflect the law that people expect? It is not always the situation. People have different expectations of law. In such case, the Marxism Class theory explains why a law usually fits the expectation of just the ruling class. Democracy is the system established by the current capitalist society, which intended to break the spell of Marxism so that people, no matter what their level wealth or social position, would be voluntarily restricted by the modern legal system. Democratic society is a society which is designed to realise the will of the majority in order to partially solve conflict between the individual and the collective no matter which class the individual is from. The will of democracy is truly good. But to realise the ideal, the democratic system based on a majority voting system should be carefully designed and the law ought to be kept in good faith so as to prevent the will of a certain group of people arbitrarily prevailing in the society. Besides the idea of majority vote, many other factors may influence the making of a decision, such as the capacity to clearly understand a certain situation of voting. Even though judging the whole political system of the EU and China is an issue which is too general to be managed in this research, the current mechanism relevant to the authorisation of the market access of TCMP must be discussed. Before beginning discussion of the system, it is better to think through how the law ought to be first, otherwise either the legislators, lawmen or people who should obey the law would easily get lost in the variety of interests being sought.

The law that ought to be can be discussed from the law's values, function and implementation. Hereinto, issues directly relating to the market access of TCMP in the EU are generally refined for a preparation of the detailed discussions later on. First, the study in this book holds that the values of law embody the demands of people, individually or collectively to Law, or stand for the value of the Law *per se*. As for the former, those values are extrinsic and affiliated to people's expectations or demands, such as living, safety, belonging, happiness, self-actualisation and so on. As for the latter, when those extrinsic values are in conflict with each other, the law sets up rules to determine their orders so to realise the effectiveness and efficiency of law. As developed so far, the values of law are embodied by notions of justice, fairness, freedom, equity and some other basic principles of law often discussed by scholars. These notions have the nature of being highly inductive, but they are too abstract to be implemented directly in life. Therefore, it is easier to start thinking of the law from the demand of people. Only the legal principle which is in line with the natural demand of people can last. The values of Law should always be carried in mind and transposed into the sources of law, and then be realised by a functional system of law. Second, law has a punitive function as well as the function of predictability, and it predicts the punitive consequence to the unlawful behaviours of people. Third, the effect of the implementation of law can be shown by the behaviour of lawmen and people who should obey the Law, and the prerequisite is transparency and accessibility of law. Therefore, finding the law that ought to be is the root for realising the sense of the existence of law.

2.2 Jural Relation Analysis

Jural relation analysis is a methodology to interpret and understand social phenomena through law. It is also a norm of legal philosophy to explore the relation between the law and the will of people and intends to clarify how law functions in society. Albert Kocourek analysed various definitions of jural relation in 1920. Along with his other publications, jural relations relating to market access of TCMP are discussed hereinafter (Kocourek 1920; Corbin 1921; Willis 1929; Clark 1922).

In *Various Definitions of Jural Relation*, Kocourek (1920) notes that the term 'jural relation' scarcely finds a place in books written in English before he wrote his article in 1920. However, Kocourek traced the available discussion relevant to jural relation back to Savigny. He noted that Savigny (1779–1861) speaks of the jural relation as 'a relation between person and persons determined by a rule of law' and '[t]his determination by a rule of law consists in the assignment to the individual will of a province in which it is to rule independently of every foreign will'. Kocourek tries to disclose the link between law and human wills, and writes that '[s]ince the law does not act directly, it must operate by means of jural relation where there are opposing or opposable human wills which may influence future facts'. Therefore, '[i]n private law, the jural relation is a fundamental concept; it is the basic idea through which the whole system of legal advantages is realised.' Kocourek commented that Savigny's opinion on jurial relation is nothing more than 'rights in the strict sense'. But indeed, it is 'one of the relatively early discussions in a field which has only in recent decades found extensive treatment'. Some American and English analysts tend to define three and sometimes four fundamental jural elements when discussing jural relation. For instance, Terry mentioned four elements including 'correspondent rights, permissive rights, protected rights and facultative right', while 'Pound finds three of such concepts—rights (corresponding to duties), powers (capacities of creating, divesting, or altering right), and privileges (immunity from liability)'. The Yale group under the leadership of Hohfeld invented a classification of 'rights, privileges, powers and immunities'. Bierling explains that the contents of jural relation are expressed by all legal norms between persons entitled and persons bound, and, therefore, consist of claims on one side and duties on the other. Finally, Koucurek concluded that:

> A jural relation is a situation of legal and material fact upon which one by his own will may restrict or claim to restrict, presently or contingently, with the aid of the law, freedom of action of another (Kocourek 1920).

Even though the above jurists tried to explain jural relation with different ideas, Kocourek call them all 'modern'. The 'modern' understanding of jural relation focuses on persons and proceeds from a starting point of a system of rights. By contrast, Kocourek noted in an essay that Puntschart reaches an entirely different conclusion from those modern opinions on jural relation. He holds that '[a] system of rights is the very cornerstone of modern theory'. However, "[i]n Roman law, while there was a definition of 'actio', there was none of 'ius'[3] in the sense of right". Kocourek (1920) comments:

> In Roman application of legal ideas, norms related to persons, to things, the relations of persons to things and to other persons, and this application of legal norms created legal

[3]Ius or Jus (Latin, plural iura) etymologically means 'that which is binding' and comes from the same root as iungere, 'to join'. In ancient Rome it was used primarily to mean a right to which a citizen (civis) was entitled by virtue of his citizenship (civitas). See, Youdao Dictionary.

bonds by which persons were gyved to persons and persons to things for define purposes within the purview of the law.

Therefore, according to Puntschart, a jural relation is a bond derived from 'juris nexus' and 'juris vinculum' rather than from a right. For instance, ownership, according to the prevailing view, is only a kind of right; but according to Puntschart, it is not a right but a legal bond between a person and a thing. As Kocourek noted, 'Puntschart seeks to find a satisfactory base for administering purpose in the law.' And one effect of Puntschart's theory is 'to emphasise duties as was characteristic of the Roman system, instead of right'. Puntschart's definition is objective, comparing to the modern understanding on a man-made definition of right. He pursues and explores the bond between a person and a thing. However, Kocourek criticised Puntschart's idea of 'juris nexus' noting that it can hardly be taken as a substitute for a jural relation by reason of its objectivity because he gave no analysis of rights. Therefore, Kocourek stressed Puntschart's opinion on the jural relation, even though, finally, he does not entirely agree with Puntschart (Kocourek 1920).

Referring to pharmaceutical law, the author would agree with Puntschart's definition of the jural relation as a juris nexus. It is important to analyse the relation between the person and the thing in pharmaceutical law. Juris nexus can be applied for clarifying the safety, efficacy and quality control duties lying in the relation between manufacturers and the pharmaceutical product as well as the supervision duty[4] lying in the relation between the administrative competent authority and the pharmaceutical product. In such cases, a balance is formed between two duties, rather than between right/obligation and power/duty. To encourage obedience of law, only public rights are affirmed, and any private rights or powers/privileges are driven from the desire to protect the public interest.

In the area of international trade law, the modern definition of jural relation is easier to apply because international trade law relates more directly to the relations between countries, instead of the relations between a country and a thing. The will of a country is a collective will of the leading group of people or the majority of people in that country. Therefore, international trade law adjusts the relation between countries, rather than adjusting the relations between persons and a thing directly. The study in this book does not conclude that the jural relation should be or must be a relation between a person and/or legal person and a thing. Obviously, the jural relation focusing on the relations between person(s) and/or legal person is meaningful, especially for establishing the link between social phenomena and law, such as when analysing the case of concession violation between the contracting parties in WTO, the case of government inaction claimed by a counterpart. However, defining the jural relation as between persons may impair the objectivity of the legal analysis.

---

[4]Some may consider the duty as a power of licensing instead of supervision duty, in that case, modern jural relation notion is applied, relation is set up between competent authority and the manufacturer, licensing is the object of the jural relation, and competent authority and manufacturer are the two subjectives.

2.3 Legal Framework Surrounding Market Access

2.3.1 Market Access in Law

Market access is the core legal concept discussed in this book. The WTO holds that 'market access for goods in the WTO means the conditions, tariff and non-tariff measures, agreed on by members for the entry of specific goods into their markets (WTO n.d.). Countries have different systems controlling the import of products through setting up tariff, non-tariff and other measures. Those measures constitute the conditions of market access (ITC n.d.).

Market access can be discussed in different situations in law relevant to TCMP. Firstly, market access for goods means the conditions, tariff and non-tariff measures, set by countries on the entry of TCMP to their markets. In WTO law, tariff commitments on goods are agreed upon and set out in each member's schedules of concessions. They are the basic rules between the EU and China to regulate the market access of the import and export of TCMP. Secondly, besides market access for goods, market access also can relate to market access for foreign investment in the other country or a service across the border of the other country (European Commission 2016; OECD 2015, p. 128). Regarding TCMP, the issue of market access to investment arises when an EU investor intends to set up an entity to join the R&D or production of TCMP in China or a Chinese investor sets up a factory to produce TCMP in the EU. However, the latter is not likely to reasonably happen because of the difficulty of market access of TCMP, as goods, to the EU. The market access of services may indirectly relate to the market access of TCMP as a goods when Chinese doctors enter the service market and provide medical service. Thirdly, market access is also discussed in pharmacoeconomics and refers to the process by which a company gets a pharmaceutical product to market so to make the pharmaceutical product available for patients. Herein, the focus will be evidence-based market access, which requires production of market access reports based on scientific, preferably peer-reviewed and referenced, material (Chris et al. 1998; Wight 2012).

The study in this book comprehensively discusses the mainstream notion of market access of TCMP in international goods. Relevantly, the study covers evidence-based market access but from the view of administrative supervision of authorisation rather than the product management of a pharmaceutical company. In addition, issues concerning to legislation on trade related services is involved when necessary. Therefore, hereinto, market access is the phase of trade before a good, service or investment can enter a market. It consists of a set of measures enacted by a state or negotiated between different states for international trade. As for the policy makers, legislators and administrative authorities, market access can be used to protect national industry or economy by setting up trade obstacles to import and export; it can be used to protect the public interest by setting up standards and conditions on the product; and internationally or regionally. SR on market access can also make the relevant administrative rules transparent, so to promote fair trade. As for the producers of goods, providers of services and investors, knowing rules on market access helps in their business operation strategy, such as applying for authorisation or a business license and properly pricing the product. Market access is the pre-authorisation phase that precedes TCMP entering the market. This is where WTO rules and EU pharmaceutical law are the most relative.

2.3.2 A General Overview of Different Legal Branches Relevant to Market Access of TCMP

The discipline of law is divided into many sub-disciplines, often called legal branches for the convenience of research and education. The criterion for a classification is based on the common natures of a group of legal phenomena. However, the division may direct the focus to be on only the common natures of that group but overlook some other unique aspects. The methodology, putting one phenomenon in one legal branch, functions well for finding out the type of relation between parties in litigation, but for a comprehensive legal research, it has obvious drawbacks. Therefore, the study in this book generally reviews all legal branches relevant to market access first and then deduces the main branches it should focus on for analysing the issue of market access of TCMP in the EU.

The issue of market access can be discussed within various legal branches. The category of legal branches is an academic classification, and it summarises the common nature of different groups of legal phenomena in which people can refine similar jural relations and principles. Due to the different legal historical development paths, the anglo-american and continental systems of law have quite different recognitions on categories of legal branches. For instance, the anglo-american system does not have a branch of administrative law, therefore, it lacks legal principles that function in such a legal branch as the continental law system (Harlow 2006). Even though a meaningful discussion can be had on which legal system is better for facing the practical legal problem by using the concept of legal branches, it is not the focus of this research. Instead, the research aims to clarify the jural relation for the issue of market access in international trade of TCMP by referencing the academic categories of legal branches, no matter in which legal system they are formed, in order to define the relations of the fundamental elements in the legal phenomena relating to market access of TCMP.

The study in this book does not involve issues of remedy in civil, tort law or criminal law, but pays attention to jural relation analysis relevant to the phase of market access of TCMP. Therefore, it considers four legal branches, including administrative law, economic law, international trade law and pharmaceutical law. The cross thinking between these legal branches on the issue of market access of TCMP helps the study review the topic from different angles and find the key issue that the study should focus on. These four branches can be divided into two pairs, pair one includes administrative law and economic law, and pair two includes international trade law and pharmaceutical law. Pair one is the more general category when compared to the second.

In the written law of the EU, legislative aims are often clarified in the beginning of consolidated legislation, and they guide the drafting of other clauses, affiliated legal documents and legal practice. Similar functional clauses can be found in constitutional law when there is no written law to pursue. The study notes that a primary legislative aim in each of the aforementioned branches can be found in current effective legislation. Coincidentally, a second goal also exists, which is the primary goal of the other branch in a pair. The primary goal and the secondary goal compose a contradiction when they lay together in one legislation. The contradiction includes unity and opposition. Unity between two goals enhances legislative efficiency while the opposition requires an order and principle to solve the conflict. Things are developed over time, moving the situation forward in a dynamic mechanism composed by unity and conflict and constantly seeking balance.

2.3.2.1 The Branch of Administrative Law vs. the Branch of Economic Law

In the study in this book, administrative law is mainly concerned within the national law domain. Accordingly, the national economic law branch is compared. Noticeably, EU and Chinese administrative laws lead to different market access standards of TCMP within their respective jurisdictions. The administration of market access of TCMP first belongs to national domestic jurisdiction and is based on specific national administrative law, unless it may be affected by some regional or international rules agreed by the state. One of the characteristics of administrative law is the managing and managed relations between the administration organisation and its counterpart, which distinguishes the jural relation of administrative law from other branches, for instance the equal relation between parties in civil law.

The economic legal branch is widely discussed with the capacity and appropriateness of the state to intervene in the market. In China, some defines the relation between the subjects of economic law to be a managing and managed relation with regard to the administrative organisation and its counterparts. They define the jural relation to be economic relations that emerge during the process by which the state effects the economic operation through identified behaviours such as harmonising, intervening, managing, adjusting, regulating and controlling. They define the goal of the law to be the state or social public interest (Xiao 2012). However, in some countries, economic law may be not emphasised as an independent branch, instead, the economic legal phenomenon may be discussed in administrative law or commercial/business law. However, along with the increase of market failures, state government has started to use legal tools to manage, adjust or intervene in the market for maintaining an efficient market economy and a fair competition environment (Stiglitz 1989; Fetter 1924; Waters 1995; Datta-Chaudhuri 1990). Economic law especially focuses on the order of market operation, which is what distinguishes economic law from administrative law.

Market access of TCMP mainly involves administrative law when discussing authorisation. However, it may also include issues of economic law, for instance whether a merger between manufacturers of the product is allowable. The study in this book discovered that the fatal obstacle to market access of TCMP in the EU is about administrative authorisation in practice, instead of an argument on the efficiency or legality of market operation in the current stage. Therefore, relevant legal issues in the administrative law branch are essential for discussing the main problem in practice faced by market access of TCMP.

2.3.2.2 The Branch of International Trade Law vs. The Branch of Pharmaceutical Law

The broad research scope of economic law includes national economic law and international economic law. The market access of TCMP closely links to the international economic law which range can be narrowed down to international trade law in this book. There are two main academic opinions on the research scope of international economic law. One claims that international economic law is a branch of international public law, which means international economic law is a set of rules dealing with the economic relations[5] between states in which international economic organisations participate. In such case, the jural relations between individuals, including enterprises and natural persons are not focused. The other opinion claims that the research scope of international economic law should also cover the jural relation between legal persons and/or natural persons in international economic business. Practically, the business relation between individuals is the non-negligible component of international economic relations. However, the study herein, only measures of the state which may form obstacles to international trade are relevant directly to market access of TCMP in the EU. Therefore, the study focuses on international trade law which covers the conditions for the state to take measures in international trade.

International agreements signed between states comprise the states' obligations and responsibilities. Treaties and agreements signed in the WTO are the main sources for adjusting market access of TCMP between the EU and China. These agreements form a restriction on regional or national laws. Hereinto, regarding TCMP, EU pharmaceutical law is the specific administrative legislation covering authorisation for market access. Therefore, market access of TCMP in the EU is a legal issue crossed between WTO law and EU pharmaceutical law.

Noticeably, there exists a conflict between the legislative aims of international trade law and pharmaceutical law. Facilitating trade is the primary goal of WTO law while the aim of protecting public health is in the priority of EU pharmaceutical law. Nevertheless, WTO law concerns public health and other state interests, while EU

[5]Hereinto, international economic relations include international trade, international investment, international finance and international taxation and so on.

pharmaceutical law also is concerned with preventing any irrational action that may impair the free movement of goods, though mainly within the EU. The conflict and harmonisation between the primary legislative aims between WTO law and EU pharmaceutical law bring difficulties to decision-making on the market access of TCMP, but the contradiction also brings a rethinking of each existing legal system for answering the same question.

2.3.3 Specific Laws Relating to Market Access of TCMP

The above is a discussion of the jural relation through an overall review of relevant legal branches surrounding market access of TCMP in the EU. Hereinafter, specific issues of international trade law and pharmaceutical law are explained. The issue of market access of TCMP can be illustrated by measurable factors in law, including the goal of the legislation, the legal subject, the legal object, the right and obligation, or power, in jural relations. Through analysing these measurable factors, the essential elements will be identified in order to answer the main question, which is refined from the practical problem.

2.3.3.1 Principles in International Administrative Law: Economic Development Should Not Be the Primary Goal of the Legislation

There is a debate on the legal attributes of market access between administrative law and economic law. The study in this book regards market access of TCMP in the EU as an issue at the intersection of administrative law and international economic law. Some also treat the latter as international administrative law when focusing mainly on the relations between states in the international economy.

Carol Harlow (2006) wrote an article titled *Global Administrative law: The Quest for Principles and Values*, discusses the principles of administrative law from the national and regional to the international. The article mentions the principles of free trade put forth by the proponents of economic liberalism. It explains the values from a good governance perspective, including 'transparency, participation and accountability' promoted by the World Bank (WB) and the International Monetary Fund (IMF), and it also discusses some values concerning human rights embodied by the due process principle in the administrative law of EU Member States (Harlow 2006, p. 187). Carol (2006, p. 191) wrote that the 'European system acknowledges the primary function of administrative law as being the control of public power'. Similar to the definition of classical administrative law on the regional and global level, international administrative law is treated as a 'legal order with fixed and stable general principles, together with formal rights of access to courts for the resolution of disputes' between states (Harlow 2006, p. 195). As an example, Harlow (2006) discusses the early days of the European Community (EC), wherein the EC obliged its Member States to ensure that their economies are organised and run in accordance with the principles of the market and competition, which reflects the capitalist model of running economies. 'Four freedoms', including free movement of persons, goods, services and capital, 'have long been read as an economic constitution coupled to an economic concept of citizenship' and secured by national systems with administrative law focused on legality and due process (Harlow 2006, p. 193). Besides the EU, '[t]he same capitalist, market, economic ideology forms the background of the values of the WTO' and other international economic organisations, such as WB and IMF.

Compared to the above classical idea which emphasises due process, Harlow (2006) lists 'the typical modern mixture of administrative law principles', including 'fairness, legality, consistency, rationality and impartiality', and comments that these principles all depend on the rule of law doctrine and address the ideals of 'good government'. The article notes that the UK has moved its emphasis from 'protected official secrecy to freedom of information legislation' (Harlow 2006, p. 193). Referencing Michael Taggart, Harlow (2006), distilled the administrative law values as 'openness, fairness, participation, impartiality, accountability, honesty and rationality'.[6]

Carol noticed that "economic liberalism is increasingly able to accept 'an ethical floor of responsibilities' applicable alike to multinational enterprises and in international rule making", which calls for principles with elements of openness, participation, transparency, and accountability for administrative law. The evolution of the 'good governance' principle transpired during the period of the world's Cold War. On that occasion, democratisation in the context of a free economy was treated as a way of compelling governments to be more accountable. Good governance was expanded to be:

> [A]n efficient public service; an independent judicial system and legal framework to enforce contracts; the accountable administration of public funds; an independent auditor responsible to a representative legislature; respect for the law and human rights at all levels of government; a pluralistic institutional structure and a free press (Leftwich 1993).

Carol (2006, p. 196) stresses that '[t]he good governance principle of transparency is a democratic right of citizenship, a kind of transparency that courts have been notably unwilling to provide'. However, 'classical administrative law systems, set up for the protection of private rights and interests, may actually characterise government information as private property, to which one has no right of access.' From this point, transparency distinguishes administrative law from private law, and administrative law needs to adjust the relation between the individual and the collection of individuals. Harlow mentions the scholars who have engaged in disclosing the relation between international administrative law and individual interests. 'Neo-liberalism' holds that the benefit of an 'economic constitution'

[6]'Public law (lat. ius publicum) is that part of law which governs relationships between individuals and the government, and those relationships between individuals with are of direct concern to society'. See, Martin (2003). E.g., constitutional law, administrative law, tax law and criminal law, and procedural law.

based on international free trade is not opposed to the protection of fundamental rights or the environment. 'Regulatory functionalism' claims that the market is an accountability vehicle under the control of governmental regulation. While Petersmann (2001) stresses the enforcement of WTO rules through recourse in domestic court proceedings, he points out that in the course of enforcement abuses to international trade by the protectionist government is restricted so that the freedom of individuals is protected.

Openness as a principle of administrative law is also highlighted as it exists almost everywhere. For instance, in the U.S., 'the AAPA opened up space to interested parties in rule-making procedures, which citizen action groups later claimed in the name of democratic participation' (U.S. 1946 Administrative Procedure Act). However, a problem came up from claiming the openness principle nationally in an international case, the WTO *Shrimp/Turtles* adjudication (WTO AB 1998, WT/DS58/AB/R). The case was about the compatibility of American legislation. Those countries most affected by the new legislation claimed that 'the [U.S.] had an obligation to apply principles of equal treatment and not to discriminate arbitrarily or unfairly against different countries'. So, they argued, this must involve a further right of participation at the rule-making stage. The AB finally required the U.S. to follow the established consultation provisions and to treat interested parties in good faith. Harlow commented that the AB has applied a 'thin' rule of law style of reasoning, so the case was only applicable within WTO procedural rules (WTO AB 1998, WT/DS58/AB/R para 16).

To sum up, economic development is stressed in Harlow's analysis of international administrative law. At the same time, Carol has noticed the contradiction between government powers and individual rights. When the contradiction happens within a country, it is a matter of national/regional administrative law, but when it involves international trade, it becomes a matter of international administrative/economic law. This book holds that economic development for the purpose of individual wealth, is just a medium to reach some intrinsic demand of humans, the law must concern other goal(s) as well. Sometimes, it is necessary to weaken the concentration on economic development to find a way out when economic development is stuck. The issue of market access of TCMP in the EU is a typical example, and the primary concern of relevant laws is public health instead of free trade as in WTO rules. The openness principle is extremely important in the course of legislation. In addition, the opinions of experts from medical science must be respected and widely collected. Lawmakers should pay close attention to the state of art on the development of ST.

2.3.3.2 An Analysis of the Legal Factors of Pharmaceutical Law and the Issue of Market Access of TCMP

The analysis of market access of TCMP now moves from a discussion of the general principles of administrative law to specific administrative law. On one hand, TCMP legislation must be linked to scientific research, because the pharmaceutical ST widely influences the law in the EU as well as at the international level. On the other hand, the law always considered and emphasizes the continued development of the pharmaceutical industry. How to combine these two is a challenge in modern pharmaceutical law. Therefore, this part of the book ascertains the aims of EU pharmaceutical law and puts particular effort into exploring the relations between the scientific research of TCMP and pharmaceutical law on the issue of market access in the EU.

2.3.3.2.1 The Purpose of Any Rules Concerning the Production and Distribution of Medicinal Products in the EU

As stated in Directive 65/65/EEC, 'the primary purpose of any rules concerning the production and distribution of medicinal products must be to safeguard public health'. However, as emphasised in the next paragraph, 'this objective must be attained by means which will not hinder the development of the pharmaceutical industry or trade in medicinal projects within the community' (65/65/EEC 1965). As illustrated in the foreword of the Directive, the attitude towards the goal of public health and the fairness of trade within the common market of the EU is clear. Under the prerequisite of safeguarding public health, fair trade must be considered within the common market. Therefore, the goal of safeguarding public health must be put in the priorities of EU pharmaceutical law in forms of Regulations, Directives, Guidance and so on.

The use of medicinal products is to cure diseases and maintain health. EU Directives relating to medicinal products have put this goal as a priority. However, law cannot cure diseases directly, and it is necessary to find out the logical chain between law and public health. Law can better serve the goal of safeguarding public health only if people ascertain the logical chain between law and public health.

Jural Relation in Pharmaceutical Law

Let's start discussion of this logical chain from the legal side. It is easier to take the 'modern' jural relation concept, first, where law belongs to social science and it adjusts certain social relations via setting up the rights and obligations of legal subjects. Jural relation analysis is for clarifying the nexus between different elements in the course of transferring the social phenomenon to the legal phenomenon. Nexus is 'a complicated series of connections between different things' (Hornby 2000). Jural relation can be analysed by measurable factors in law, including legal subjects, legal objects, rights and obligations, or power and duty.

Social relations, hereinto, refers to the relations formed between persons and during the time people produce, exchange, allocate and consume products and products' materials. Therefore, if we analyse a legal issue, we must ascertain what social relation we are talking about; based on that, we can summarise with whose

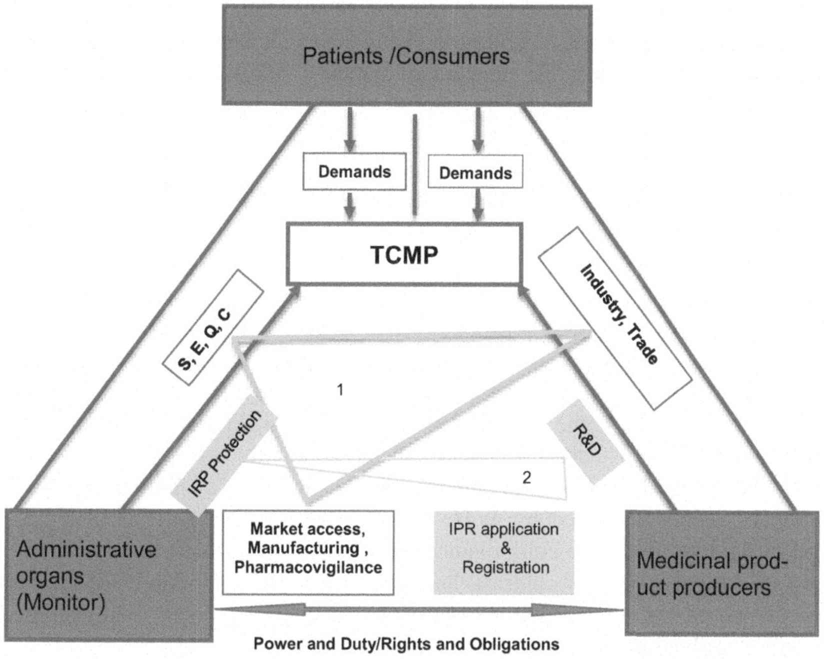

[Note] S, E, Q, C: Safety, Efficacy, Quality, Consistency; R&D: Research and Development

Fig. 2.1 Jural relations relevant to market access of TCMP

rights and obligations we are concerned and what the rights and obligations are in the social relation. Then, we can talk about how to adjust the relation.

What Is the Social Relation We Are Talking About?

We are discussing the issue of market access of TCMP. Basically, it is an issue arising before the phase of exchanging medicinal products in the market. In this phase, producers want to put their products on the market for a return of value, the primary goal. By contrast, patients, who are the consumers of the medicinal product, only need the products which can fulfil their demand, which is to cure certain diseases and safeguard their health. Along with the supervision role of the administrative organ illustrated in the next question, the social relation is comprised of patients, producers and administrative organs. It is embodied by the outmost triangle in Fig. 2.1.

Who Can Help Find the Balanced Interest Between Producers and Consumers?

The administrative organ functions through its staff. In the case of market access of TCMP, the staff of the administrative organ is a group of people who can serve the public interest in the period of market access of medicinal products, specifically through evaluating, authorising and supervising the medicinal products to make sure that the product can meet the demand of patients. Social relations refer to the relations between people in society. The jural relation is a social relation in the legal framework. When the jural relation is discussed in the issue of market access of TCMP, it mainly refers to a dynamic mechanism composed of rights and obligations borne by administration organs and products' providers including manufacturers, distributors, pharmacies and practitioners.

Different Interests of Various Stakeholders Make the Issue Complicated

The situation surrounding market access of TCMP in the EU is complicated due to the different interests and concerns of various stakeholders. First, the premise represented in Fig. 2.1 is the existing legal rules as provided by law. The affiliation of the jural relation of market access is debated nationally between administrative law and economic law. However, internationally, the issue of market access of a product is mainly governed by WTO law, and market access is affiliated to a different jural relation. The consequence is that different affiliations raise different focuses for legislatures. By contrast, legal practice in this area is not so confusing when compared with the academic discussion, since any argument in litigation can be easily dissolved by application of the proper law.

Second, the authorisation of market access is the first valve for safety control, and the authorisation is given by specific administrative departments in different countries. The centre of the graph, triangle 1, shows the essential administrative legal nexus of market access of TCMP. The patient's need is the TCMP which can effectively cure the diseases, while the TCMP producers has the first intention to make profit through trade of the product.[7] Therefore, one of the important functions of pharmaceutical law is to find coherence between the goals of the drug producers and the patient with the law authorising the relevant function to administrative organs. The competent authority ensures public interests through monitoring the safety, efficacy, and quality of the pharmaceutical product in the phase of market access.

Third, internationally, authorisation for market access is an administrative procedure which may result in non-tariff barriers to trade. Therefore, both importing and exporting countries are trade-related parties. Encouraging free trade is the primary goal of WTO law. The trade of TCMP brings the possibility of accessing the product to the patient. At the same time, free trade has been proven to be in favour of an efficient economy globally by either the doctrine of absolute advantage or the doctrine of comparative advantage (Smith 1776, 1908; Wikipedia 2020). The authorisation controls market access of TCMP together with other administrative

[7] In practice, TCM practitioners can provide TCMP as well. Here the situation mainly discussed refers to the medicinal product produced through manufacturers.

organs, such as customs and inspection and quarantine institutions in international trade.

To make the research situation simpler, the study in this book treats the three groups of subjects, including patients, producers and administrative organs in a single framework instead of two actors in a jural relation. Any of the three is different with a third party in law, and they are weighed as equally important in the framework. The graph illustrates the essential administrative legal relation as well as other relations relevant to market access of TCMP. This helps in a comprehensive analysis of the whole affair. It also reflects the relation between patients, administrative organs and producers by setting up the position of TCMP in the centre, where rights and obligations are the nexus in law. It presents the relation between TCMP and each of these three subjects, where the relation between TCMP and the patient contains the primary goal of pharmaceutical law, to protect public health. This leads to legal concerns about the relation between the administrative organ and TCMP and the relation between providers and TCMP.

The essential elements that can describe or adjust relations by law are shown by two triangles of Fig. 2.1. Triangle 1 designates the essential issues surrounding market access of TCMP. Where, authorisation, safety/efficacy/quality control and trade are the essential issues, and public health is the primary concern for each. Triangle 2 frames intellectual property rights (IPR) protection. The system of IPR protection is created and inclines to encourage or protect the interests of drug providers. Triangle 1 highlights the jural relation between the administrative organ and producers, where their power or rights and obligations directly point to TCMP. Therefore, market access of TCMP is a thing covered by the jural relations between two of the three subjects. IPR protection is implicated when the aim of the pharmaceutical law is fulfilled, whereas *vice versa*, well-operated authorisation system and IPR protection systems ensure better achievement of the primary goal of pharmaceutical law for regulating the social relation between the three subjects.

The Debate on Affiliating Market Access with Economic Law or Administrative Law

The study first holds that administrative law mainly adjusts the jural relation between administrative organs and their counterparts, simultaneously taking into account the third party's interests. The third party's interest, as a whole, is the public interest, which is the essential goal of administrative law. By contrast, domestic economic law mainly adjusts the relation between the monitor of the market and the participants in the market, while WTO law, as an international economic law, adjusts the relation between the contracting parties.

Second, the object of the general administrative jural relation can be very wide and narrowed by the power of the administrative organ and the right and obligations of the counterpart. It can be a behaviour, tangible or intangible property. The object of economic law also can be a behavior, tangible or intangible property. But it is pointed by specific economic relations.

Finally, the rights and obligations obtained by adhering to administrative law and economic law are quite different. Regarding market access of TCMP, pharmaceutical law is a typical administrative law concerning safety, efficacy and quality control of pharmaceutical products, even though it noticeably concerns pharmaceutical economic issues, such as free trade and the development of industry within the EU (Directive 2001/83/EC 2001). The main issue for market access of TCM within the EU more closely relates to pharmaceutical law. By contrast, the issue for international trade of TCMP is between the EU and China rather than an issue only within the EU. In addition, WTO law is a part of economic law, but mainly for adjusting international trade relations between its Members, which relates to international trade between the EU and China. Therefore, market access of TCMP is a cross-sector issue between EU pharmaceutical law and WTO law.

Rights/Power and Obligations/Duty

When applying for market access of a new medicinal product, the competent administrative organ and TCMP producer are the main legal subjects, while patient(s) are related interested party. Specifically, the administrative organs monitor the market order of medicinal products in the phases of production, market access and sales of medicinal products. The administrative counterpart is drug providers, and they must properly operate their business according to pharmaceutical law and under the supervision of administrative organs. In the course of the application process, rights of the applicant mainly exist in the procedural aspects. By contrast, the applicant has an obligation to behave in compliance with the law in order to gain market access; and the applicant needs to sufficiently provide the information required by law for obtaining the license. Therefore, decision-making power is held by the competent authority and is difficult to be challenged by the applicant. The substantive power includes setting up standards, judging the risk assessment data and materials provided by the applicant, making decisions on the approval and so on. Therefore, it is important to set up the mechanism for checks and balances of that power. Within the mechanism, the public interest decides the core function of the power, and the professional experts provide scientific advice for either setting up the technical standards, providing legal proposals on guidelines or assisting in implementing the power in each individual case.

Legal Object

Regarding the rights/obligations of the applicant and the power/duty of the administrative authority, the legal object generally points to an act or non-act of the competent authority in market access of TCMP. For example, to access the market, the medicinal product must be authorised by the administrative authority, and in such case authorising or not authorising the license is the object. From the view of providers, they have the right to ask for the act of issuing a license for their medicinal products to enter the market and have the obligation to provide sufficient information for the assessment. From the view of the administrative authority, to issue or to reject issuing the license based on the published legislations, standards or guideline is the object of the power.

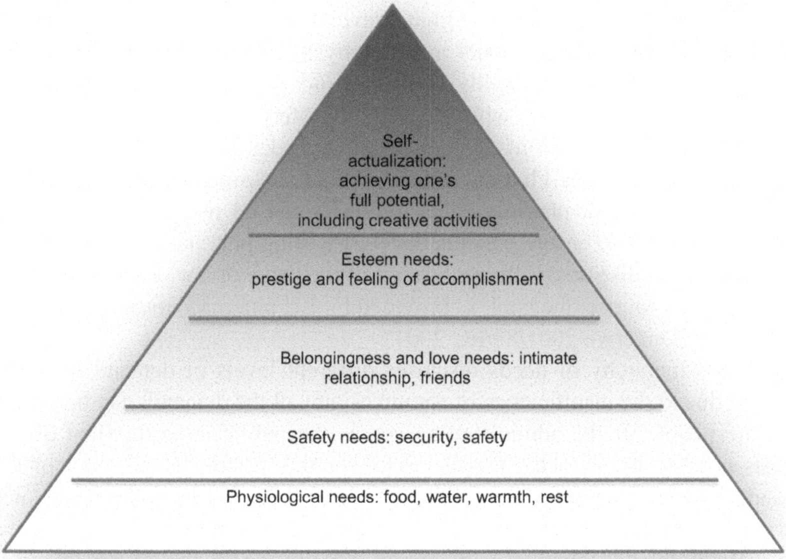

Fig. 2.2 Maslow's hierarchy of needs

What Is the Role of TCMP in the Jural Relation?

In the jural relation of market access, TCMP is not directly impacted by the contradiction and unity of the right/power and obligation/duty. However, when judging the rationality and fairness of the approval criteria in technical regulations, standards and guidelines, it becomes an essential object. Once again, Puntschart's opinion on jural relation, which focuses on the relation between person and thing, is more applicable hereinto. Understanding the legal concept of TCMP becomes one of the key issues to reach a decision of act or non-act for the competent authority.

Patient in the Jural Relation

Patients are not the legal subject in the jural relation of market access of TCMP, but the study agrees with the current EU pharmaceutical law that their demand is a reflection of the public interest in health which is the primary legislative goal. So, protecting the public interest is the basis for setting up the administrative authority as well as enacting pharmaceutical law.

Maslow's hierarchy of needs provided an analysis on the demands of people. As shown in the Fig. 2.2,[8] the most basic need of humans is for physical survival, including physiological needs and safety needs. Psychological needs and

[8]Information in the figure is referenced to *A Theory of Human Motivation* (Maslow 1943).

self-fulfilment needs are higher level demands. One must satisfy lower level deficit needs before progressing on to meet higher level growth needs' (Mcleod 2017). The basic needs in the five-stage model include physiological needs and safety needs. Physiological needs include bodily comforts, such as needs for air, food, drink, shelter, warmth, sex and sleep, while the need for safety seeks to keep humans out of danger, such as protection from elements, security, order, law, stability, and freedom from fear (Mcleod 2017). Pharmaceutical products help people meet the needs of safety, so, the need for pharmaceutical products can be put in the second layer. Understanding how to ensure patients' safety by using pharmaceutical products, in the case of curing diseases, is the realisation of the value of law. Therefore, law sets up a mechanism to meet the goal, as provided by EU pharmaceutical law, to protect public health (Directive 2001/83/EC 2001).

Maslow's hierarchy of needs discloses different levels of demand for people. However, due to the insufficiency of resources, not all the demands can be achieved by all the people. If the administration serves the public interest, when different interests need to be protected the hierarchy roughly references an order of those demands for law to achieve. It is in line with nature to make the upper layers' needs give way to the lower layers' needs when there is a conflict of interest between people. When the development of economy is claimed as a goal of law, a question should be borne in mind for what purpose? If the trade issue touches the first layer of needs, it should always be given priority. But a pure economic goal for enlarging wealth cannot be a proper or meaningful goal. Indeed, trade should be facilitated. Since trade is a link to fulfilling need(s) in modern society, facilitating trade should be concerned with fulfilling needs. In addition, law has territoriality—it focuses on the people's need, locally or regionally. Therefore, it is possible to have different standards or demands in play between states. The study holds that national law and standards should be fully respected, since national law is supposed to reflect the proper needs of the state, ideally the local people.[9] Internationally, the higher standards that individuals hold should not be lowered to meet the demands of trade, even though the individuals have the opportunity to implement a lower standard. If a lower standard is implemented, the producers in a state holding the higher standard of the product find it easier to trade in the state with lower standard. Therefore, the study in this book advocates for the self-restriction of trade by countries for economic balance and sustainable development as concerned between states.

Until this point, a logical link between the administrative authority's work and public health has been found for market access of TCMP. The administrative authority primarily represents and protects the benefit of patients, which is the essential reason that the administrative authority exists. The legal factors, including

[9]In practice, it is often not the truth. Since not many people, enterprises or states would undertake non-profitable business in international trade for only concerning the public interest of the importing state. The state concerns the interest of the state the most, ideally the majority of people in the society.

subject, object and right/obligations and power/duty have been discussed in a legal framework. Now, we can move to the next question: How can the jural relation, framed by triangle 1 in Fig. 2.1, be adjusted.

How Do We Adjust the Jural Relation?

When we discuss this question, the reason for setting up an administrative authority between drug producers and patients must be kept in mind: public health. With that, the main task becomes determining the conditions in which the administrative authority can issue a license, considering the public health. Protecting public health is the primary goal of pharmaceutical law, but it is not the measurable indicator of law. Therefore, pharmaceutical law requires measurable indicators to be set up for an administrative authority to make a decision. Where does the law find the indicators, then? Medical science provides clues. Safety, efficacy and quality control are the factors people use to evaluate a medicinal product in the pharmaceutical scientific area for the consideration of public health. Each factor is defined and assessed by measurable indicators through using risk assessment tools. By enacting legislation and publishing guidelines and standards, the concept of public health is conveyed to law by defining relevant concepts of pharmaceutical science in law.

Pharmaceutical law can regulate the legal relations between the administrative authority and medicinal products' producers. Law requires the producers to provide information that is consistent with the standards set up in medical scientific area for the consideration of public health, and the administrative authority is able to evaluate the information and consider whether or not to authorise a license for market access for a new medicinal product.

The Jural Relation Involving Patients

Patients are users of medicinal products. Their interest has been treated as the priority by pharmaceutical law, which is summarised as public health. Regarding the market access of TCMP, the administrative authority does not set up the relation with patients directly but holds the aim of executing the administrative regulations to protect patients' interests. Consequently, its power is monitored by the patients. By contrast, there are direct legal relations between producers and patients/consumers once the latter obtain the medicinal product from the former. The relations between producers and patients/consumers can be directly adjusted by civil law or commercial law, and some other administrative laws, such as the law on protection of the rights and interests of consumers, can intervene as well. Among all types of administrative law, pharmaceutical law is an important legal source which has a significant effect on the relation between these two. For instance, non-registered medicinal products are banned from accessing patients/consumers except otherwise provided by law. In the case where a medicinal product causes serious injury to a patient, criminal penalties might be applied. Therefore, a broad understanding of pharmaceutical law as a set of rules—instead of one piece or one kind of—law is necessary.

IPR Protection vs. Authorisation of Pharmaceutical Product

Legislators should consider both the interest of consumers/patients and the drug producers when regulating TCMP access to the market, which forms a dynamic legal framework. On one hand, the advanced technology can be sold and bought via an IPR trading system. An IPR protection system encourages the development of technology via advocating fair and efficient competition. A well-functioning IPR protection system guarantees a return on the discovery or innovation of the medicinal product. Patent registration is not compulsory for the authorisation of market access, but it is always spontaneously done by the producers. On the other hand, it is notable that patent protection focuses more on the utility, novelty and inventiveness instead of safety, efficacy and quality control. But safety, efficacy and quality control are the essential factors of public health. Therefore, risk assessment is compulsory in the phase of market access authorisation. Safety, efficacy and quality control are abstract concepts, and they can be assessed by science only if the factors are identified. In addition, the risk assessment's approach and its results should be expressed clearly and accurately by using legal terms in the form of either hard law or soft law.

Above all, the market access of TCMP in the EU lies in a complicated net of a jural relation composing rights/power and obligation/duty between the administrative authority and medicinal product producers, wherein the patients'/consumers' interest centres on perceptions. However, considering that the difficulty of market access of TCMP to the EU composes the main, current practical problem, it is proper to focus on the legal position of TCMP in EU pharmaceutical law and analyse the administrative organ's power in approving market access in order to seek the reason and solution for difficulties.

2.3.4 Legislative Techniques for Transferring the Concept of Public Health Into Law

Pharmacy, short for pharmaceutical science links directly to public health. It is a subject based on medical science, and it treats the human body as the research subject. It is patient-oriented, and its research focuses on the medicinal product as a way to prevent and cure human diseases (Men 2016, p. 3).

Medicinal products are used to cure diseases and maintain health. EU directives relating to medicinal products have set safeguarding public health as a primary goal of pharmaceutical law (Directive 2001/83/EC 2001, Preamble, Recital 2). The problem is that law adjusts the behaviours of legal subjects or the relation between subject and thing, but law cannot cure diseases directly. Therefore, policymakers should concern themselves with the development of scientific status and use legislative techniques for transferring the concept of public health into law.

Pharmaceutical law can realise the regulation of public health through three legislative techniques: (1) ascertain and define the basic terms relating to the medicinal product; (2) set up reasonable standards for medicinal products according to the state of development of medical science; and (3) adjust the behaviours of manufacturers, distributors and administrative organs which are the main legal subjects of pharmaceutical law. Among these three, the first two provide the more substantive content of the law related to the phase of market access of TCMP, while the third one deals with procedural rules.

2.4 Theories in WTO Law and Pharmaceutical Law

This part summarises some detailed legal theories provided by WTO law and pharmaceutical law. These theories make up the legal framework and are the bases to analyse the legal question central to the study in this book.

2.4.1 WTO Law Theories

International Trade Law theories include Fair Competition, Non-Discrimination, Transparency and so on. They are agreed upon by WTO Members, so they form restrictions on national law based on the legal custom *pacta sunt servanda*. Furthermore, specifically, the precautionary principle in Agreement on the Application of Sanitary and Phytosanitary Measures (SPS) and technique regulations in TBT pertain directly to the issue of market access of TCMP in the EU.

The Fair Competition principle requires that all members and exporters should not take any unfair trade measures in international trade competition or take any measure which may generate undue distortions.

The non-discrimination principle includes General Most Favoured Nation Treatment (MFN) and NT. The former means 'any advantage, favour, privilege or immunity granted by any contracting party to any product originating in or destined for any other country shall be accorded immediately and unconditionally to the like product originating in or destined for the territories of all other contracting parties' (WTO 1994b, GATT, art I); the latter essentially means treating foreigners/foreign products and local products equally within the territory of a state. NT is a core principle for assessing the legality of the pharmaceutical rules applied to TCMP in the EU.

Transparency requires members of the WTO to publish their legislations promptly and sufficiently, and ensure easy access of such legislations to foreigners as well (WTO 1994b, GATT, art X).

The 'precautionary principle' is a notion that provides basis to take protective action if scientific proof of a risk is uncertain. In other words, 'action should not be delayed simply because full scientific information is lacking' (European Parliamentary Research Service 2015). The principle gives countries importing TCMP a basis on which to set obstacles on international trade when necessary (WTO 1994a, SPS, art 5, para. 7).

WTO legislation on market access of medicinal products is a dynamic procedure, in other words, it is the result of the development of contradictions between NT and the precautionary principle. The application of NT and the precautionary principle should be consistent with the rule of WTO law. This is further explained in Chapter V.

In addition, principles of the diffusion of law from a perspective of globalisation can be considered when discussing the possibility and feasibility of deferring to the original legal system of TCMP in the EU. 'Diffusion' expresses the phenomenon of the spread of one liquid throughout a second liquid, thereby transforming the character of both (Westbrook 2006). Integration between Western conventional medicine and TCM is ongoing in the scientific research arena. It is meaningful to take a global view in considering the development of TCM through pushing the establishment of international standards. The EU and China both have their own concerns and legal framework for TCM, whilst they also have the same regulative targets—safeguarding the health of the patient, better supervising the traditional medicine market and developing medicinal science. The common goals make diffusion between laws possible. However, the divergence between the EU and China clearly exists in culture, medical practice and law, further compared in Chapter IV for the purpose of assessing EU pharmaceutical law.

2.4.2 Legal Theories Relevant to Pharmaceutical Law

The study of this book directly connects with pharmaceutical law. However, principles of public health set out in EU fundamental law and legal theories in the branch of medical law set up the umbrella principles of pharmaceutical law.

2.4.2.1 The General Regulatory Goals on Public Health in the EC Treaty

The issue of public health is mentioned in Article 152 of Part three of the EC Treaty (TEC 2002, art 152). The EU tries to ensure a high level of human health protection. The field of action includes improving public health, preventing human illness and diseases and obviating sources of danger to human health by promoting research into their causes, their transmission and their prevention, as well as health information and education (645/96/EC 1996). The goals on public health reflect the basic demand of people in life and give the basic demand primary consideration in legislation.

2.4.2.2 Legal Theories in Western Medical Law

A discussion of medical law theories requires a discussion of medical ethical theories. In the West, it often involves the following aspects. First, teleological theories, which include theories that are goal-orientated or consequentialist. In teleological theories, pleasure, knowledge, virtue and justice are considered as utilitarian when applied to medicine. Some philosophers introduced deontological principles. Deontological principles concern autonomy, beneficence, non-maleficence, justice and veracity. Moreover, religion, contractarianism and feminism also put effects on medical law. Second, among these theories, autonomy is highly relevant to the issue of market access of TCM hereinto. Referring to the ethical principle of autonomy, it includes freedom of action, freedom of choice and effective deliberation. It requires that the person who makes a choice in medicine be mature both in age and mentality. And the action is intentional, based on an understanding of circumstances without controlling influence. The principle gives people the basic right to choose TCM, and the law should respect the basic right of the patients. Third, beneficence and non-maleficence refer to a doctor's obligations to ensure the medical benefit for the patient with as little harm as possible and with respect for an autonomous person's deliberated choices for themselves via professional consultations. Fourth, referring to justice, all patients should have an equal chance to access assistance for their illness, avoiding the consequences brought by differences in level of poverty or social status and so on. Fifth is veracity, a controversial principle, which is often connected with therapy instead of the medicinal product *per se*. Finally, a publicly funded, publicly administered, and publicly delivered system is widely required to be equally available for both the treatment and pharmaceuticals (Maclean 2001, p. 250).

2.5 A Reflection on the Issue of Market Access from Economic and Political Angles

Market access has traditionally been analysed from a narrow international trade perspective. From this perspective, it links to conditions, tariff and non-tariff measures, set by countries for the entry of specific goods, foreign direct investment or services into their markets. Noticeably, the WTO provides a platform for negotiating the market access issue of trade and trade-related investment, service and IPR protection. Some hold a broad economic view on market access and claim that market access is a broad concept that can be manifested in three sets of separate but interrelated elements. It 'results from an economy possessing the right set of public institutions, an appropriate regulatory environment, and the requisite network industries' (Hugo 2006). Under the broad conceptualisation, the goals in the research of cross legal sector between administrative law and economic law are to prevent bureaucracy and to increase the efficiency of administration (Turkel and Turkel

2016). Market access is also discussed as pharmacoeconomics and refers to the process by which a company gets a medicinal product to market. Hereinto, the study in this book adopts the narrow concept of market access and discusses the issue mainly from the international trade law perspective, as well as the most relevant national pharmaceutical law legislation. Since TCMP has not yet been possible to meet the scaled manufacture in the EU, the current debate on market access of TCMP to the EU focuses more on the scientific consideration of safety and efficacy instead of market competition, fairness and the bureaucracy of administration.

Generally, three theories on administrative governance, which actually reflect political views, are widely discussed. One is traditional public management theory which aims at limiting corruption and bringing expertise to administration by establishing a more autonomous legal rational organisation. A second theory is new public management focusing almost exclusively on 'sharply reducing public bureaucracy through measures and organisational practices based on economic efficiency'. The third is public value theory that 'aims at reinvigorating the role of publicly formed values' by noticing the, sometimes, unavoidable market failure (Turkel and Turkel 2016, p. 1). Legal values undertaken by administration—including economy safety, social responsibility, fairness and so on—the attention placed on public value and on making up for the deficiency of the market economy in economic theories. However, the study in this book focuses on the substantive rules of administrative authorisation on market access of TCMP in the EU, rather than discussing the justification and efficiency of the governance. Governance and economic concern are not essential issues, unless they directly affect the authorisation of market access for TCMP in the EU. However, indeed, they compose the external environments.

2.6 Chapter Summary

Whether the Anglo-american system of law or continental system of law, a system of law will have reason to exist so long as it serves the general demand of people. Maslow's hierarchy of needs discloses different levels of demands of people. However, due to the insufficiency of resources, all of those demands cannot be met for all people. The hierarchy references an order by which law should achieve those demands. Therefore, law is supposed to discourage anything or any behaviour which is contrary to the basic demands of humans. Herein, regarding the specific case of applying EU pharmaceutical law and WTO law to market access of medicinal products, it is proper to set public health as the primary goal, while taking trade facilitation second.

To achieve the primary goal of pharmaceutical law, the relation between law and ST must be paid attention to. Medicinal science provides measurable indicators for assessing the safety, efficacy, and quality control of market access of TCMP. Law transforms those technical criteria so that they are accessible and transparent to the public, and at the same time it takes into account the uncertainty of science on judging market access of certain medicinal products.

Through this analysis, EU pharmaceutical law and WTO law are deduced as the essential laws addressing the issue of market access of TCMP in the EU, which frame the legal research scope of the main question. This chapter also has explored the jurisprudential methodologies for answering the question, and many scholars are engaged in dissecting the jural relation. Indeed, jural relation analysis comprises the unique methodology of analysing the social relation through law. Thereinto, relations between persons and/or legal persons lying in the social phenomenon can be split into measurable factors for the application of law. Subsequently, legal responsibilities in national law or sanction/retaliation provided by international law can be placed upon the rights and obligation of the legal subjects. It also can be employed in analysing the rights and obligations of Members of the WTO. However, the methodology is not good enough to lead to a satisfying result for analysing the case of the market access of TCMP since it loses sight of the significance of exploring the relation between a thing and a person(s). Recalling the original meaning of the jural relation in Roman law, drawing attention to the legal nexus between the thing and person is meaningful for approaching the legislative goal in the case of market access of TCMP. Therefore, the study in this book places the emphasis of the following chapter on TCMP in law.

References

65/65/EEC (1965) 65/65/EEC of 26 January 1965 on the Approximation of Provisions Laid down by Law, Regulation or Administrative Action Relating to Proprietary Medicinal Products. OJ 022: 369–373

645/96/EC (1996) Decision No. 645/96/EC of the European Parliament and of the Council of 29 March 1996 Adopting a Programme of Community Action on Health Promotion, Information, Education and Training within the Framework for Action in the Field of Public Health (1996 to 2000). OJ L 95:1–7

Baldwin GB (1966) Law in support of science: legal control of basic research resources. Georgetown Law J 54:559–592

Bix B (2010) Natural law theory. In: Patterson D (ed) A companion to philosophy of law and legal theory, 2nd edn. Blackwell Publishing Ltd, London, pp 209–227

Chris LP et al (eds) (1998) Health care cost, quality and outcomes: ISPOR book of terms, 1st edn. Princeton, ISPOR Lexicon

Clark CE (1922) Relations, legal and otherwise. Illinois Law Q 5(26)

Coleman JL, Leiter B (2010) Legal positivism. In: Patterson D (ed) A companion to philosophy of law and legal theory, 2nd edn. Blackwell Publishing Ltd, London, pp 228–248

Corbin A (1921) Jural relations and their classification. In: Faculty scholarship series. Yale Law School, Paper 2873, pp 226–238

Cornforth M (1967) Marxism and the Linguistic Philosophy. Lawrence & Wishart, London Part II Chap. 7, pp 245–263

Datta-Chaudhuri M (1990) Market failure and government failure. J Econ Perspect 4(3):25–39

Directive 2001/83/EC (2001) Directive 2001/83/EC of the European Parliament and of the Council of 6 November 2001 on the Community Code Relating to Medicinal Products for Human Use. OJ L 311:67–128

European Commission (2016) Services and Investment in EU Trade Deals Using 'Positive' and 'Negative' Lists
European Parliamentary Research Service (2015) The Precautionary Principle—Definitions, Applications and Governance
Fetter FA (1924) The economic law of market areas. Q J Econ 38(3):520–529
Feynman RP (1963) The Feynman Lectures on Physics, New Millennium edn. California Institute of Technology, Vol. I Chap. 1
Gardner JA (1961) The sociological jurisprudence of Roscoe Pound. Villanova Law Rev 7 (1):165–192
Garner BA (ed) (2004) Black's law dictionary, 8th edn. Thomson/West Group, p 1217
Gibbons H (1981–1982) The relationship between law and science. Idea 22:43, 47, 51
Harlow C (2006) Global administrative law: the quest for principles and values. Eur J Int Law 17 (1):187–214
Hart HLA (1983) Essays on jurisprudence and philosophy. Clarendon Press, Oxford, pp 49–87, cited in Patterson D (1996, 1999) Philosophy of law and legal theory. Blackwell Publisher Ltd., U.S. & UK
Hornby AS (2000) Nexus. In: Oxford advanced learner's dictionary, 6th edn. Oxford University Press, Oxford, p 857
Hugo S (2006) Jay Squalli and Kenneth Wilson, What Explains Market Access? The World Economic Forum, Working Paper No. 06-08: 3
ITC (n.d.) Market Access Map. http://www.macmap.org/Default.aspx
James W (1891) The moral philosopher and the moral life. Int J Ethics 3(344):346
Kocourek A (1920) Various definitions of jural relation. Columbia Law Rev 20(4):404
Leftwich A (1993) Governance, democracy and development in the third world. Third World Q 14 (3):611
Liu B (2002) Ren Lei Ren Shi Fa Zhan Ben Xing Yu Jie Fang Si Xiang (The Nature of Human's Awareness and Ideological Emancipation). She Hui Ke Xue Yan Jiu 3:41–46
Maclean A (2001) Briefcase on medical law. Cavendish Publishing Limited, London, p 250
Mao T (1937) On contradiction. In: Selected works of Mao Tse-tung. Foreign Languages Press, Peking, Vol. I. In marxists.org (2004) Mao Tse Tung Internet Archive. https://www.marxists.org/reference/archive/mao/selected-works/volume-1/mswv1_17.htm
Martin EA (2003) Oxford dictionary of law, 7th edn. Oxford University Press, Oxford
Maslow AH (1943) A theory of human motivation. Psychol Rev 50:370–396
Mcleod S (2017) Maslow's Hierarchy of Needs. Simply Psychology. https://www.simplypsychology.org/maslow.html
Men R (2016) Yao Shi Guan Li Xue (The Discipline of Pharmacy Administration), 4th edn. China Science Publishing & Media Ltd., Beijing, p 3
OECD (2015) Entrepreneurship at a Glance 2015. OECD Publishing, Paris, p 128. eBook, https://doi.org/10.1787/entrepreneur_aag-2015-en
Olsen F (1984) Socrates on legal obligation: legitimation theory and civil disobedience. Georgia Law Rev 18:929
Oxford Living Dictionaries, Theory. https://en.oxforddictionaries.com/definition/theory
Packer M (2010) Science of qualitative research. Cambridge University Press, London
Patterson D (1996, 1999) Philosophy of law and legal theory. Blackwell Publisher Ltd., USA & UK, pp 241, 243, 245
Patterson D (2010) A companion to philosophy of law and legal theory, 2nd edn. Blackwell Publisher Ltd, London
Petersmann E (2001) European and international constitutional law: time for promoting cosmopolitan democracy in the WTO. In: De Burce G, Scott J (eds) The EU and the WTO. Bloomsbury Publishing PLC, Oxford, p 81–110
Pound R (1923) Interpretation of legal history. Cited in Gardner JA (1961) The sociological jurisprudence of Roscoe pound. Villanova Law Rev 7(1):165–192

Pound R (1950) New paths of the law. Cited in Gardner JA (1961) The sociological jurisprudence of Roscoe Pound. Villanova Law Rev 7(1):165–192

Sacred Lotus (n.d.-a) Yin & Yang in Chinese Medicine. https://www.sacredlotus.com/go/foundations-chinese-medicine/get/yin-yang

Sacred Lotus (n.d.-b) The Five Element Relationships in Chinese Medicine. https://www.sacredlotus.com/go/foundations-chinese-medicine/get/5-elements-relationships

Sacred Lotus (n.d.-c) General Symptoms and Their Meaning in TCM. https://www.sacredlotus.com/go/diagnosis-chinese-medicine/get/symptoms-patterns-tcm

Smith A (1776, 1908) An inquiry into the nature and causes of the wealth of nations. Routledge, London, E. P. Dutton, New York. eBook, https://www.gutenberg.org/files/3300/3300-h/3300-h.htm

Stiglitz JE (1989) Market failures, and development, papers and proceedings of the hundred and first annual meeting of the American economic association. Am Econ Rev 79(2):197–203

TEC (2002) Treaty Establishing the European Community (Nice Consolidated Version). OJ C 325:33–184, art 152

Trotsky L (1942) In defence of marxism. In: Woods A, Grant T (eds) (1995) Reason in Revolt—Marxist philosophy and modern science, 1st edn, 8. eBook. https://www.marxist.com/reason-in-revolt-marxist-philosophy-and-modern-science/contents.htm

Turkel E, Turkel G (2016) Public value theory: reconciling public interests, administrative autonomy and efficiency. Rev Pub Adm Manag 4(2)189:1–7

U.S (1946) Administrative Procedure Act. 60 Stat 237, as amended by 80 Stat 378 (1966) and 81 Stat 54 (1967)

Waters M (1995) The thesis of the loss of the perfect market. Br J Sociol 46(3):409–428

WebMD (n.d.) Slideshow: What Your Nails Say about Your Health. http://www.webmd.com/skin-problems-and-treatments/ss/slideshow-nails-and-health?ecd=wnl_wmh_043017&ctr=wnl-wmh-043017_nsl-ld-stry_1&
mb=Y3QLDnLIVCmqGOMs6y6tDZAyWFWqf9PLvZHVlfOijmI%3d

Weiss R (1998) Socrates dissatisfied: an analysis of Plato's Crito. Oxford University Press, New York, p 157

Westbrook DA (2006) Theorizing the diffusion of law in an age of globalization: conceptual difficulties, unstable imaginations, and the effort to think gracefully nonetheless. Harv Int Law J 47(2):489–505

Wight C (2012) The True Meaning of Market Access?, PMLiVE. http://www.pmlive.com/pharma_intelligence/the_true_meaning_of_market_access_422511

Wikipedia (2020) Comparative advantage. https://en.wikipedia.org/wiki/Comparative_advantage#cite_ref-econbook_6-0

Willis HE (1929) Jural relations, by Albert Kocourek. Indiana Law J 4(6):431–435. http://www.repository.law.indiana.edu/ilj/vol4/iss6/5

Woods A, Grant T (1995) Reason in Revolt—Marxist philosophy and modern science, 1st edn. eBook, https://www.marxist.com/reason-in-revolt-marxist-philosophy-and-modern-science/contents.htm. pp 8, 26

WTO (1994a) Agreement on the Application of Sanitary and Phytosanitary Sanitary Measures, (SPS), art 5, para 7

WTO (1994b) General Agreement on Tariffs and Trade (GATT), art I, X

WTO (n.d.) Market Access for Goods. https://www.wto.org/english/tratop_e/markacc_e/markacc_e.htm

WTO AB (1998) WT/DS58/AB/R. India, Malaysia, Pakistan, Thailand v. the U.S., U.S.—Shrimp

Xiao J (2012) A study on the Chinese academic history defined by economic law— focus on the objects adjusted by economic law. J Peking Univ (Philos Soc Sci) 49(5):115–123

Yuan R, Lin Y (2000) Traditional Chinese medicine: an approach to scientific proof and clinical validation. Pharmacol Therapeut 86(2):191–198

Zhang W (2007) Fa Li Xue (Jurisprudence), 3rd edn. Law Press China, Beijing, p 99

Chapter 3
The Conceptualisation of TCMP in Law

TCM includes diagnosis and therapies, of which TCMP is one type of TCM therapies. The nature and development of TCM significantly influences the use of TCMP. So, TCM should first be well-understood when studying the concept of TCMP. However, considered by the West to be only one of many CAMs, it is not recognised by law in a separate system apart from Western conventional medicine. It is difficult to understand the nature of TCM through referencing the knowledge of Western conventional medicine. TCMP is often misunderstood in the West, and consequently, this misunderstanding leads to confusion in legislation. Therefore, this chapter moves from the theoretical aspect of the study to a legal and practical part. It aims at eliminating the misunderstanding of TCM and TCMP and clarifying the position of TCMP in law.

3.1 Understanding Traditional Chinese Medicine from a Semantic Perspective

The mainstream opinion of Western conventional medicine often treats TCM as a non-science-based medicine. Some have put forth criticisisms that TCM was based only on anecdotal information due to the difficulties in figuring out the complexities of biology, physiology, anatomy, biochemistry, genetics, infection and disease pathophysiology and epidemiology. However, much effort has been put in finding scientific evidence of the safety and efficacy of TCMP by scientists as the book reviewed in Chap. 1. Successful cases of using TCMP are too numerous to be mentioned one by one in practice. For instance, a non-quinine-based drug called Artemisinin used for treating advanced cerebral malaria was used in 1979, and the drug was a crudely distilled antimalarial pill based on Artemisinin (WHO/Cui 2009). Today, scientists at the Shanghai Institute of Materia Medica, where Artemisinin was first isolated, have further refined the compound into the most effective

S. Wang, *Market Access of Traditional Chinese Medicinal Product in the EU under WTO Legal Framework*, Economic and Financial Law & Policy – Shifting Insights & Values 5, https://doi.org/10.1007/978-3-030-52848-5_3

antimalarial drug (Gu et al. 1999). The team leader, Ms. Youyou Tu, was honoured with the Nobel Prize in 2015 for this work (Tu 2015). It has been a long time since Chinese physicians started to combine Western conventional and Chinese traditional medicines together to look for solutions for fighting different kinds of diseases (Jiang 2005).

3.1.1 Traditional Medicine vs. *Western Conventional Medicine*

Dr. Anna MacIntosh (1999) initiated an online discussion on many general terminologies of different types of medicines in the West. She discussed conventional, orthodox, allopathic, and biomedical medicine as one group and CAM, natural and holistic medicine as the other. Her discussions provide clues for this book to approach TCM and describe it as if it were an alien compared to Western conventional medicine.

Dr. MacIntosh (1999) set out that the synonymous of conventional medicine in the U.S. included allopathic, orthodox and traditional, biomedical medicine, and explained that the first appearance of the word 'allopathic' was in the late 18th century in reference to the use of therapeutic modalities which were based on the assumption that symptoms need to be treated. The word 'allopathic' is more appropriate when describing this characteristic of conventional medicine in the current Western world since '[t]he focus on treating symptoms appeared to have developed as one of the guiding treatment principles in orthodox medicine'. However, 'conventional' and 'orthodox' were given a 'high degree of credibility'—even though they do not appropriately describe the practice the term refers to—so these terminologies are still widely used in practice. As Dr. MacIntosh noted the power of these terms are so great that to some extent they lead to negating the existence of any other system of medicine.

Dr. MacIntosh (1999) noted that traditional medicine was often used synonymously with orthodox medicine in the West, but '[i]n the sense that allopathic medicine would claim its basis to be scientific, rather than cultural or spiritual, traditional medicine should not be used synonymously with orthodox medicine'. Dr MacIntosh (1999) also compared the term 'biomedical' with 'conventional' and noted that biomedicine was also often used to refer to conventional medicine due to its accurate, scientific and proven feeling attributed to the word by Western medicine doctors (Benjamin et al. 1997, cited in Macintosh 1999).

Therefore, recalling the wording of TCM, it is not difficult to understand why TCM is linked to Chinese cultural rather than a possible medical science in the West. However, if 'traditional' means 'the handing down of opinions, doctrines, practices, rites, and customs, especially by oral communication' as Dr. MacIntosh wrote, TCM would not be 'traditional' medicine. Not only does TCM include knowledge of diagnosis, but also it is a therapeutic method in contrast to allopathic medicine. Many

Chinese ancient books and current scientific research record the rational and scientific essence of TCM. The rational essence encompassed by TCM is continuously explored and researched by scientists. Regarding the entirety 'traditional medicine' as a counter-scientific phenomenon could be just a linguistic game played by people who flaunt Western conventional medicine.

3.1.2 Complementary and Alternative Medicine

It is difficult to define CAM. Since CAM is a general term covering numerous diagnostic and therapeutic methods that exist the outside of the system of orthodox medicine. Therefore, most definitions 'describe CAM by what it is not rather than by what it is' (Ernst et al. 2004). For instance, some explain CAM as:

> [D]iagnosis, treatment and/or prevention which complements mainstream medicine by contributing to a common whole, by satisfying a demand not met by orthodoxy or by diversifying the conceptual frameworks of medicine (Ernst et al. 2004).

CAM is a predominantly private medicine and not often reimbursed within the official healthcare system; the providers of CAM may lack medical training. Non-medical CAM providers generally have their own licensing laws, or frequently operate outside medical licensing laws. The safety and efficacy of many forms of CAM therapy are under-researched according to the standards currently adopted in Western conventional medicine. The *WHO Traditional Medicine Strategy 2014-2023* (WHO Strategy) notes that CAM may be termed as TM, non-conventional medicine, or complementary medicine (WHO 2013). Selectively, the WHO Strategy calls CAM traditional and complementary medicine. Therefore, it is very difficult to unify the scope of CAM, which is in the similar situation of giving a common name. 'CAM' is more like a name often used in the conversation of medical practice than a formal legal term used in binding legislation. Also, different states define the scope of CAM differently. For instance, in Europe, people distinguish acupuncture, anthroposophic medicine, Ayurveda, Chiropractic, herbal medicine/phytotherapy, homeopathy, massage, naprapathy, naturopathy, neural therapy, osteopathy and TCM. Among those, most EU Member States recognise only some of them as legal medicine in their territories (Wiesener et al. 2012). By contrast, TCM is widely used and well recognised both by law and practice in China as a conventional medicine. Some CAMs may be not repelled in Chinese official or people's opinion, but practically they are not regulated in a formal and legal way. No matter in the EU or in China, the ambiguous legal position of the non-regulated CAMs either stops the trade or service of such non-regulated CAMs or brings uncertainty for them accessing the market.

Dr. MacIntosh (1999) discussed whether Alternative medicines were just therapies instead of diagnostic procedures in reality. She suggested that "if the term 'alternative medicine' is simply used to mean therapies, which can be used to treat illness, but are not the 'standard of care', then the paradigm for practice of alternative medicine is the same as orthodox medicine." Complementary medicine was defined to be like alternative medicine, but its efficacy was given more recognisable, so it is often used in conjunction with allopathic therapy. While, the term alternative medicine stands for some medicines that are more controversial in practice. By contrast, the use of complementary medicines was tolerated more even though they are non-standard treatment in the West, either.

In medical practice of China, TCM is not only about therapies, but also includes a series of diagnostic procedures. Ancient TCM books have recorded abundant knowledge on diagnosing symptoms which are profound regarding health checks and have raised wide attention in the West, such as *Huang Di Nei Jing* (See: Unschuld 2011). In addition, to provide a prescription of TCMP must consider the TCM diagnostic mechanism. Chinese people have developed a theoretical basis and system for TCM in a very long period of development of TCM. Of course, China and the West have different attitudes to categorise TCM either in orthodox or CAM group based on many influential factors, such as the practice of using TCM, the knowledge of TCM held by professionals and patients, the developmental level of TCM and so on.

3.1.3 Natural and Integrated Medicine

Natural medicine was considered as 'the science and art of preventing, curing or alleviating ill health using treatment modalities in harmony with the laws of nature' (MacIntosh 1999). Naturopathic medicine, synonymous with natural medicine, began in the U.S. in the early 1900s by German-born healer Benedict Lust. Homeopathy, developed by Samuel Hahnemann, MD in the late 1800s, is treated as another type of natural medicine. Dr. MacIntosh (1999) objectively analysed that homeopathy was one of the natural medicines and had both a systematized theoretical and therapeutic basis. The main theory in homeopathy is to set up a system pursuant to diseases and patients' illness status through, first, ascertaining the substance causing the disease; second, extracting the substance via dilution and succession from somewhere; and third, treating the diseases by using very little dosage. Samuel Hahnemann believed that the substance which causes the disease was the one which can cure the disease (Buie 2020). But this healing method is also criticized and controversial due to its slow remedy's potency (NIH 2018). From this point, TCM is not natural medicine in the West, even though it also focuses on the relationship between nature and human health.

Dr. MachIntosh also explained the term holistic medicine and thought it was an archaic and confusing term. She argued that natural medicine was probably a more appropriate term since there was no system of medicine known as holistic medicine. However, holistic thinking is one of the main theories in TCM. It guides the doctor to treat and adjust the body's health as a whole instead of only on the target spot and raises more attention of people on the philosophical dissection behind TCM. Not only does TCM concern the relationship between nature and the human body but it also observes the relationship between different parts of the body itself.

Therefore, there could be different understandings when using the term TCM between Western and Chinese people. TCM can be categorised as traditional and holistic medicine. In Western people's mind, TCM is not orthodox medicine due to the lack of scientific basis. By contrast, in China, it is orthodox medicine based on experimentalism as well as scientific evidence for curing diseases. Nowadays, more and more TCM doctors combine TCM and Western conventional medicine. Usually, they read the check-up report produced via armamentaria, as well as use the traditional diagnostic methods, including observation, auscultation, interrogation, and palpation, to decide the symptoms and syndrome (Wang and Xu 2014).

3.2 Forms of Existence of TCMP

The WHO defined TM as:

> [T]he sum total of knowledge, skills and practices based on the theories, beliefs and experiences indigenous to different cultures that are used to maintain health ......as well as to prevent, diagnose, improve or treat physical and mental illnesses (WHO/EDM/TRM/2000 2000)

The description of TM in WHO covers the characteristics and different aspects of TCM well. As one type of TM, TCM is a traditional diagnostic method as well as a therapeutic method based on traditional Chinese knowledge. Sequentially, it relates to TCM practitioners who practice the TCM diagnostic method and use TCMP to cure the diseases for patients alongside other Chinese physiotherapies such as acupuncture, Zhong Yi Qigong and massage. However, the definition of TM provided by WHO is still too general and far from enough to comprehensively illustrate the various scenarios of TCM.

3.2.1 Classifications of TCMP

The term TCM is generally used in many situations, but TCM *per se* can stand for either a diagnostic mechanism or a therapeutic method. Referring to the therapeutic method, TCM can be classified into physiotherapy and drug therapy. The former is for instance acupuncture and massage, while the later includes different TCMPs. TCMPs can be classified from different angles. For instance, according to the function of the medicine, TCMPs can be classified into products for detoxification, products for clearing heat, products for regulating the flow of vital energy and removing obstruction, and products for promoting blood circulation and removing blood stasis among others. Depending on the part(s) of the plant used by producing the TCMP, the herbal medicinal product can be classified as a drug made by the root of plants, the leaf of plants, the flower of plants and the skin of plants among others. Depending on the nature of raw materials, TCMPs can be classified into herbal medicine, animal medicine, mineral medicine and so on.

The above classifications contribute mainly to the medical research area. They are important for physicians and practitioners who apply TCM to cure diseases, and also important for pharmacists who distribute TCMP in the market. However, regarding the legal research, TCM as a whole is not a legislative object of current EU law, TCM practitioners and various TCMPs are under the government of different regulations.

In law, TCMPs can be classified as registered or non-registered. They can be dispensed either by pharmacists or practitioners. Registered TCMPs, and even non-registered TCMPs dispensed by registered medicine practitioners, are legally used medicines. Registered medicine can be divided into Proprietary medicinal products and Generic Drugs. Proprietary medicinal products are '[a]ny ready-prepared medicinal product placed on the market under a special name and in a special pack' (Directive 65/65/EEC 1965). It is normally still in the protection period based on patent law if a patent is pending. Therefore, it is also sometimes called a patented medicinal product. However, many traditional Chinese medicinal products may not be applied for patent, instead the TCM practitioners prefer to hold the formulas as secrets. Then, under such circumstances, the trademark law or other IPR protection provisions can be applied. A generic drug is 'a pharmaceutical product, usually intended to be interchangeable with an innovator product that is manufactured without a licence from the innovator company and marketed after the expiry date of the patent or other exclusive rights' (Alfonso-Cristancho et al. 2015). Both proprietary medicinal products and generic drugs include ethical drugs and OTC drugs. An ethical drug is a drug that can be dispensed only with a doctor's prescription, while an OTC drug is a drug that is prepared and packaged for the public's immediate use, and it has been found 'to be safe and appropriate for use without the supervision of a health care professional such as a physician' (U.S. FDA 2015). Non-registered TCMP may be legally used as well. Many herbal medicines might be sold or imported in the form of raw materials or preparations, since Chinese doctors can combine several herbal materials or preparations to cure the disease based on the principles of formulating prescriptions. Under such circumstance, either the doctor or practitioner should have licence to do so.

3.2.2 *Terms Used in Chinese Legislation*

The Drug Registration Regulation of the PRC (SFDA of the PRC 2007) was promulgated according to the Drug Administration Law of the PRC (NPC Standing Committee of the PRC 1984) and the Regulation for the Implementation of the Drug Administration Law of the PRC (State Council of the PRC 2002) to ensure the safety, efficacy and quality control of drugs and standardise drug registration in the mainland of China. It uses 'Chinese Medicine' to represent the TCM discussed in the study herein in order to distinguish TCM and Western medicine. The use of 'Chinese medicine' reflects a perception that TCM is derived from tradition but has been developed to meet contemporary standards.

State council of the PRC published a circular (2003) noted three concepts relating to TCMP which well represent the forms of TCMP often seen in the market. These concepts are Chinese Crude Drugs, Traditional Chinese Medicine Decoction Pieces, and *Zhong Cheng Yao*.

Chinese crude drugs are the raw material of traditional Chinese Medicine decoction pieces and *Zhong Cheng Yao*. People can call it a drug instead of a plant or parts of the body of the animals or mineral materials because all crude drugs need to be sorted, washed, cut and finished so that the part of plant, animal body or mineral material functioning as drugs may be separated efficiently (SDA of the PRC 2002).

Decoction pieces are processed crude drugs that can be used by doctors to formulate a TCMP for patents. They can be given to patients for decocting or be used for producing *Zhong Cheng Yao*. It is notable that Decoction Pieces can only be used under the supervision of Chinese doctors based on the principle of formula of TCM. The way of processing the decoction pieces is regulated in Chinese Pharmacopoeia (Pharmacopeia of the PRC 2015), and processing is aimed at guaranteeing the safe use of TCMP means that crude drugs need to be cleaned, cut, qualified and prepared into small pieces ready for the decoction. A formula granule is a typical decoction piece which is popularly used in current practice. Active ingredients are extracted and processed to make a formula granule from one substance as well as for the convenient use of patients.

In addition, *Zhong Cheng Yao*, or sometimes simplified as *Cheng Yao*, are processed and ready to use products. *Zhong Cheng Yao* is affiliated with proprietary medicine in the Hong Kong Chinese Medicine Ordinance (1999). In other words, from the legal aspect it can be protected via patent law and trademark law. TCMP includes *Zhong Cheng Yao*, as well as prescriptions. In the market, it is important to put OTC on the package of the *Zhong Cheng Yao* if a certain kind of *Zhong Cheng Yao* can be sold without the doctor's prescription. *Zhong Cheng Yao* can be either patented medicinal products or generic drugs.

3.2.3 The Understanding of TCMP in Chinese TCM Practice

A case was recorded for a better understanding of the practice of TCM in China. The patient was a 7-year-old Chinese boy. His symptoms were cough, wheeze in the lungs, accompanied by coryza. The case was recorded in December 2014 in China. An interview with doctor in charge—Guo Xiaoyue—was taken on 9 March 2016 in Zhonglu Hospital of Shandong University of Traditional Chinese Medicine.[1]

[1]Doctor Guo has more than 50-year experience of combined therapy of Chinese and Western medicine. She is expert in curing Children pneumonia. At the very beginning she studied Western

The symptoms were confirmed by the doctor via using TCM diagnostic methods, including observation, auscultation, interrogation, and palpation. Notably, in China, integrative medicine is encouraged; in other words, TCM doctors do not exclude allopathic or Western conventional medicine to treat patients. However, in this case, the doctor did not conduct an X-ray, since she confidently confirmed the symptoms via auscultation and palpation. Another detail: the parents were told that the boy needed to be observed carefully. If the symptom of wheezing was getting worse, IV would be needed. Usually the patient can get the check-up result by using the armamentaria in addition to the traditional diagnostic methods in TCM if the doctor feels it is necessary.

Doctor Guo issued a prescription after the diagnosis in the case, including two *Zhong Cheng Yao* and a dose of decoction pieces, in the EU it is more likely to be called a magistral formula. The period of using the prescription was 5 days.

Firstly, ten substances in a specific amount for each day were given in the form of decoction pieces to compose the dose, including liquorice, Bulbus fritillariae cirrhosae, Radix Ophiopogonis and Fried ephedra processed with honey and so on. With the instruction, they were put into a casserole, immersed in cold water for 30 min. After 30 min, the water with the ingredients was boiled for 15 min the first time, then the boiling water was poured out into a container. More cold water was added in and boiled a second time for another 20 min, and then the water from each boil was mixed together for use.

Secondly, two *Zhong Cheng Yao* were prescription-only medicine, both in the form of granule. One is for clearing the cough and wheeze and the other is for curing coryza, and they are both compound formulas. The original ingredients of granules cannot be identified individually anymore, but all ingredients are listed in the specification of the products. In this case, the granule was put into the boiling water and dissolved for use. In practice, in addition to granule, *Zhong Cheng Yao* can be in the form of a capsule, pill, unguent, liquid and so on.

The crude herbal substance is rarely given to the patients directly since it is difficult for patients to control the use of dose and they are not prepared as ready for use. But not deniable, some crude herbal substances can be used directly as ingredients, especially when there is no precise requirement on usage dose, such as certain number of dates or a piece of ginger. In EU practice, Chinese decoction pieces should be encouraged and used by TCM practitioners, since they are well selected and clean compared to raw materials.

Two more things need to be noted. Firstly, in the example case, the TCM was chosen because by using IV the bronchitis easily relapsed, and the child needed to be brought to the hospital every day, risking cross-infection. Secondly, with the treatment, the child recovered soon after using the TCMPs, which means TCM functioned in the case.

---

conventional medicine in China and gradually exploited the way of combined therapy (Shangdong Xin Zhonglu Zhong Yi Yuan n.d.).

TCM practitioners may provide different services, such as acupuncture, massage or GP. For each type of service, a specified market access licence is needed, and professionals need to be trained and educated in TCM subjects in China.

3.3 The Understanding TCMP in EU Pharmaceutical Law

Patients can access TCM through pharmacies or Chinese practitioners. For the former, only registered products can be sold in pharmacies, and the EU has very explicit regulations in EU legislation. However, for the latter, Chinese practitioners, Member States of the EU enact more detailed regulations in national law (EHTPA n.d.). It is necessary to read the definition of an herbal product in EU law, then the common official understanding of TCMP in Europe can be further explored (Directive 2001/83/EC 2001).

3.3.1 Definition of Herbal Medicinal Product in EU Pharmaceutical Law

Article 1 of Directive 2001/83/EC (2001), paragraphs 30, 31 and 32 define herbal medicinal product, herbal substances and herbal preparations respectively. An herbal substance is the raw material of herbal preparations and herbal medicinal products, and herbal substance and preparation can be used to produce herbal medicinal products. According to EU law, herbal substances include whole or only part(s) of plants, algae, fungi, and lichen, which are normally in dried forms and unprocessed, but sometimes fresh. Herbal substances are normally subject to specific treatments, but exudates without special function might also be considered as herbal substances (2001/83/EC, 2001, art. 1 para. 31). Herbal preparations are processed substances, the ways of process include extraction, distillation, expression, fractionation, purification, concentration or fermentation. The forms of herbal preparations include 'comminuted or powdered herbal substances, tinctures, extracts, essential oils, expressed juices and processed exudates' (2001/83/EC, 2001, art. 1 para. 32). An herbal medicinal product is composed by one or more herbal substances or/and preparations containing active ingredients (2001/83/EC, 2001, art. 1 para. 30).

In addition, Directive 2004/24/EC (2004) provides for THMP, which comprises a part of the consolidated Directive 2001/83/EC (2001). A registered THMP must fulfil the conditions laid down in Article 16a(1) of the Directive. The products provided by Directive 2004/24/EC (2004) mainly points to OTC products, and the criteria laid down in Article 16(a) and (c) for traditional use medicinal product include: (1) the function of the traditional medicine is for use without the supervision of a medical practitioner for diagnostic purposes or for prescription or monitoring of treatment; (2) they are exclusively for administration in accordance with a specified strength and posology; (3) the preparation form can be oral, external and/or inhalation; (4) they must have been used throughout a period of at least 30 years, and at least 15 years in EU; (5) they need to comply with the standards of safety and efficacy.

Therefore, Directive 2001/83/EC (2001) mainly covers herbal medicinal products. However, TCMP in practice can compose either a single component or a combination of herbal substance(s), animal origin(s) and/or mineral material. In addition, non-registered TCMP can also gain access to the EU market under certain circumstances. Therefore, TCMP in practice covers more categories than the regulated types of traditional use herbal medicinal products in EU pharmaceutical law. Chinese medicine practitioners may legally provide non-registered TCMP in the EU. Article 3(1) of Directive 2001/83/EC (2001) states that '[a]ny medicinal product prepared in a pharmacy in accordance with a medical prescription for an individual patient, 'commonly known as the magistral formula', is not covered by the Directive.

3.3.2 The Issue of Homology of Medicine and Food

A 'medicinal product' is defined either in relation to its medicinal presentation or to its medicinal function (Walker 2015). According to EU law:

(1) Any substance or combination of substances presented as having properties for treating or preventing disease in human beings;
(2) Any substance or combination of substances which may be used in, or administered to, human beings, either with a view to restoring, correcting or modifying physiological functions by exerting a pharmacological, immunological or metabolic action, or to making a medical diagnosis (Directive 2001/83/EC 2001, art. 1).

The European Court of Justice (ECJ) has confirmed that falling under either of these definitions is sufficient to classify a product as a medicinal product. Case law has determined that the definition must be applied on a case by case basis (ECJ C-211/03 2005; MHRA 2020).

In practice, many foods are given therapeutic functions, which happens both in the EU and in China. TCMP is rendered with characteristics of nature, and people are impressed by its close relationship with food. But cases have shown that TCMP has side-effects because of the toxicity of ingredients, sometimes serious.

The case of TCMP is complicated in China. When TCMP is discussed by Chinese people in daily life, it can be either the raw material of a food product, a processed food product as understood by the West, or a pharmaceutical product as provided in EU pharmaceutical law. Therefore, TCMP as described by a Chinese person may be understood to be an entirely different product in the West. The concept of a product in business or in Chinese people's opinion is not always the accurate concept of the product in law. The confusion does not cause too many difficulties in Chinese

Society, since Chinese people accept the idea of food therapy and spontaneously use some of the theories of TCM in their daily life. So, naturally they treat the food used in line with TCM philosophy as TCMP. However, the ambiguous concept can cause chaos for a new product to enter a market.

Obviously, the historical development of TCMP is much longer than the establishment of the current Chinese legal system. The tolerance of this inaccurate naming by Chinese people in practice is because of the trust to TCM. However, some pros and cons appeared in course of the spread of TCM philosophy in folk. On one hand, TCM philosophy and techniques are well disseminated and trusted, so TCM, as the collection of a wise of ancient people and a part of long-standing traditional Chinese culture, can be continued and developed generation by generation in Chinese society. On the other hand, the citizens have not enough capacity to relate the scientificity of TCM knowledge diffused by the society or their parents' generation, so TCM's effect is exaggerated sometimes and the TCM philosophy becomes more mysterious.

The cons are not in line with the spirit in law and science. Law requires good faith, honesty and credibility, and for understanding and utilising science, science calls on transparency, accessibility and stringency. Therefore, TCM should not be more and more mysterious, but entirely the opposite way. However, as a typical diagnostic and therapeutic method distinguished with the Western conventional medicine, TCM, as well as its unanswered mysteries on TCMP, should be studied and explored. TCM should be developed. And indeed, the scientists continually putting forth effort on its research. The practice of TCM and TCMP calls for more precise regulations in both the EU and China.

Then, the next question comes to how to reach the goal of assessing the scientificity of TCM knowledge. Science clarifies techniques, where law sets up the regulations to encourage the development of knowledge in science. But at the same time law controls the risk(s) raised from the uncertainty of science by using legislative techniques.

If the mystery of TCM is still ok in Chinese society, the confusion that TCM brings to the West becomes unacceptable in international trade. Since customers or patients in the West normally have little knowledge of TCM and rarely give trust to TCMP at all, more caution is used when considering market access of the product. Is it proper to use the original evaluation system to assess something exotic to the system? This is the case of the EU with the market access of TCMP, and before entirely understanding the 'something', it might still be reasonable. However, this knowledge should not always stay undeveloped, especially in cases where the development of the knowledge has been shown to be restricted. The Western world would ask, what does TCMP really mean? Is it a food or a medicinal product? How do we solve the confusion between TCMP as expressed by the title composed of 'M' and other TCMP in form of food as claimed in practice by the Chinese? Actually, in international trade, it is not difficult to tell the difference between the attributes of a food product and drug. The customs code can help clarify the attribution of the product in export or import, but the customs code is claimed by exporters. The problem comes to EU customs again, which is, how to properly supervise clearance of customs. However, it is not a question that EU customs can answer if the administrative law cannot clearly and accurately clarify and define TCMP.

EU pharmaceutical law treats TCMP as the same product as THMP. It reflects that the EU does not distinguish between these two and does not recognise their difference, even though the discussion, no matter in medical practice or in the medical legislation sphere, has lasted for a long time. In March 2020, Medicines and Healthcare Products Regulatory Agency (MHRA) produced a Guidance to explain how, and on what basis, the MHRA decides whether products are medicines or not. MHRA explains[2]:

> There are many herbs with known medicinal uses and at the same time uses as either foods or cosmetics. When considering the status of a herb that does have various uses the Agency will make a judgement as to which is the dominant function and pays particular regard to the purpose of the herb's inclusion in a product. In very general terms the Agency does not usually regard products containing culinary herbs to be medicines unless included for their medicinal properties or claims to treat or prevent disease are made for them. Some herbs, however, have well-known medicinal effects and would usually only be found in products for a medicinal purpose (MHRA 2020, p. 11).

Any claim to state that a food has the property of preventing, treating or curing human disease is not permitted for either the labelling or advertising of food. However, the MHRA likely consider products using claims such as 'maintain' or 'help to maintain', 'dietary maintenance' or 'support health or a healthy lifestyle' not to be medicinal, unless such claims are clearly made in relation to healthy bodily functions or organs for treating disease (MHRA 2020, p. 12).

The borderline between food and medicine is hard to be clarified even just considering the THMP in the EU. A document produced by EUROCAM (2017) mentioned a ruling produced by the European Food Standards Agency (EFSA 2013).[3] In this ruling, a herbal product containing 6 herbs including rhubarb root which contains anthraquinones with a proven laxative effect could be considered a food supplement and marketed as such with health claims. In addition, EUROCAM mentioned BELFRIT list of botanical food supplements with accepted health claims created by Belgium, France and Italy, and thought the list blurred the borderline between food and medicine. Therefore, EUROCAM called for a coherent strategy from EFSA and the Herbal Medicinal Products Committee (HMPC) to clarify the therapeutic scope and differences as well as the borderline between herbal products marketed as food supplements and herbal medicines.

[2]A notification is given by MHRA that '[t]his MHRA Guidance Note should not be taken as a complete or definitive statement of the law. It is not intended as a substitute for legal or other professional advice' (MHRA 2020).

[3]EUROCAM is a European platform for organisations representing patients, medical doctors, veterinarians and practitioners in the Complementary and Alternative Medicine sector.

3.3.3 TCMP vs. *Food Supplements & Novel Food in the EU*

Food supplements is a type of food products under the regulation of food law, which may be easily mixed with medicinal product. It is an addition to a normal diet and in the form of concentrated sources of nutrients (or other substances) with a nutritional or physiological effect. The food supplements can be marketed in 'dose' form, such as pills, tablets, capsules, liquids in measured doses, etc. Directive 2002/46/EC on food supplements aims to protect consumers against potential health risks from those products and to ensure that they are not provided with misleading information. With respect to the safety of food supplements, the Directive lays down a harmonised list of vitamins and minerals that may be added for nutritional purposes in food supplements (in Annex I to the Directive). Annex II of the Directive contains a list of permitted sources (vitamin and mineral substances) from which those vitamins and minerals may be manufactured. The Directive Article 6.2 clearly sets up a line between food supplements and Pharmaceutical products, it reads '[t]he labelling, presentation and advertising must not attribute to food supplements the property of preventing, treating or curing a human disease, or refer to such properties'. Food supplements containing substances other than vitamins or minerals are foodstuffs within the meaning of Article 2 of Regulation (EC) No 178/2002. Such foodstuffs are in the form of 'substance or product, whether processed, partially processed or unprocessed, intended to be, or reasonably expected to be ingested by humans' (Regulation No. 178/2002 2002, art. 2). Substances in food supplements for the use of scientific evidence purposes should be distinguished from those of vegetable origin, such as plants or plant extracts. Features of substances, for instance amino acids, are listed in the Annex to Commission Directive 2001/15/EC, which may be added to food for specific nutritional purposes or for particular nutritional uses.

The EU decentralised the authorisation on the safety of food supplements to national legislatures, except for vitamins and minerals. Many Member States have drafted positive and negative lists of substances in food supplements in the form of technical conditions, such as maximum limits, type of extract or combination of ingredients. Entry of new substances onto these lists is liable to be subject to an assessment (COM (2008) 824 final).

Even though the EU Commission explicitly states some substances, in particular certain herbal extracts, used both in food supplements and proprietary medicinal products (COM (2008) 824 final). The practice still faces the difficulties on distinguishing the use of the herbal extract between food supplements and medicinal products. Therefore, it gives clear guidance for distinguishing food supplements and medicinal products from the perspective of business practice, SR, the Court of Justice and the functions of the product. In business practice, any substance or combination of substances presented as having properties for treating or preventing diseases in human beings, for instance labelling in the product specification, must be classified as a medicinal product. Regarding SR, Article 2(2) of Directive 2001/83/EC, as amended by Directive 2004/27/EC lays down that:

> [I]n cases of doubt, where, taking into account all its characteristics, a product may fall within the definition of a 'medicinal product' and within the definition of a product covered by other Community legislation, the provisions of the legislation on medicinal products shall apply (Directive 2004/27/EC 2004).

In legal practice, the ECJ recognises that the incomplete status of SR is the reason for difficulty in the classification of a product between medicinal products and foodstuffs. Therefore, it concluded that "a product which satisfies the definition of 'medicinal product' within the meaning of Directive 2001/83/EC must be held to be a medicinal product and be made subject to the corresponding rules even if it comes within the scope of the other" (Case C-219/91 Ter Voort 1992, ECR I-5485, para. 19, cited by ECJ 2007, C-319/05, I-9855, para. 38). In light of its function, medicinal product means, as aforementioned in Directive 2001/83/EC:

> [A]ny substance or combination of substances which may be used in or administered to human beings either with a view to restoring, correcting or modifying physiological functions by exerting a pharmacological, immunological or metabolic action, or to making a medical diagnosis (Directive 2001/83/EC 2001, art. 1).

It is noticeable, that the physiological effect is also contained by the concentrated source of substances in food supplement. However, the ECJ has given strict interpretation on such definition of medicinal product by function. It ruled that the pharmacological properties on the human body should be scientifically observed, and substances should not be treated as having a medicinal function if they do not significantly affect metabolism and thus do not strictly modify the functioning of the human body, even though it may have some effect on the human body (ECJ 2007, C-319/05). Nevertheless, the scientific evidence on the function of food supplements to the health of the human body should be provided, which may focus more on preventing diseases ('reduction of disease risk') or improving health conditions (Regulation (EC) No. 1924/2006 2006).

Novel food is the other type of food products that may be easily mixed with medicinal product. It covers foods and food ingredients with a new or modified primary molecular structure. It can consist of or be isolated from micro-organisms, fungi or algae and so on.[4] It also covers foods or food ingredients with significant changes in the composition or structure which affect their nutritional value, metabolism or level of undesirable substances (Regulation (EC) No 258/97 1997). If there are no specific Community provisions, food shall be regarded as safe (Regulation (EC) No. 178/2002 2002). However, when it is a novel food, a safety assessment is necessary (Regulation (EC) No 258/97 1997). The extract from herbs may fall in this situation when it is defined as 'novel food', when a plant extract was not on

[4]The EMA Action Plan for herbal Medicines 2010–2011 notes that: 'A possible extension of the scope of Directive 2004/24/EC has been proposed by the European Commission and is supported by the Herbal Medicinal Products Committee (HMPC), i.e. the simplified registration procedure could be opened to other traditional products of a long-standing tradition in the EU, including certain products of animal origin'(Cited in EUROCAM 2017, p. 13).

Community market, or not produced, as at the date of entry into force of Regulation on 27 January 1997.

3.3.4 Safety and Efficacy Concern

Even though test on toxicity of food product is not compulsory for market access except otherwise provided by law, food product faces similar difficulties with TCMP for the attestation of safety when needed. Foods normally contain chemical compounds which should be safe when consumed. The safety assessment of such chemically complex food matrices (CCFMS) is usually difficult, expensive and time-consuming. Simple methodology for reducing the difficulties, have been explored by scientists. For instance, TON.NL provides ideas for changing the current approach which focuses on full identification to a complex matrix safety assessment strategy (CoMSAS) which focuses on toxicological relevance (TNO 2017).

Medicinal products face stricter rules on characteristic instruction and safety assessment. The difficulties of the safety assessment are generally faced by the most TCMP, especially in the case of compound products. A guideline on summary of pharmaceuticals characteristics issued by the EU requires that the active ingredients in the medicinal product must be expressed qualitatively and quantitatively, and the pharmaceutical form and the contents by weight should also be stated (European Commission 2009, SmPC, p. 4; also see: Council Directive 92/27/EEC 1992, art. 1 para. 2; EUR 2017). But the compound formulas comprise many active ingredients, even some unknown substances. The situation is more difficult for TCMP than other European herbal medicinal products, since less TCMP substances or formulas are recorded by the European Pharmacopoeia (Ph. Eur.) due to the lack of recording materials on the safety use.

The tools to assess risk of compound medicinal product are developing, even though far from enough. The chemical reflection between substances in a compound medicinal product are difficult to be controlled and expressed by using the same risk assessment tool as for conventional medicine. For instance, research on anti-fibrotic drugs is generally based on two distinct but interactive strategies: one strategy is based on mechanism studies and the other is based on exploring efficacy. The former ‘begins with identification of molecular targets through mechanistic studies, and then development of inhibitors or enhancers targeting the molecules’; while the later ‘starts with screening drug candidates in disease models to identify activities and efficacy, with less reliance on analysis of mechanisms of action’ (Xu et al. 2012, p. 337). Due to the complexities of the compound TCMP, it is difficult to adopt the mechanism studies on the safety assessment. However, efficacy-based strategies have been employed in finding activities from traditional medicinal products by Qihe Xu et al., King’s college London. A knowledge-based approach, namely to screen candidate objective believed to be beneficial in treating fibrotic disease based on the theory and practice of TCM, was adopted in the research (Xu et al. 2012). This research demonstrated that the tools on assessing risk are developing. The editorial group of a scientific publication *The Art and Science of Traditional Medicine* noted that besides the integrated toxicological approaches, 'newer's omics technologies and poly-pharmacokinetics will also play an increasing role in bridging the gap between the personalised approach of Chinese medicine theory and modern clinical research methodology' (Fan et al. 2014).

The efficacy of the extract as a preparation of TCMP is also criticised in practice, since the efficacy may not be ensured if only the deemed active ingredients are extracted from TCMP raw material or plant decoction pieces based on the chemical efficacy analysis. Such perception mainly comes from empiricism in practice, but it is also led by the lack of scientific research on the efficacy of the product, especially the production techniques which influence the chemical reactions between substances.

3.4 A Comparison on the Concept of TCMP in EU Law and Chinese Law

'Traditional medicinal product' mainly points to those herbal products which have been registered under Chapter 2a of Directive 2001/83/EC in EU pharmaceutical law. This article requires sufficient evidence of the medicinal use of the product throughout a period of at least 30 years, including at least 15 years in the EU. Therefore, a TCMP can be approved as a traditional use medicinal product only if it is registered by following article 16a of 2001/83/EC. Even though EU pharmaceutical law regulates medicinal substances and preparations, only herbal products can be approved on the market access for patient use. Therefore, Chinese medicinal substances and preparations which are directly used to cure diseases drop out of the regulative scope of EU pharmaceutical law.

In TCM practice in China, TCMP includes Chinese crude drugs, traditional Chinese medicine decoction pieces and *Zhong Cheng Yao* (State Council of the PRC 2003). All three forms can be used directly by the Chinese doctor to treat a patient. First, Chinese crude drugs are raw materials of TCM and can be linked to herbal substances in EU law. It can be animal origins and/or mineral materials besides herbs. Comparably, animal origin is also a possible source of medicinal product in EU law, but the registration for traditional use drug mainly focuses on herbal medicinal products currently. Second, TCM decoction pieces are drugs that can be used by doctors to formulate a TCMP for patients; they are processed drugs and can be linked to herbal preparations in EU law. Thirdly, *Zhong Cheng Yao* is a type of TCMP with either a compound formula or consist of individual herbal substances. Registered herbal *Zhong Cheng* Yao—namely traditional Chinese herbal medicinal product—can be linked to herbal medicinal products in EU pharmaceutical law. It can be either prescription-only medicine or OTC in China but is only available in the EU in the form of OTC if it is registered as THMP.

In addition, market of the extract of TCMP has been flourishing over the past several years (Liu et al. 2016). However, the understand of application, standards of extracting, and efficacy in medicinal products are not unified. Extract of TCMP can be used for the preparation of TCMP, and it is also possible to be used in food supplement, for either traditional foods or novel foods. Using an extract as the TCMP preparation or substance of novel food faces similar challenges in the safety assessment. Such issues are addressed by COM (2008) 824.

3.5 Chapter Summary

First of all, currently, TCM notions and theories are difficult for the West to understand and accept, since Western conventional medicine has pursued an entirely different philosophy to develop the diagnostic and therapeutic system. Modern TCM derives from tradition, but scientific research continues putting efforts on finding the evidence for its safety and efficacy.

Secondly, EU pharmaceutical law defines a recognisable traditional medicinal product based on sufficient evidence of the medicinal use of the product throughout a period of at least 30 years, including at least 15 years in the EU. Therefore, the way that the EU defines the traditional medicinal product does not put emphasis on traditional knowledge and/or any specific and unique processing techniques. Instead, the following elements are considered relevant to the traditional use medicinal product: (1) it must have 30 years of being used in practice; (2) it must have at least 15 years of use within the EU; (3) sufficient evidence to prove the safety and efficacy must be provided; (4) mainly herbal medicinal products are covered at the current stage; (5) it must be an OCT product. Therefore, the biggest difference in the understanding of TCMP sits in the recognition of TCM. China recognises TCMP as a medicinal product formulated under rule of TCM. TCM is not well known and understood in the EU, so it is difficult for the EU to follow China's way of defining TCMP. Then, question comes down to whether the current understanding that the EU has of TCMP is proper, which is answered along with the settlement of the main question of the study in the following chapters. The study in this book observes that EU pharmaceutical law was drafted based on a full understanding of conventional EU medicinal products and its THMP instead of TCMP.

Thirdly, from a legal research aspect, legislation relating to TCM in the EU can be divided into two groups: one to regulate practitioners and the other to regulate TCMP. Two kinds of legislation, then, should be expected to be further developed. TCMP should also be divided into two groups in regulations, one group should consist of crude Chinese drugs and decoction pieces delivered with prescription, and the use of such TCMPs must be regulated together with Chinese medicine practitioners. The other group refers to *Zhong Cheng Yao*. The administration of *Zhong Cheng Yao* is regulated by EU pharmaceutical law. Basically, all crude Chinese drugs and decoction pieces should be used by well-trained doctors and under the supervision of trained doctors. While the specifications on the syndromes and symptoms of using *Zhong Cheng Yao* are accurate, the properties of the product *per se*, and the side effects need to be labelled properly on the package.

Fourthly, the chapter does not give enough attention to the registration of TCM practitioner, but the issue of registration of TCM practitioner is also important. Different types of services should be regulated by different market access rules. Acupuncture has been comparatively better accepted and regulated in the West, but the TCM practitioner, as the executor for realising the combination between diagnostic and therapeutic functions of TCM, is hardly to be regulated due to the heavily insufficient TCM knowledge. If TCMP cannot be well accepted by the EU, it is difficult to effectively accept the Chinese practitioners too.

Finally, in China, TCM does not mean undeveloped heritage. Instead, the merit of TCM contributes to an innovative future of medicinal products. The theory lying in TCM will push the R&D of new products continually. However, EU THMP does not pursue a theoretical system as that which TCMP is based on. The insufficient knowledge on TCM leads to the misunderstanding of TCMP in the EU. It also leads to the difficulties of regulating TCMP by law and restricts the scientific development of TCMP.

References

Alfonso-Cristancho R et al (2015) Definition and classification of generic drugs across the world. Appl Health Econ Health Policy 13(Suppl 1):5–11

Benjamin S et al (1997) Exploring the other health care systems. Patient Care:133–169

Buie TL (2020) Classic Homeopath. In: History of Homeopathy. https://classichomeopath.com/history/

Chinese Medicine Ordinance (1999) Hong Kong, c 549, s 2

COM (2008) 824 final. European Commission (2008) Report from the Commission to the Council and the European Parliament on the Use of Substances other than Vitamins and Minerals in Food Supplements

Council Directive 92/27/EEC (1992) Council Directive 92/27/EEC of 31 March 1992 on the Labelling of Medicinal Products for Human use and on Package Leaflets, OJ L 113, pp 8–12

Directive 2001/83/EC (2001) Directive 2001/83/EC of the European Parliament and of the Council of 6 November 2001 on the Community Code Relating to Medicinal Products for Human Use. OJ L 311:67–128

Directive 2002/46/EC (2002) Directive 2002/46/EC of the European Parliament and of the Council of 10 June 2002 on the Approximation of the Laws of the Member States Relating to Food Supplements. OJ L 183:51–57

Directive 2004/24/EC (2004) Directive 2004/24/EC of the European Parliament and of the Council of 31 March 2004 Amending, as Regards Traditional Herbal Medicinal Product, 2001/83/EC on the Community Code Relating to Medicinal Products for Human Use. OJ L136:85–90

Directive 2004/27/EC (2004) Directive 2004/27/EC of the European Parliament and of the Council of 31 March 2004 mending Directive 2001/83/EC on the Community Code Relating to Medicinal Products for Human Use. OJ L 136:34–57

Directive 65/65/EEC (1965) Directive 65/65/EEC of 26 January 1965 on the Approximation of Provisions Laid down by Law, Regulation or Administrative Action Relating to Proprietary Medicinal Products. OJ 022: 369–373

ECJ (2007) C-319/05, European Commission v. Germany

ECJ, C-211/03 (2005) HLH Warenvertriebs GmbH v. Bundesrepublik Deutschland

EFSA (2013) Scientific Opinion on the substantiation of a health claim related to hydroxyanthracene derivatives and improvement of bowel function pursuant to Article 13 (5) of Regulation (EC) No 1924/2006

EHTPA (n.d.) Medicines Legislation. http://ehtpa.eu/medicines_legislation/index.html

Ernst E, Cohen MH, Stone J (2004) Ethical problems arising in evidence based complementary and alternative medicine. J Med Ethics 30(2):156–159

EUR (2017) Labelling and Package Leaflets for Medicinal Products. In EUR-Lex. http://eur-lex.europa.eu/legal-content/EN/TXT/?uri=LEGISSUM:l32006

EUROCAM (2017) The Regulation of Herbal Medicines in the EU. Brussels

European Commission (2009) A Guideline on Summary of Product Characteristics (SmPC). p 4

Fan T et al (2014) Integrating traditional medicine into modern health care. In: Fan T et al (eds) The art and science of traditional medicine, the Science/AAAS Custom Publishing Office, p S4

Gu J et al (1999) The radical transformation in artemisinin: a DFT study. J Phys Chem A 103 (46):9364–9369

Jiang W (2005) Therapeutic Wisdom in traditional Chinese medicine: a perspective from modern science. Trends Pharmacol Sci 26(11):558–563

Liu Y et al (2016) 2015 Nian Zhong Yao Shang Pin Jin Chu Kou Fen Xi (Analysis of TCM Import & Export Trade in 2015). Zhong Guo Xian Dai Zhong Yao (Modern Chinese Medicine) 18 (2):228

MacIntosh A (1999) Understanding the Differences between Conventional, Alternative, Complementary. Townsend Letter for Doctors and Patients. http://tldp.com/medicine.htm

MHRA (2020) A Guide to What is a Medicinal Product, UK, Guidance Note 8

NIH (2018) Homeopathy. http://nccam.nih.gov/health/homeopathy

NPC Standing Committee of the PRC (1984) Yao Pin Guan Li Fa (The Drug Administration Law of the PRC) (revision 2019). Order of the President of the PRC No. 31

Pharmacopeia of the PRC (2015 Edition) Chinese Pharmacopoeia Commission, Part one

Regulation (EC) No. 1924/2006 (2006) No. 1924/2006 of the European Parliament and of the Council of 20 December 2006 on Nutrition and Health Claims Made on Foods, OJ L 202:9–25

Regulation (EC) No. 258/97 (1997) Regulation No. 258/97 of the European Parliament and of the Council of 27 January 1997 Concerning Novel Foods and Novel Food Ingredients. OJ L 43: 1-6, Art 3

Regulation No. 178/2002 (2002) Regulation No.178/2002 of the European Parliament and of the Council of 28 January 2002 Laying down the General Principles and Requirements of Food Law, Establishing the European Food Safety Authority and Laying Down Procedures in Matters of Food Safety. OJ L31:1–24

SDA of the PRC (2002) Zhong Yao Cai Sheng Chan Zhi Liang Guan Li Gui Fan (Shi Xing) (Good Agricultural Practice of Traditional Chinese Medicinal Product Materials). Order No. 32

SFDA (2007) Yao Pin Zhu Ce Guan Li Ban Fa (Drug Registration Regulation)

Shangdong Xin Zhonglu Zhong Yi Yuan (n.d.) Introduction of Guo Xiaoyue. http://www.sdzhongluyiyuan.com/team_show.asp?id=4982

State Council of the PRC (2002) Regulation for the Implementation of the Drug Administration Law of the PRC (revision 2019). Order No. 360

State Council of the PRC (2003) Circular on Printing and Issuing the Measures for Administration of the Good Agricultural Practice for Chinese Crude Drugs Inspection (For Trial Implementation) and the Evaluation Standards for GAP for Chinese Crude Drugs Inspection (For Trial Implementation), Guo Shi Yao Jian An [2003] No. 251

TNO (2017) Safety Assessment of Complex Food Products. In TNO.NL. https://www.tno.nl/media/2649/safety_assessment_complex_food_products_tno_13_5897.pdf

Tu Y (2015) Youyou Tu—Biographical. https://www.nobelprize.org/nobel_prizes/medicine/laureates/2015/tu-bio.html

U.S. FDA (2015) Drug Applications for Over-the-Counter (OTC) Drugs. In U.S. Food & Drug Administration. https://www.fda.gov/drugs/developmentapprovalprocess/howdrugsaredevelopedandapproved/approvalapplications/over-the-counterdrugs/default.htm

Unschuld PU (2011) Huang Di Nei Jing Su Wen—An Annotated Translation of Huang Di's Inner Classic-Basic Questions. University of California Press, Auckland
Walker DR (2015) Report on the Herbal Medicines and Practitioners, DC's Improbable Science
Wang Y, Xu A (2014) Zheng: a systems biology approach to diagnosis and treatments. In: Fan T et al (eds) The art and science of traditional medicine, the Science/AAAS Custom Publishing Office, Part 1: TCM Today—A Case for Integration, p S13
WHO (2013) WHO Traditional Medicine Strategy: 2014-2023
WHO/Cui W (2009) Bulletin of the World Health Organization. Past Issues 87(10):733–804
WHO/EDM/TRM/2000 (2000) General Guidelines for Methodologies on Research and Evaluation of Traditional Medicine
Wiesener S et al (2012) Legal status and regulation of complementary alternative medicine in Europe. Forsch Komplementmed 19(Suppl 2):29–36
Xu Q et al (2012) Knowledge-based discovery of anti-fibrotic and pro-fibrotic activities from Chinese materia medica. In: Kuang H (ed) Recent advances in theories and practice of Chinese medicine. eBook, https://www.intechopen.com/books/recent-advances-in-theories-and-practice-of-chinese-medicine

Chapter 4
Assessing the Issue of Market Access of TCMP in EU Pharmaceutical Law

Traditional medicine has been regulated in the EU since Directive 2004/24/EC came into force. However, since then very rarely have TCMPs been registered in practice. This chapter focuses on exploring the legal reasons for the current situation and assesses the legal environment of market access of TCMPs in the EU. It reviews the historical development of EU pharmaceutical legislation and standards relevant to TCMP. It analyses the market access rule for non-registered TCMP as well as current registration status of registered TCMP. It introduces the institutional framework of the approval of market access of TCMP in the EU by comparing it with that of China. Thereinto, systematology and its relevancy to the study is introduced, and one of its tools, the network, is employed. Finally, the chapter concludes the difficulties of EU pharmaceutical law to regulate TCMP and provides some recommendations to close the loophole in the current EU pharmaceutical law.

Notably, the UK is in a very special situation as a Member State of the EU, since the results of its 2016 referendum supported Brexit. However, the UK has profoundly influenced the development of legislation on THMP in the EU. Therefore, the chapter covers the development of TCM related legislation in the UK.

4.1 Historical Review of the Development of TCMP Related Legislation in the EU

Regulations relating to the market access of TCMP in the EU are under the legal framework of EU pharmaceutical law. EU pharmaceutical law is under the umbrella of EU law. EU law sets up the basic rules for affairs within the EU, including political as well as economic affairs, and EU members are authorised to enact detailed regulations under their common understanding of the EU treaty. Herein below, the book reviews the general legal system of EU law and stresses the most relevant EU Directives to market access of TCMP.

S. Wang, *Market Access of Traditional Chinese Medicinal Product in the EU under WTO Legal Framework*, Economic and Financial Law & Policy – Shifting Insights & Values 5, https://doi.org/10.1007/978-3-030-52848-5_4

4.1.1 Overview of EU Law

4.1.1.1 EU Law

Up to now, four treaties have been signed by EU members since the first treaty, the Maastricht Treaty, entered into force in 1993. Over time, these treaties gradually set up the current functional and theoretical framework of the EU. The latest consolidated version of the EU treaty is the Treaty of Lisbon. It was signed on 13 December 2007 and entered into force on 1 December 2009. It is treated as the constitutional legal document of the EU (Wessel 2003; Europa 2017a).

Title XIV of the consolidated EU treaty sets out the issue of public health and is an outline for EU Member States to follow. Therefore, any legal discussion relating to TCMP should pursue all principles set up under this Title (TFEU 2012). In addition, the EU legal system establishes many fundamental rules for regulating certain issues in the form of regulations, directives and decisions (TFEU 2012, art. 288). They are all binding legislations. Moreover, the EU authorised its Member States to enact more detailed rules that fall within the ambit of its fundamental law (Mathijsen 1995).

4.1.1.2 EU Soft Law Acts As Guidance for Administrative Practice

Soft law is the term applied to EU measures, such as guidelines, recommendations, declarations and opinions that are not binding on those to whom they are addressed (Eurofound 2011). These are seen quite often in the pharmaceutical regulatory area, especially relating to technical standardised issues. The obligation of the European Commission to apply its own soft law is based on the principle of equal treatment and of protection of legitimate expectation (TFEU 2012, art 290).[1] In addition, measures provided by the soft law of the European Commission has external effect

[1]TFEU Article 290 provides,

1. A legislative act may delegate to the Commission the power to adopt non-legislative acts of general application to supplement or amend certain non-essential elements of the legislative act. The objectives, content, scope and duration of the delegation of power shall be explicitly defined in the legislative acts. The essential elements of an area shall be reserved for the legislative act and accordingly shall not be the subject of a delegation of power.
2. Legislative acts shall explicitly lay down the conditions to which the delegation is subject; these conditions may be as follows:

   (a) the European Parliament or the Council may decide to revoke the delegation;
   (b) the delegated act may enter into force only if no objection has been expressed by the European Parliament or the Council within a period set by the legislative act.

   For the purposes of (a) and (b), the European Parliament shall act by a majority of its component members, and the Council by a qualified majority.

3. The adjective 'delegated' shall be inserted in the title of delegated acts.

when they are addressed to EU Member States and their national administrative authorities to implement EU law. By addressing the national authorities of EU Member States, the European Commission seeks to push EU Member States to harmonise their respective administrative approaches. Soft law measures guide national authorities in their day-to-day application and interpretation of EU law. Furthermore, although soft law acts can only impose limitations on the European Commission itself, the competent national authorities would apply the soft measures in their administrative practice in order to avoid inconveniences or even a proceeding for breach of contract pursuant to Article 258 TFEU (2012).[2]

4.1.2 EU Directives Most Relevant to the Issue of the Market Access of TCMP

Directives to regulate THMP, food supplements and novel foods may relate to the import of TCMP, since many of the TCMPs exported to EU market are under the categories of food, health products, or pharmaceutical ingredients, instead of medicinal product (Fan et al. 2012). In addition, there is a set of rules functioning to control TCMP. Not only are special regulations used to restrict herbal medicinal products, but also rules in civil law, intellectual property law and criminal law can be applied in other situations other than for market access. Even more, environmental law and animal protection law must also be considered in selecting the materials of TCMP and in drug disposal.

This book focuses on the market access phase of medicinal product among TCMPs. Where, Directive 2001/83/EC (2001) and Directive 2004/24/EC (2004) are the most relevant regulations on market access of TCMP in the EU. The latter was enacted for amending the former as regards THMP for Human Use. The simplified registration procedure set out in Chapter 2a of Directive 2004/24/EC is recommended as a fast track for authorisation. But very rarely have Chinese companies applied under this Directive. A principal of Beijing Tong Ren Tang, one of the biggest Chinese pharmaceutical companies in China, expressed that a lack of funds was the main obstacle and evidence on sales for 30 or 15 years was difficult to obtain. Beijing Tong Ren Tang eventually obtained a GMP certificate in the EU in 2016, a process it began in 2010 (Tong Ren Xuan 2016).

Therefore, 2004 was the turning point for the regulation of TCMP in the EU, and from then on, the EU restricted conditions to authorise TCMP. Actually, even

[2]TFEU Article 258 provides 'If the Commission considers that a Member State has failed to fulfil an obligation under the Treaties, it shall deliver a reasoned opinion on the matter after giving the State concerned the opportunity to submit its observations. If the State concerned does not comply with the opinion within the period laid down by the Commission, the latter may bring the matter before the Court of Justice of the European Union'.

earlier, from 1999, the demand for strengthening the legislation of CAM has been shown in the EU because of the reporting of side effects of TCMP (See: Sect. 1.1.2).

4.1.3 The Historical Development of TCM Legislation in the UK

The discussion on the legislation of TCM and TCMP in the UK has been ongoing since the House of Lords provided the Six Report on CAM in November 2000 (hereinafter called the Six Report) (UK House of Lords Select Committee 2000). Reading the historical development of the legislation on TCMP in the UK help reveal the regulative path of the EU on TCMP. Until now, there is still an argument as to whether there should be a unique and separate regulatory system for TCM and TCMP beyond the Western conventional medicine regulatory system in the EU.

4.1.3.1 Influence of Brexit on the EU

The negotiation of Brexit is ongoing between the EU and the UK. The Medicines and Healthcare products Regulatory Agency (MHRA) is working with the Government of the UK to analyse the options and opportunities available for the safe and effective regulation of medicines and medical devices after the Brexit referendum, though, in the course of the negotiation, the UK still retains full rights and obligation of EU membership (MHRA 2016).

Regarding the regulations on medicine, the UK asserts that it will continually contribute in both the centralised and decentralised regulatory procedures of the EU until an agreement is reached between the EU and the UK for Brexit. Until then, the UK will maintain its programmes for implementing EU legislation as required by its obligations as a Member State and will also remain fully engaged in European and national scientific advice services and in delivering its EU inspection-related duties (MHRA 2016).

4.1.3.2 The Six Report

The Six Report was ordered by the House of Lords and printed on 21 November 2000 in the UK. It assessed the risk of CAM and was passed almost 20 years ago. However, many issues the report addressed still remain today (UK House of Lords Select Committee 2000). The Six Report drew an outline for the regulation of CAM in the UK and the EU. All CAM were divided into three groups in the report. Group 1 includes medicines that have well-developed regulatory structures considered by the Report; therapies, in Group 2, were supposed to be the complementary medicine; while the efficacy of alternative medicines, in Group 3, was questioned due to the absence of a credible evidence. TCM was defined as using a number of treatment methods to restore the balance of *Yin qi* and *Yang qi* in the Report. In practice it includes acupuncture, herbal medicine, massage and the exercise technique Qigong. Among those methods, acupuncture was categorised in Group 1, and it was treated as a well-regulated therapy by the report. However, TCM was classified in Group 3, while it is defined as a tradition of medicine used for thousands of years in China and a way to use combinations of herbs to address a wide range of health problems (UK House of Lords Select Committee 2000, Chap. 2, Box 1).[3] The report was used to comprehensively document the problems of CAM and not only TCM, but it clearly held that TCM must have evidence on efficacy. Some concepts of TCM given in the Report are baffling. For instance, *Yin qi* and *Yang qi*, are complicated and mysterious concepts even in China.

The Six Report mentions that the difference in philosophy between CAM therapies and conventional medicinal therapies lies in that most CAM therapies distinguish little between the body, mind and spirit in distinct sources of disease. Most CAMs are lacking in scientific evidence of the type pursued by the Western conventional medicine system. Therefore, patient satisfaction and placebo effect are discussed as empirical evidence to combat negative reviews related to the non-scientificity (UK House of Lords Select Committee 2000, Chap. 3). The Six Report discussed the difficulties of and a design for integrating CAM practitioners into the GP system. Thereinto, Dr. David Peters described six stages to integrate CAM into general practice. Indeed, one of the difficult parts of integrating CAMs into the Western health care system is that GPs lack knowledge of CAMs. Moreover, the UK Six Report has given two general methods to regulate CAM in its Chap. 5: one is to regulate by SR and the other is to use single voluntary regulatory bodies which operate in a professional manner.

The Report on the Experience Acquired as a Result of the Application of the Provisions of Chapter 2a of Directive 2001/83/EC (introduced by Directive 2004/24/EC) on Specific Provisions Applicable to Traditional Herbal Medicinal Products reflected the current status of regulations on Chinese traditional herbal medicine in the EU (European Commission 2008). It pointed out that without expert knowledge on different medical traditions in Europe it is very difficult for the Committee on Herbal Medicinal products (HMPC) to work in this area. Indeed, expert knowledge is necessary if EU citizens are to benefit more from traditional herbal medicine.

---

[3]Group 1 defines a kind of herbal medicine, synonyms for phototherapy, as '[a] system of medicine which uses various remedies derived from plants and plant extracts to treat disorders and maintain good health'. However, it excludes TCM. Group 3a, paragraph 3 states TCM as '[a] tradition of medicine used for thousands of years in China, which has its own system of diagnosis. Uses combinations of herbs to address a wide range of health problems'. (UK House of Lords Select Committee 2000, Chap 2, Box 1).

4.1.3.3 The Historical Development of TCM Legislation in the UK

Legislations on TCM has experienced ups and downs in the UK. The article, *Review on the Course of Chinese Medicine Regulation in the UK of the Last 10 Years* published by Cheng and Shen (2010), reviews well the history of legislation on TCM in the UK. It reflects the attitude of the UK toward TCM and TCMP. Among various CAMs, TCM is a typical example that has existed in the UK for a long time. For instance, explained by Cheng and Shen, acupuncture began to be developed in the UK more than 40 years ago. Since TCM practitioners emerged there in the 1980s, the quantity of TCM practitioners has been growing and rose to more than 1000 in the year 2010. Also, many universities provide educational courses on TCM. However, the development of the practice of TCM and the lack of regulation formed a sharp contrast, which brought a practical problem. Cheng and Shen mention that the UK National Health Service (NHS) had ever taken a relaxed restriction on CAM (including TCM) before the year 2000. However, some practitioners used the relaxed restriction and provided unqualified services, which damaged the reputation of TCM in the UK. The Medicines Control Agency (MCA) (now, MHRA) reported two cases that arose alleging damage to kidney function due to the use of TCMP containing Aristolochia in 2001. The case created anxiety about TCMP in the EU.

Therefore, Before MCA officially reported the cases, the Six Report had already catalogued TCM—including TCMP—into Group 3, where the safety and efficacy of the products were heavily questioned, while TCM acupuncture was put into Group 1 and treated as having a better regulatory structure (UK House of Lords Select Committee 2000). However, TCM has been developed as a medicine having completed diagnostic and therapeutic knowledge and system including acupuncture in China. This grouping by the Six report demonstrates that TCM conceptualised in Chinese medical practice is disintegrated. Thus, it is understandable that the UK—as well as the EU—is considering the practice of CAM instead of only TCM. Possibly for the convenience and efficiency of an administrative concern, acupuncture was separated from TCM, which would lead the TCM practitioners and acupuncture practitioners were treated differently under the legislation. However, guidance on a completed TCM system should be provided. Such as in China, acupuncture belongs to the TCM system in Chinese medical practice but, similarly, is regulated separately.

In September 2001, the Committee on the Safety of Medicines (CSM) and the MCA announced TCM cases in which side effects occurred and reminded the public to use TCM cautiously. Cheng and Shen (2010) note that even though the negative cases in the report of TCMP decreased the reputation of TCM in the public, the UK government still had the intention to push specialised legislation on TCM at that time. Non-governmental organisations made great efforts for developing TCM, which include the Register of Chinese Herbal Medicine (RCHM), The Association of Traditional Chinese Medicine (UK) (ATCM) and the British Society of Chinese Medicine (BSCM, merged into ATCM in 2003). In 2002, the Herbal Medicine Regulatory Working Group (HMRWG) and Acupuncture Regulatory Working

Group (ARWG) were set up and started the preparation work of legislation on herbal medicine and acupuncture practice. HMRWG was established by the UK Department of Health (DH), the Prince's Foundation for Integrated Health (FIG), and the European Herbal Medicine Practitioners Association (EHPA, now is European Herbal and Traditional Medicine Practitioners Association (EHTPA n.d.)) for preparing herbal medicine regulatory work (UK Department of Health 2003). Some other public representative organisations, including RCHM and BSCM also joined the work. At that time, EHPA had been preparing the EU herbal medicine legislation for more than 10 years and had designed a unified herbal medicine legislation system. It had decisive influence on the later THMP legislation in the EU. ATCM and BSCM strongly claimed the independent status of TCM, and they received the support of EHPA at the beginning. Therefore, the report of HMRWG provided the conceptualisation of independent registration by a CAM Council in 2003. ATCM proposed the registration of TCM practitioners (Cheng and Shen 2010). Besides HMRWG, many other organisations have endeavoured to set up a separate statutory system on CAM in the EU, such as AEWG 2003 and the UK DH 2004 (The King's Fund 2009). For instance, the UK DH put forward a proposal for SR of herbal medicine and acupuncture in 2004. It followed the legislative suggestions made by HMRWG. Unlike the House of Lords, it supported non-registered herbal remedies in the UK made up to meet the needs of individual patients. It recommended that acupuncturists and herbalists, practitioners of TCM and other traditional medicine systems practised in the UK should be included in a SR (EU Department of Health 2004).

However, Cheng and Shen (2010) note that the recommendation of the title of TCM Doctor and its registration did not receive the support of UK acupuncture professionals as UK acupuncture professionals preferred to set up an acupuncture council instead of a CAM council, within which they intended to register the title Acupuncturist. The Acupuncture Council was set up 3 months after HMRWG. It comprises both the Chinese acupuncture school and Western acupuncture school. And its representatives are mainly from British Acupuncture Council (BACC), established in 1990s. As Cheng and Shen (2010) explain, the CAM Council vanished gradually, and in 2006, the Health Professions Council (HPC) took over the work of drafting the health care professions registration. HPC was set up in 2001 by the UK government, and currently, it is in charge of the legislative affairs of health care professions (Health & Care Professions Council 2017).

Also mentioned by Cheng and Shen (2010), among the non-governmental institutions, ATCM is set up formally and contributes the most for pushing the development of TCM in the UK. Indeed, it provides a curriculum and publishes a Code of Practice to define the hygiene and safety standards relating to the practice of TCM as well as a Code of Professional Conduct for guidance and for the protection of patients in relation to the practice of TCM. It also updates research issues continually and actively responds to the UK government's calls for public comments on TCM or CAM legislation (Cheng and Shen 2010).

The enacting of Directive 2004/24/EC reflects that the EU legislation absorbed market access of TCMP into the administrative system of EU THMP. TCMP was finally put together with Western herbal medicinal products and regulated as THMP in Directive 2004/24/EC. Cheng and Shen ends with a review of a response collected and submitted by ATCM to the UK HD consultation on the SR of TCM of September 2009. It shows that the endeavour to statutorily regulate TCM practitioners and relevant non-registered TCMP continues. Based on the 2009 consultation, the UK HD published an analysis reporting on the SR of Practitioners of Acupuncture, Herbal Medicine, Traditional Chinese Medicine and Other Traditional Medicine Systems Practised in the UK in 2011 (UK Department of Health 2011). The perceived harmful result from unregulated practices of acupuncture, herbal medicine and traditional Chinese Medicine was addressed. A majority of responses (85%) were in favour of SR for ensuring qualified practitioners and a safe practice, while voluntary regulation was voted as the second best and a licence to practise was also mentioned as an option.

To sum up, the evolution of SR on CAM and TCM in the UK represents the understanding of the EU on TCMP. Even though Chinese medical law also regulates TCM practitioner, TCMP and acupuncturist separately, China relies on a theoretical mechanism of TCM based on TCM's historical development and current clinical practice. Theoretically, those three are all covered by the TCM system. In Western medical science, however, TCM is not recognised as a complete mechanism and is not well understood, which is echoed in legal practice, rendering law helpless to better regulate TCMP.

4.2 Analysing the Legal Framework Through Application of Systematology Theory

Hereinto, the EU law implementing mechanism on market access of TCMP is introduced along with a comparison to China's. Systematology theory is used for bridging the relation between the legal rules/principles and market access of TCMP.

4.2.1 Systematology

Systematology theory is well developed in the natural sciences for building the bridge between some principles in the discipline of philosophy and complex natural scenarios (Wei 2013). This Chapter uses the methodology to illustrate how EU rules function on the issue of market access. Indeed, the core issue of the study herein closely relates to this phase of legislation. It is necessary to review the lawmaking process so to further understand and assess the content of a law. Hereinto, administration of medicinal products is a general concept, and it is relevant to the governance of public health affairs based on law and policy (Cambridge Dictionary n.d.).[4] The governance of public health affairs is in the domain of politics (European Consortium for Political Research 2017),[5] and it is realised by the administrative system. In the system, the policymakers publish policies and provide guidelines and standards for managing affairs in case the law has not provided detailed rules (Europa 2017b, c, d).[6] Even though the policymakers have no right to make law, they do influence lawmaking widely because they deliver proposals for making law when needed.[7] Therefore, ensuring the quality of the proposal becomes extremely important for meeting the demand of public interest or of stakeholder interest in the law.

Thereinto, the general public interest or stakeholder interest are normally positioned as the legislative aim or legal principles. Once the legislation proposed by the policy makers are approved by the European Parliament (EP) and adopted by the Council of the EU, the rules or principles provided by the legislation can function in many individual cases. This mirrors the relationship between principles in the discipline of philosophy and complex natural scenarios in the original design of systematology.

[4]Per Cambridge Dictionary (online): 1. Administration is 'the arrangements and tasks needed to control the operation of a plan or organisation' 2.'Policy is a set of ideas or plan of what to do in particular situations that has been agreed to officially by a group of people, a business organisation, a government or a political party'.

[5]Politics is the activities associated with the governance of a country or area, especially the debate between parties having power.

[6]In the EU, (1) the European Council is composed by heads of state or government of EU countries, European Commission President, High Representative for foreign Affairs and Security Policy. It defines the general political direction and priorities of the European Union. It was established in 1974 as an informal forum, received formal status in 1992 and became an official EU institution in 2009. (2) The Council of the EU adopts EU laws, coordinates EU policies, develops the EU's foreign and security policy, based on European Council guidelines, concludes agreements between the EU and other countries or international organisations, and jointly with the European Parliament adopts the annual EU budget. It is the main decision-making body of the EU together with European Parliament. (3) European Commission promotes the general interest of the EU by proposing and enforcing legislation as well as by implementing policies and EU budget. It proposes new laws for protecting the interests of the EU and its citizens on issues that cannot be dealt with effectively at national level and getting technical details rights by consulting experts and the public.

[7]The European Parliament is the EU's law-making body. Currently, it has 751 Members representing different parties in Europe. It was established in 1952 as Common Assembly of the European Coal and Steel Community and in 1962 became the European Parliament. Its first direct election was in 1979. In addition, the Council of the European Union was established in 1958. It negotiates and adopts EU law, together with the European Parliament, based on proposals from the European Commission. The Council of European Union represents the voice of EU member governments and is composed by the government ministers from each EU country, according to the policy area to be discussed (Europa 2017e).

After a law is enacted, the power of interpreting law is delivered to the judges. In the custom of the common law system, the legal principles and rules are delivered through precedents. In applying legal principles and rules in cases, the law is interpreted and further developed, and in this way, judges also make law.

The EU is composed of states with either the tradition of a civil law system or a common law system. Even though a great amount of SR has been enacted, the ECJ impacts legal practice through its power of interpretation of law and its discretion (Europa 2017f). In such a design of checks and balances, policy and administrative power are checked and balanced by law. Although written law is driven by policy makers, in practice it should reject the interruption of policy makers once it has been approved, as designed, by the parliament or people.

4.2.2 *Validity and Incentive Analysis of Using Systematology in Social Science*

Systematology was originally designed for the use of natural science. Hereinto, the validity and incentive analysis discuss the rationality and sense of applying the methodology to the legal issue discussed by the study.

In the course of applying systematology in natural science, it is noticeable that the rules of philosophy in nature are objective and that the natural scenario is materially existing as well. However, even though the rules of philosophy in nature are objective, they are refined by thought. The object of natural science is to seek the true objective regulation of nature through the subjective analysis of a human. It is quite possible that an illustration of the rules of philosophy does not reflect an objective relationship. Nevertheless, scientists use systematology theory to bridge the two objective ends, so to prove natural regulation. *Vice versa*, natural regulation can be used in practice for other innovations. The course of illustrating the system is also the process to deduce or prove the applicability of the rules of philosophy.

By contrast, law in society *per se* is a system based on thought. However, the goal of law can be objective and law in society can last as long as the dominant objective goal prevails in the society. A social scenario can be deemed as objective from the historical perspective. In this case, it makes sense to assess the rationality of the application of social law between an objective goal of law and a historically objective social scenario. Accordingly, law in society is assessed while at the same time keeping as far as possible away from the rules of humans. Legislation with an objective goal(s) can break through the limitation of class to a certain extent.

The above logic can be put into the specific situation of market access of TCMP in the EU presently. The goal of pharmaceutical law is determined by the objective demand of people on safety. While market access of TCMP in the EU is a request objectively existing in reality based on the historical development of TCM in Europe, the right of autonomy held by patients or any other possible ethical reasons must be taken into account. Of course, there might be some other material reason(s) that stop TCM's existence in Europe. Therefore, if man-made law forms the obstacle and puts influence on a natural evolution of TCM in Europe, it is necessary to assess the rationality and appropriateness of the existence of the rule. Tools in systematology provide the methodologies to analyse the relationship between these two objective ends.

Market access of TCMP is initiated by the applicant. The relation between TCMP and the protection of public health needs to be confirmed by law. An ideal law is one in which the rules in law are objective, goal-driven and embody a system to ensure the realisation of the goal. Throughout the duration of analysing the system there is a process to evaluate the applicability of the existing principles and rules of the social scenario—hereinto, market access of TCMP in the EU standing on the legislative goal of protecting the public health.

Moreover, the system in the original design for natural science is objective. While it is illustratable and stands firmly between the principles and the existing scenario, scientists can still explore the possibility of changing the system for the use of human beings. Similarly, even though the EU system of administration is manually designed, it was already in existence before the issue of market access of TCMP arose in the EU. Therefore, it is meaningful to explore the applicability of the system to market access of TCMP by using systematology theory.

4.2.3 Some Traits of Complex Systems

OECD published the report Applications of Complexity Science for Public Policy in 2009 (OECD Global Science Forum 2009). It discussed the question of '[h]ow can the insights and methods of complexity science be applied to assist policymakers as they tackle difficult problems in policy areas such as... public safety' and the notion of 'complex system' in science was thereby introduced into the public policy arena. The report summarised some traits of complex systems to describe the nature of the complex system as well as the control of it. Below are listed some traits that guide the research.

- Adaptability[8]

The decision-making system of market access of TCMP is like a complex system that is formed by some independent subsystems. These independent subsystems interact with each other and cooperate with each other through sharing data in an information system, thus realising the transparency of rules and adapting to the development of science.

---

[8]Adaptability is defined as 'complex systems [that] are formed by independent constituents that interact, changing their behaviours in reaction to those of others, thus adapting to a changing environment' (OECD Global Science Forum 2009).

- Emergence[9]

Emergence should raise the attention of policymakers or legislators. TCMP has generally fit into the category of THMP. However, it is an alien product to the EU, therefore, emergent properties should be observed for testing the adaptation of the fundamental system to TCMP.

- Self-organisation[10]

As a whole, the system adaptation to market access of TCMP is a self-organisation. Each independent sub-system should have its own dynamic system, and then all the constituents come together to form the dynamic mechanism of the whole system. Therefore, any of the inefficient factors in each independent sub-system may influence the efficiency of the whole system.

- Attractors[11] and Self-Organised Criticality[12]

Attractors and self-organised criticality show the difficulties of making a change in an existing complex system. The system for controlling market access of medicinal products has set up standards or used some tools for assessing and managing risk. On one hand, the efficiency of the standards and tools used might have been well-proven. On the other hand, it might not be that flexible for those that are new and emergent. Therefore, creating a new constituent might be a way to adapt to the emergent. Otherwise, either the emergent would be very difficult to fit in the existing system or it might be difficult for the emergent to keep its inherent properties. This is the situation TCMP faces in the EU.

4.2.4 *Overview of the Tool of Network Analysis*

After illustrating the traits of the complex system, the report listed some of the most important complexity tools used in public policy domains for transmitting such a

[9]Emergence is explained as 'novel patterns that arise at a system level that are not predicted by the fundamental properties of the system's constituents or the system itself are called emergent properties' (OECD Global Science Forum 2009).

[10]'A system that is formed and operates through many mutually adapting constituents is called self-organising because no entity designs it or directly controls it. Self-organising systems will adapt autonomously to changing conditions, including changes imposed by policymakers' (OECD Global Science Forum 2009).

[11]Attractors means '[s]ome complex systems spontaneously and consistently revert to recognisable dynamic states known as attractors'.... 'if the pendulum of a grandfather clock is given a random nudge, it may move about erratically for a short time, but will soon settle back into its customary regular beat' (OECD Global Science Forum 2009).

[12]Self-organised criticality 'a complex system may possess a self-organising attractor state that has an inherent potential for abrupt transitions of a wide range of intensities. Because the state is an attractor, the system will, eventually, and spontaneously, return to it after each transition' (OECD Global Science Forum 2009).

complex system (OECD Global Science Forum 2009). Among them, network analysis is the one employed hereinafter. Network analysis can well present complex systems.

The issue of market access of TCMP is covered by a pharmaceutical law system applied to the medicinal product. Hereinto, the pharmaceutical law system is a complex and intricate whole formed by a set of interacting or interdependent subsystems or constituents (SCRATCH n.d.). First, both China and the EU have a specific administrative system which manages affairs relating to traditional medicinal products. The administrative system is based on an institutional framework. In the case of the approval of a new TCMP for market access, the competent authority operates along with other relevant institutions to make the decision. Second, safety, efficacy and quality control are the factors that the technical regulations and standards need to define for assessing the risk of the product. Therefore, identifying the standards of safety, efficacy and quality control is a task for the law, and the technical standards as a whole is a constituent of the complex system. Third, the system's efficiency is based on the level of perfection of an information system. Fourth, impact from the external environment should be assumed in legislating pharmaceutical law. Fifth, the legislative intent should be clarified. Legislative intent is not a constituent of the system, but it is the soul that drives respective constituents running on a single track. Therefore, four important constituents with a common legislative intent are shown in Fig. 4.1, which represents the important factors impacting the administrative system of market access of TCMP.

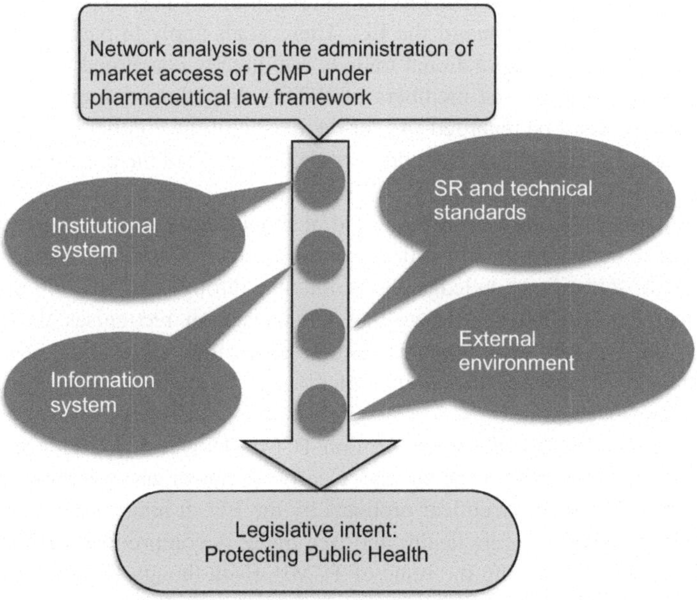

Fig. 4.1 Network analysis on the administration of market access of TCMP under pharmaceutical law framework

4.3 Comparison of the Legal Frameworks for Market Access of TCMP in the EU and China

Network analysis is employed hereinto for analysing the legal framework of market access and its impact factors. The legislative intent and each constituent in the network are analysed respectively by using a comparative study between the EU and China.

4.3.1 Legislative Intent

In the EU, Recital 2 of the Preamble of Directive 2001/83/EC states that '[t]he essential aim of any rules governing the production, distribution and use of medicinal products must be to safeguard public health'. However, from the expressions in Recital 3, one may not deduce with certainty that the consideration for public health will always prevail in industry development and trade when there is conflict between them. It leaves discretion to judges and national administrations to make a decision when there is a conflict between public health and the pharmaceutical industry and/or trade. Precisely two different goals are included in Recital 3 of the Preamble: one goal is to protect the development of the pharmaceutical industry, and the other goal is to protect trade. Considering the interest of each member of the Community respectively, the protection of a member's national industry may impair cross-border trade between Members States of the EU. These goals apply to partnership within Community. Therefore, international trade is not directly concerned with EU pharmaceutical law. However, as members of WTO, obligations committed to in the WTO agreement shall be regarded. As for the reason of the conflict between public health and pharmaceutical industry and/or trade, recital (7) of the preamble states the criteria to examine the harmfulness and therapeutic efficacy of the pharmaceutical product. Where risk assessment is requested, it should result that 'the potential risks are outweighed by the therapeutic efficacy of the product'. The result should relate to the progress of scientific knowledge and is obtained through examination in relation to each member. Recital (7) shows that the legislation recognises the possible limitations of scientific development, acknowledges that side effects of the drug may exist, and emphasises the weight of efficacy (Directive 2001/83/EC 2001, Preamble (2), (3), (7)).

EU pharmaceutical law does not mention TCMP. However, EU pharmaceutical law covers all medicinal products and clearly demonstrates scientific attitudes toward approval of pharmaceutical products by the EU. It hints at the significance of the balance between public health and free trade. A compromise between these two is necessary when facing the issue of TCMP. Even though EU pharmaceutical law does not give absolute priority to either of them, safeguarding public health is called 'the essential aim'.

The preamble stresses the issue of homeopathic medicinal products in Recital 21 to Recital 25. Comparably, herbal medicine is not highlighted therewith.

Chapter 2 of Directive 2001/83/EC is about the specific provisions applicable to homeopathic medicinal products, while specific provisions applicable to THMPs were added to Chapter 2a of Directive 2001/83/EC by 2004/24/EC. The numbering of Chapters 2 and 2a are bit odd. The relationship between homeopathic products and herbal medicinal products is not clarified. They are both treated as natural medicine comparing to conventional medicine. However, Chapter 2 includes articles 13 to 15, whereas chapter 2a only has article 16a but includes subsections a to i. It easily brings about confusion if Chapter 2a is a sub-chapter of Chapter 2. Homeopathy and traditional herbal medicine are different, and it is better to separate them according to each of their characteristics identified by law. Therefore, the EU legislator and the law executor may claim an entire separation between Chapter 2 and Chapter 2a. But the numbering reflects the evolution of EU pharmaceutical law on these two types of medicines. That is, the EU recognises these two medicines as a similar type when comparing them with Western conventional medicine, and they are both treated as CAM.

The Drug Administration Law of the PRC, Chapter I sets out the task of the law and grants administrative power to drug administration institutions (NPC Standing Committee of the PRC 1984). Article one states that the law is enacted for strengthening drug supervision and administration, ensuring good quality of the drugs, protecting the safety of human beings, and maintaining people's health and their rights to use the drugs. The specific law on TCM and TCMP in China—Law of Traditional Chinese Medicine and Medicinal Product of the PRC—provides the goals of legislation, including inheriting and developing TCM, ensuring and pushing the development of TCM undertakings, and protecting public health (NPC Standing Committee of the PRC 2017, art. 1).

Essentially, both China and the EU put public health as the legal objective of their pharmaceutical law. In addition, they both published GAP, GLP, GMP, GCP as well as Pharmacopeia for assessing and managing the risk. The comparison hereinto does not go into the details of all the similarities and differences between each of them. But noticeably, regarding the approval of new products, Chinese law divides TCMP into more types. Besides *Cheng Yao*, the part of the plant, animal body or mineral containing active ingredient(s) can be registered as a product. In addition, the TCMP for which the administration route or dosage form has been changed can be registered. Chinese law requires the clinical trial report for registering new TCMP (SFDA 2007; SAMR 2020). National Medical Products Administration (NMPA) published an announcement regarding the simplified registration procedure for registration of the TCMPs deriving from famous and classical ancient compound formulas (NMPA 2018). Strict conditions are provided to apply to this procedure and clinical trial research materials can be exempted in such application (NMPA 2018, art. 5).[13] In

[13]Article 3 of this announcement provides that to apply to simplified procedure should fulfill 7 conditions: (1) the formula does not contain any incompatibility, and does not contain highly or strong toxicity or any toxicity proved by modern toxicology; (2) there are national standards for materials in the prescription to follow; (3) the producing method comply with the records in ancient literature; (4) except decoction can be produced in form of granule, other forms should comply with

addition, Chinese doctors are allowed to give prescriptions of TCMP based on formula composing principle of TCM in practice. Comparing with EU traditional-use medicinal product, TCMP is more widely accepted in China based on both records of ancient literature and clinical practice of TCM.

4.3.2 Institutional System

4.3.2.1 EU's Institutional System

As mentioned before, the European Commission was established in 1958. It is responsible for drawing up proposals for new European legislation, and it implements the decisions of the EP and Council of the EU (Sect. 4.2.1). The European Commission includes many departments that are called Directorates-General (DG). Market access of TCMP is an affair under the management of the DG Health and Food Safety. The DG Health and Food Safety is assisted by the European Medicines Agency (EMA) in its undertaking of the responsibility of the administration of public health.

The EMA began operating in 1995. It provides scientific advice for the European Commission to authorise medicinal products through a centralised procedure (European Commission n.d.-a). It evaluates applications for marketing authorisation, monitors the safety of medicines across their lifecycle, and also provides information to healthcare professionals and patients (EMA 2017a). Of course, the majority of medicines available in the EU are authorised at national level (EMA 2017a). Nevertheless, the EU institutional system for centralised authorisation is the main focus of discussion hereinto.

The EMA has seven scientific Committees, some working parties and other groups which conduct the scientific work of the Agency. The committees work independently with an advisory function. Among them, the Committee on Herbal Medicinal Products (HMPC) is responsible for compiling and assessing scientific data on herbal substances, preparations and combinations to support the harmonisation of the European market. To support EU Member States, the HMPC focuses on two main tasks: (1) to establish EU monographs 'covering the therapeutic uses and safe conditions of well-established and/or traditional use for herbal substances and preparations' and (2) to draft 'an EU list of herbal substances, preparations and combinations thereof for use in traditional herbal medicinal products' (EMA 2017b). HMPC has some working parties and other groups which work on scientific issues relating to their particular field of expertise, and it delegates certain

---

the records in ancient literature; (5) administration route should comply with the records in ancient literature, and daily dosage should be equal to the dosage set out in ancient literature; (6) the function of the drug should be described by using terminologies of TCM, and accord with the records in ancient literature; (7) drugs going through simplified registration procedure cannot be used by groups of people of infectious, pregnant and infant.

tasks to them associated with the scientific evaluation of applications or drafting and revising scientific guidance documents (EMA 2017c). The EMA has the Pharmacovigilance Risk Assessment Committee (PRAC), and it also coordinates the affairs of pharmacoepidemiology and pharmacovigilance across Europe with the European Network of Centres for Pharmacoepidemiology and Pharmacovigilance (ENCePP) (Blake et al. 2012). The divisions of EMA undertake the daily administrative work led by the Executive Director as a whole with the support of scientific committees, groups and agencies, where each division also pursues a chief executive responsibility system (EMA 2017d). Among the Divisions, the Human Medicines Division is responsible for activities related to the scientific, regulatory and procedural management of human medicines evaluation.

EMA maintains a public list containing details of European experts who are involved in the Agency's work in the context of the authorisation, supervision and maintenance of medicinal products for human use. Those European experts serve as members of the Agency's scientific committees, working parties and other groups, and fall within the scope of the policy on handling affairs relevant to the interests of scientific committees' members and experts. They are nominated by Member States or by the Agency itself and are made available by the national competent authorities as well (EMA 2017e).

4.3.2.2 China's Institutional System

Prof. Li from China Renmin University made a presentation in a seminar organised by the OECD to support the work of Regulatory Reform Review in China. Specifically, she introduced the evolution of the Chinese pharmaceutical governance system, the main governmental institutions and their functions, the working content of the governance, the governance regulations and methods and so on. There are also some other journal articles and research outcomes in China which analyse the evolution of the Chinese pharmaceutical governance system (E.g. Hu et al. 2009). These resources traced the evolution of Chinese governance of public health. Overall, the governance system was initially set up from 1949 to around 1978. A second phase took place between 1979 and 1998, in which the Chinese governance system on pharmaceutical products was recovered from the Great Cultural Revolution. A third phase, the institutional reformational period began in 1998. And since March 2018 to present, China has been in a new phase, in which the arrangements of some administrative institutions have been adjusted and many pharmaceutical regulations have been amended.

4.3.2.2.1 Understanding the General Legal Framework of TCMP in China

In mainland of China, legislation has a strict hierarchy. The lower level legislations shall not conflict with the upper lever legislations. First, the Constitution Law (NPC of the PRC 1982) is on the top of the hierarchy. It provides the fundamental rights and obligations of citizens. Sanitary and hygienic legislation should not conflict with Constitutional law in China. Second, legislations enacted by the National People's Congress (NPC) and its standing committee are in the second level of the hierarchy. For instance, referring to TCMP, these legislations include the Drug Administration Law of the PRC (NPC of the PRC 1984) and its implementing regulation, the Law of Traditional Chinese Medicine and Medicinal Product of the PRC (NPC of the PRC 2017), and the Tort Liability Law (NPC Standing Committee of the PRC 2010). Third, administrative regulations enacted by central and local administrative institutions are in the third level and fourth level respectively, such as Provisions for Drug Registration (SFDA 2007, 2020), and Measures for the Reporting and Monitoring of Adverse Drug Reactions (Ministry of Health of the PRC 2011).

In addition, Hong Kong, hereinto taken as an example of one of the Special Administrative Regions of China, has a highly autonomous jurisprudence and legislative power. It applies the common law legal system, which contrasts with the civil law system followed by the mainland of China, in practice. However, it has a written administrative law, the Chinese Medicine Ordinance that functions for TCM administrative affairs. The Chinese Medicine Ordinance ensures the safety of TCMP in Hong Kong. The Chinese Medicine Council of Hong Kong (2017) is responsible for the administration of TCM.

Even though mainland China and Hong Kong have separate legal frameworks (NPC 1997), both legal frameworks aim at ensuring the safety of the pharmaceutical product and protect public health and interest. Hereinafter, the mainland pharmaceutical law system is explained to further discuss the administrative institutional system of TCMP in China.

4.3.2.2.2 Evolution of the Administrative Institutions and Their Functions

Phase One The Ministry of Health of China was set up in 1949.[14] It set up the *Yi Zheng Ju* (Medicine Administrative Bureau) to manage medicine-related and pharmacy-related affairs. The Ministry of Health set up the *Zhong Yi Si* (Department of Chinese Medicine) in 1954, and the *Zhong Yi Si* had sub-departments in charge of the science and technology of TCM, diagnosis of TCM, education on TCM and integration of TCM and Western medicine (Shang 2016). The general policy of quality control in 1954 was that the producers guaranteed quality, while the health administrative department monitored drug safety through spot tests (Li 2008). In 1957, *Yao Zheng Guan Li Ju* (Drug Administrative Bureau) was formed. It was responsible for product, selling and using of medicinal products. Accordingly, some local administrative organs were gradually set up as well (Li 2008).

Phase Two The second phase of this evolution was between 1979 and 1988, after the Great Cultural Revolution, and many things needed to be done to reach a revival

[14]The Ministry of Health of PRC merged with the Family Planning Committee to become the National Health and Family Planning Commission in 2013 (Xinhuanet 2013).

of the Chinese economy. In 1979, ratified by the State Council, the State Medicine Administrative Centre Bureau was set up, led by the Ministry of Health. The affairs of the trade in medicinal products were gathered together under the control of the Centre Bureau. In 1982, the leading power of the State Medicine Administrative Centre Bureau was transferred to State Economic Commission, and the Centre Bureau was renamed the State Medicine Administrative Bureau. Accordingly, many medicine administrative offices were established at the provincial and municipal level and were mainly in charge of the manufacture and selling of medicinal products and medical devices in China. In 1986 *the Zhong Yi Guan Li Ju* (Administrative Bureau of Chinese Medicine (ABCM)) was set up by the State Council. In 1988, ABCM was abolished, and *the Zhong Yi Yao Guan Li Ju* (National Administration of Traditional Chinese Medicine (NATCM)) was set up by the State Council (Shang 2016; Xinhuanet 2013). It carried on the responsibilities of *Zhong Yi Si* in phase one and focuses on the development of TCM.

Phase Three The Third phase was from 1998 to 2018. In 1998, China merged bureaus—the Medicinal Administrative Bureau led by the State Economic Commission and the Pharmacy Administration Office led by Ministry of Health—into the State Drug Administration (SDA). The SDA was in charge of a wide range of administrative affairs including pharmaceutical R&D, authorisation, manufacture, circulation and consumption. In 2003, the State Food and Drug Administration (SFDA) replaced the SDA, and its administrative supervision was extended from only pharmaceutical products to food, cosmetics, health care products. It was affiliated to the State Council between 2003 to 2008. In 2008, SFDA changed its affiliation and started to be led by the Ministry of Health (Gov.cn 2008). In 2013, SFDA and the State Food Safety Commission merged, becoming the China Food and Drug Administration (CFDA) (Xinhuanet 2013). CFDA became an affiliation of the State Council again but directly led by the National Health and Family Planning Commission (NHFPC). NHFPC was created from a merger of the previous Ministry of Health and the State Family Planning Commission. It was responsible for national healthcare, health services, family planning and other public health affairs (NHFPC 2013). In addition, the NATCM was led by the NHFPC as well, and it focused on the supervision of TCM in the domain of diagnosis (SATCM 2017).

Apart from the above-mentioned institutions, the National Development and Reform Commission (NDRC), the State Administration for Industry and Commerce of the PRC (SAIC) and Ministry of Finance were relevant to the development of TCMP in the third phase. NDRC engaged in the management of the macroeconomy of Chinese society, including enacting the strategy and long-range plan for economic development. SAIC related to the supervision of the manufacturing of pharmaceutical products, licensing of the pharmaceutical enterprises, trademark, advertising, and restricting unfair competition behaviours. In addition, the Ministry of Finance involved in issues of inspecting fees and other expenses relevant to administrative supervision.

Phase Four The fourth phase is from 2018 to present. In March 2018, the State Council announced its latest institutional restructuring (State Council of the PRC

2018). While the NDRC was maintained, the NHFPC, CFDA and SAIC do not exist anymore. NDRC still monitors the market, while some functions relating to the administration of medicine, medicinal products and food of those removed units are taken by the National Health Commission of the PRC (NHC), the State Administration for Market Regulation of the PRC (SAMR), and National Healthcare Security Administration (NHSA). The NHC is a department of the State Council, and the SAMR and the NHSA are direct affiliations of the State Council. The NHC leads the National Administration of Traditional Chinese Medicine (NATCM) that focuses on the supervision of TCM, including practice registration of TCM medical institutions. It includes seven departments and covers functions such as drafting the health insurance directory and payment standards, drafting the policy on government procurement of pharmaceutical products in the health insurance directory and monitoring the implementation of the policy and so on. The SAMR covers the responsibilities of the cancelled CFDA and leads a newly established bureau called the National Medical Products Administration (NMPA) in charge of the safety of medicinal products including TCMP.

4.3.2.2.3 The Coordination and Distribution of Responsibilities

In practice, research institutions or R&D departments of manufactures work on R&D of medicinal product; manufactures also work on the naming, quantity control, specification, storing, and distribution of the medicinal product; hospitals and pharmacies sell medicinal products to patients; while, doctors provide prescriptions to patients who buy and use the drug. Accordingly, a drug may go through four stages, including R&D, manufacture, circulation and consumption. First, R&D involves safety and efficacy tests, quality control, clinical trial quality control and drug authorisation. Second, once a drug is authorised for market access, it enters the second stage, manufacture. The manufacture procedure must be conducted according to Good Manufacturing Practice (GMP). Pharmaceutical enterprises should have rules on management of employment, internal administration, plant, facilities, equipment, raw materials, manufacturing techniques, archives, monitoring systems, and sales of the product. Third, in the stage of circulation, China has the Good Supply Practice (GSP) regulation to supervise the bid, drug e-commerce, physical distribution, retail sales through internet or franchising. Certain percent of drugs are covered by the national healthcare system and collected in a catalogue of drugs for basic national medicinal insurance through bidding procedures. Fourth, consumption relates to the use of drugs. There are committees for checking the list and purchase plan and for pharmacovigilance. At the same time different levels of drug administration bureaus organise the spot check on the drug in the market, and the result of the spot check and invalid drugs with poor quality, poor safety and low efficacy are announced publicly in the supervision of the fourth phase (Li 2008). Drug administration institutions take the administrative responsibility in these four stages. Professor Zhen Li ever used a flowchart to explain the coordination and distribution of responsibilities among all relevant administration institutions in

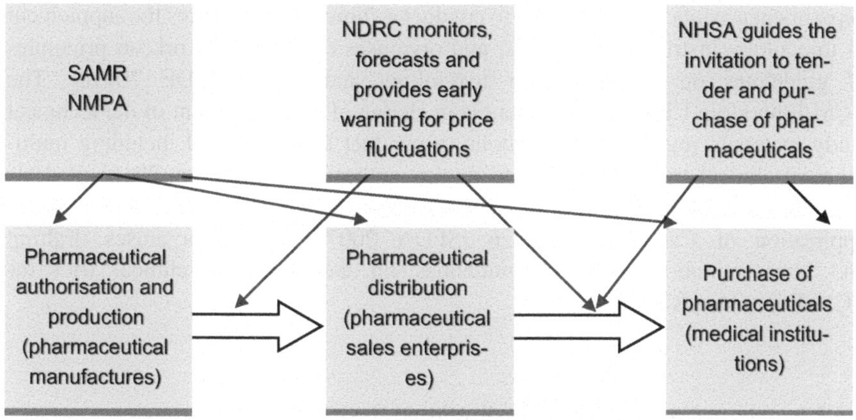

Fig. 4.2 Flowchart of the supervision on pharmaceutical product in China

charge of different affairs in phase three. Along with the changings in phase four, Fig. 4.2 is produced. NMPA authorises market access for pharmaceutical products, and it supervises and monitors the safety, efficacy and quality control of the pharmaceutical products; NDRC monitors the market and the fluctuation of prices of medicinal products; and NHSA guides the tender and purchase.

The NMPA took over the Department of Drug Registration (DDR) and the Centre of Drug Evaluation (CDE) which belonged to CFDA in phase three. DDR organises the drafting of the national pharmacopeia, technical standards and essential drugs list and supervises the implementation of these technical standards. The CDE continues working on accepting applications for market access of medicinal products and being responsible for the technical review. The CDE's day to day management is guided by the Chief Scientist. Besides some of its administrative departments, such as office, personnel, and financial department, its work is mainly driven by ten pharmaceutical departments, among them, the TCM/Ethnodrug Pharmacy department, the Pharmacology and Toxicology department and the TCM/Ethnodrug Clinical Trial department are directly relevant to market access of TCMP.

The TCM/Ethnodrug Pharmacy department is in charge of technical assessment of the study materials submitted for the authorisation of market access as well as the application to conduct clinical trials. It deals with the assessment and authorisation of clinical trials of Categories 7 and 8 in the registration classification on TCMP and natural medicinal products (SFDA 2007),[15] market access affairs of Categories 7, 8 and 9, and some other work assigned by CDE (CFDA 2017). The applicant can apply for administrative review or initiate administrative lawsuits in case they disagree with the decisions of CDE. The Pharmacy Pharmacology and Toxicology

[15]Category 7 is the registration application for TCMP/natural medicinal product with the changed administration route; Category 8 is the registration application for TCMP/natural medicinal product with the changed dosage form; Category 9 is generic medicinal product.

department accepts the application to conduct a clinical trial, requires the supplement of toxicology instruction materials, and organises the drafting work on principles of guidelines on assessment of toxicology and so on (CDE 2017a). The TCM/Ethnodrug Clinical department is in charge of the assessment of the technical study materials regarding applications to conduct a clinical trial including multi-regional clinical trials (MRCT) and market authorisation (Shenoy 2016). It deals with the clinical trial applications of Category 6 and the market authorisation application of Categories 1 to 6 (SFDA 2007). It also organises drafting and implementation work of guidelines on assessing the clinical trial for TCM/Ethnodrug (CDE 2017b).

4.3.2.3 Short Comparison of Institutional Systems

Regarding the administration of traditional medicine, China has a specific and more sophisticated administrative framework on TCM and TCMP with which the EU cannot compete. Although, the EU does have independent and quite strong scientific working groups to support the medical and pharmaceutical administration system.

4.3.3 Information System

For meeting the goal of transparency of law, the EU has a well-designed information system for the communication between the public and itself. The EU recognises the citizens' right to access the EU decision-making process. It is noted that,

> [t]he more open the process is, the easier it is to ensure balanced representation and avoid undue pressure and illegitimate or privileged access to information or to decision-makers (Europa 2017g).

The EU has a transparency register platform in place to answer core questions (Europa 2017g). Citizens can register individually or in groups, such as professional consultancies, non-governmental organisations, think tanks, research and academic institutions and other types of groups. In addition, the DG Health and Food Safety of European Commission builds up the EU Health Policy Platform to ease communication between the Commission's services and health stakeholders. The objectives of the EU Health Policy Platform include ensuring transparency through health policy dialogue, contributing to building knowledge and expertise on public health issues, and gathering and circulating research outcomes and so on (European Commission n.d.-b). The EU Health Policy Platform operates in two ways: through an IT platform enabling online discussion and collaboration and through a face-to-face meeting hosting targeted thematic discussions. DG Health and Food Safety heads the secretariat of the EU Health Policy Platform (European Commission n.d.-b).

Chinese administrations also concern themselves with the transparency of public information (See: State Council of the PRC 2007, 2019 revision). The technological development of internet has made the disclosure of public information timely and prompt. For instance, the website of the CDE has a portal for Public Information for disclosing registrations of clinical tests and new drug applications, evaluation and decision of administration, and a window of Law and Regulations for publishing the Technical Regulations such as ICH. It also has a portal for Clinical Trial Registration for guiding the applicant's registration, and other web links for public communications. The Website of SAMR also has similar links for disclosing public information. In addition, consumers can also report fake medicines and inferior medicines to different levels of food and drug administrative institutions and industrial and commercial bureaus.

4.3.4 Statutory Regulations and Technical Standards for Medicinal Products

The SRs and technical standards for market access of TCMP are instruments of drug administration. Drug administration follows regulations in the supervision of all pharmaceutical production chains. The production chains include R&D, production, pricing, circulation, consumption, advertising and so on. The issue of market access involves safety, efficacy and quality control of medicinal products. Pharmaceutical law sets up the authorisation system for medicinal products to monitor safety, efficacy and quality, so to secure people's health. Medical science has played a vital and decisive role in the lawmaking process. Standards set up a buffer zone between SR and science in case the law is ambiguous.

Standards are soft law, and they play an important role in regulating the technical target. They create a bridge between law and science. Agreement on Technical Barriers to Trade (TBT) in the WTO clearly distinguishes technical regulations and standards. It treats a technical regulation as a:

> Document which lays down product characteristics or their related processes and production methods, including the applicable administrative provisions, with which compliance is mandatory. It may also include or deal exclusively with terminology, symbols, packaging, marking or labelling requirements as they apply to a product, process or production method (WTO 1994).

TBT puts standards into technical requirements just as with technical regulations, but it defines standards as a kind of voluntary requirement. Standards are certain medicinal normative documents that are formatted and enacted with a common recognition within a scientific area or profession. Standards normally are approved by relevant WTO Members based on science, technology and experience and can be repeatedly and commonly used by people. Law and standards are two methods which guarantee the proper and effective running of the market. Standards *per se* are not law, but they can be mandatorily implemented via being cited or regulated by laws. Therefore, the main difference between standards and technical regulations is that the former is voluntarily implemented, and the latter is mandatorily implemented (Motaal 1998). Regarding TCMP, the Ph. Eur., known as the Community herbal monographs, and the Chinese pharmacopoeia have drawn very broad attention to and have placed big influence on market access of medicinal products.

4.3.4.1 General Comparison of the Regulations Between the EU and China

Figure 4.3 shows important laws, regulations and technical standards on deciding market access of pharmaceutical products in the EU and in mainland China. This part of the book does not aim to analyse either the EU technical standards or China's in detail, however, it will show the general framework of SR and standards on assessing the safety, efficacy and quality control of medicinal products. Both the EU

	Law and technical standards of the EU	Law and technical standards of the mainland of China
Essential aim of pharmaceutical law	Directive 2001/83/EC, Title I (2), (3)	Yao Pin Guan Li Fa, Article 1 (Drug Administration Law of China)
GAP	EMEA/HMPC/246816/2005	Zhong Yao Cai Sheng Chan Zhi Liang Guan Li Gui Fan (Chinese GAP)
GLP	ICH Topic S 7A, 2004/9/EC, 2004/10/EC, OECD GLP	Yao Wu Fei Lin Chuang Yan Jiu Zhi Liang Guan Li Gui Fan (Chinese GLP)
GMP	91/356/EEC amended 2003/94/EC, 91/412/EEC	Yao Pin Sheng Chan Zhi Liang Guan Li Gui Fan, Yao Pin Sheng Chan Jian Du Guan Li Ban Fa (Chinese GMP)
GCP	The 'Clinical Trial Directive' 2001/20/EC, the 'GCP Directive' 2005/28/EC	Yao Pin Lin Chuang Shi Yan Zhi Liang Guan Li Gui Fan (Chinese GCP)
Registration	Directive 2001/83/EC Directive 2004/24/EC	Yao Pin Zhu Ce Guan Li Ban Fa (Provisions for Drug Registration)
Pharmacopoeia	European Pharmacopoeia	Chinese Pharmacopoeia
[Note]: GAP: Good Agricultural Practice; GLP: Good Laboratory Practice; GMP: Good Manufactural Practice; GCP: Good Clinical Practice		

Fig. 4.3 Comparison of EU and China's Legislations Governing TCMP

and China have rules of GAP, GLP, GMP and GCP—China has more specific rules on TCMP, whereas the EU covers TCMP mainly as a herbal medicinal product. Even though both China and the EU have similar frameworks on assessing the risks of market access of TCMP, they have distinct standards. For instance, Chinese pharmacopeia has recorded more herbal substances or compound formulas, but the EU has quite different monographs. China does not have a rule such as that for traditional-use medicinal product registration as the EU provided in the Directive 2004/24/EC. But China has simplified procedure for registration of compound Chinese medicinal product deriving from ancient famous and classical formulas (NMPA 2018). In practice, a large number of TCMPs developed from the famous and classical formulas have been registered in China.

In addition, the internationally harmonised rules are worth mentioning. The EU follows the rules of the International Council for Harmonisation (ICH) which was initially founded by the EC, the U.S. and Japan in 1990 (ICH 2017a). The ICH, formerly the International Conference on Harmonisation (ICH), was established as an international association, with the nature of a legal entity under Swiss law, on 23 October 2015. The idea for harmonising rules regarding medicinal products was conceived as early as the WHO Conference of Drug Regulatory Authorities in Paris in 1989 (ICH 2017b). Soon afterwards, the International Federation of Pharmaceutical Manufacturers and Associations (IFPMA) was approached to discuss a joint regulatory-industry initiative on international harmonisation, therewith ICH was conceived (ICH 2017b). A major achievement of ICH is that it has established an over-arching governing body with the aim of focusing on global pharmaceutical regulatory harmonisation. ICH's mission is to help increase patient access to safe, effective, and high-quality pharmaceuticals and ensuring that pharmaceuticals are developed and registered efficiently. China became a member of ICH in May 2017 (ICH 2017a). It stands to reason that China is meeting the international standards of pharmaceuticals. On one hand, the membership of China in ICH pushes China to strengthen safety, efficacy and quality control and grants Chinese pharmaceutical products and industry easier access to the markets of other members of the ICH. On the other hand, the standards of ICH may challenge the R&D and market access of TCMP. In its Guideline on Quality of Herbal Medicinal Products/Traditional Herbal Medicinal Products the EU clearly notes that "[a]nalytical procedures not given in a Pharmacopoeia should be validated in accordance with the ICH guideline 'Note for guidance on validation of analytical procedures: text and methodology' (CPMP/ICH/281/95) or the corresponding VICH guideline (CVMP/VICH/591/98), unless otherwise justified" (CHMP 2006).

4.3.4.2 An Overview of EU Legislation and Standards Regarding TCMP

Notably, TCMPs have very rarely been registered in practice in the EU, so this discussion is focused on the market access phase. The issue of market access of TCMP is mainly regulated in EU pharmaceutical law in the form of ST and technical standards, and sometimes precedents. The law is primarily to protect public health through ensuring the safety, efficacy, and quality of medicinal products, while also taking economic interests into account (EU 6655/7/08 REV 7 2012). To reach this goal, the law regulates the manufacture, trade and use of medicines through the activity of competent authorities. Hereinto, the right to know, the right to be educated on pharmaceutical information and the right to freely select medicine should be ensured and considered. Pharmaceutical regulations and standards provide technical rules for assessing safety, efficacy and quality (EU 6655/7/08 REV 7 2012).

4.3.4.2.1 The Development of EU Pharmaceutical Legislation

EU pharmaceutical law does not regulate TCMP as a therapy of a specific type of medicine, therefore the clue to pursue the legal developmental path of TCMP is from the reform of the pharmaceutical law which is applied to TCMP. The preamble of the consolidated edition of Directive 2001/83/EC offers a clue for teasing out the legal developmental context. It reflects that the development of EU pharmaceutical legislation relevant to TCMP can be divided into three stages. The first stage was from 1965 to 2001; the second stage from 2001 to 2011; and the last stage from 2011 up to now. Hereinto, 2004 is a very important year because of the enacting of Directive 2004/24/EC.

As stated in the preamble of Directive 2001/83/EC, the relevant legislation can be traced back to Directive 65/65/EEC of 26 January 1965 on the approximation of provisions laid down by law, a regulation or administrative action relating to medicinal products. It established the legal bases and general regulative structure for the registration of medicinal products in the EU. In Directive 65/65/EEC, TCMP can be imported or produced by Chinese practitioners according to Article 1 (4) and (5) and Article 2(3). Article 2(3) excluded the application of the Directive to herbal medicinal products provided by Chinese doctors for individual use. This article has been absorbed into Directive 2001/83/EEC. Even though Article 2 (3) of Directive 65/65/EEC did not clearly mention herbal medicine, the application to herbal medicine can be deduced from the definition clause. In detail, Article 1 (4) defined the 'magistral formula' as 'any medicinal product prepared in a pharmacy in accordance with a prescription for an individual patient', whereas Article 1 (5) defined the 'officinal formula' as 'any medicinal product which is prepared in a pharmacy in accordance with the prescriptions of a pharmacopoeia and is intended to be supplied directly to patients served by the pharmacy in question'. Taken together, the exemption clause and the definition clause make it possible for Chinese practitioners to produce TCMP or import TCMP from the third parties for the indicated use of individual patients.

Strictly speaking, according to Directive 65/65/EEC, medicinal products must be registered when entering the EU market, except for in situations mentioned in Article 2. Therefore, it will be illegal if any Member State of the EU imports 'any substance or combination of substances presented for treating or preventing disease in human beings or animals' or '[a]ny substance or combination of substances which may be administered to human beings or animals with a view of making a medical diagnosis or of restoring, correcting or modifying physiological functions in humans' without an official registration. The rule is strengthened by Directive 2001/83/EC and its amendment, Directive 2004/24/EC. According to Directive 2004/24/EC Article 2 (2), even no medicinal product material of TCMP is permitted to be imported to EU market without a legal registration. Indeed, there is an exception for the import of the non-registered TCMP through Chinese practitioners, but the legal conditions to use the exception clause tend to be stricter as well.

4.3.4.2.2 Standards Relevant to TCMP

EU soft law was covered in the early part of this chapter. The Ph. Eur. established by the HMPC is highlighted in this part. It states the scientific opinion of the HMPC on the safety and efficacy of the specific herbal substance and its preparations intended for medicinal use (EU HMPC 2007). The substances and preparation, for the use of application for well-established use medicinal product and traditional use medicinal product, are recorded in the Ph. Eur., including their medicinal product name, qualitative and quantitative logical properties, pharmaceutical particulars, and compilation/last revision dates (EU HMPC 2005). These data provide a very important gist for evaluating the safety and efficacy of herbal products for registration. The European Directorate for the Quality of Medicines and Healthcare publishes technical Guides for the elaboration of monographs (European Directorate for the Quality of Medicines and HealthCare 2017).

In addition, the Chinese Pharmacopoeia is an important official document in China for collecting data on TCMP, which is compiled by the Chinese Pharmacopoeia Commission (2015). It gives descriptions and information on the standards of purity, testing, dosage, precautions, storage, and the strength of compound formulas as well as substances and preparations (CFDA of the PRC 2010, No. 43). According to Qu et al. (2014), until 2014, 'there [were] 10 herbal substances in HMPC herbal substance assessment inventory which have the same congruent genus, species, and plant part origins as used in Chinese traditions determined by Pharmacopoeia of the People's Republic of China' (EU HMPC 2017). A press release of 30 May 2016 showed that 66 Chinese herbs had undergone strict examination and discussion and were approved by 37 signatory states, so that they are listed in the European Pharmacopoeia (Xinhua 2016).

4.3.4.3 An Overview of Chinese Administrative Legislation and Standards Relevant to TCMP

In general, regulations on pharmaceutical affairs of the PRC include law, administrative regulation and its implementation, administrative department rules, national standards, local administrative department rules and international treaties. Law includes constitutional law and laws enacted by the National People's Congress (NPC) and its Standing Committee (Zeng and Wang 2009). Among these laws, China's constitutional law is on the top of the Chinese legislative hierarchy, followed by laws made by the NPC and its Standing Committee. China's constitutional law is similar to the EU's primary legislation which covers general principles and people's fundamental rights (Hameed 2012; EUR-Lex 2017). Laws enacted by NPC and its Standing Committee align with the relevant principles established in China's constitutional law and explicitly set out rights and obligations in the various legal branches. As for the pharmaceutical administrative legislation, on one hand, they set out the power and duty of the administrative organs as a whole, or they sometimes impose individual responsibilities in situations in which the individual bears obligations to certain administrative positions. On the other hand, they guide and regulate the administrative counterparts' activities in application, and manufacturing, selling and other marketing behaviours. These laws are primary legal sources in China, but similar to EU secondary legislation which enables the EU to exercise its powers. The local Chinese governmental departments can also make regulations and rules relating to respective local affairs. Comparing to the highly independent EU Members States, Chinese local governments operate their legislative power under the supervision of the central government, except in certain areas including Hong Kong, Macao and Taiwan, in which the local governments have large autonomy. All administrative regulations should comply with rules set out by laws. In addition, national standards on pharmaceutical products are very important guidance for producers and for the R&D of pharmaceutical products. They are considered soft law and are widely influenced by and develop along with the scientific research of medicine.

The issues of TCMP range from safety, efficacy and quality control, to manufacture, and finally to the use of the product. Thereto, various legislations are applied. The Drug Administration Law of the PRC was introduced in 1984 (NPC Standing Committee of the PRC 1984, Order of the President No. 31). It has been revised many times, and the latest edition was published in 2019. It is the law that generally regulates all the chains of the administration of medicinal products. It has twelve chapters. Chapter I sets out the task of the law and grants administrative power to drug administrative institutions. Article 1 states that the law is enacted for strengthening drug supervision and administration, ensuring good quality of the drugs, protecting the safety of human beings, and maintaining people's health and their right to use these drugs. Chapter II to IV set out the administrative rules on entities involved in manufacturing, distribution and medical institution. Chapter V to Chapter IX regulate the selling, packaging, price monitoring, advertising, storage and supply of drugs, and pharmacovigilance. Chapter X sets out the supervision of fake medicine and inferior medicines. Chapter XI states some obligations on the person or entity that breaches the rules, mainly involving administrative and criminal responsibilities. The last chapter includes some miscellaneous items. Accordingly, the State Council issued the Regulations for the Implementation of the Drug Administration Law of the PRC in 2002 and the last revision was published in 2019 through the State Council in the Decision of the State Council on Amending

Certain Administrative Regulations (State Council of the PRC 2002, Order No. 360; State Council of the PRC 2019, Order No. 709). The Drug Administration Law of the PRC and its implementing regulation cover administrative affairs of all pharmaceutical products, but they do not emphasise any specific type of product.

The Standing Committee of the National People's Congress (NPC) issued the Law of China on Traditional Chinese Medicine and Medicinal Products (hereinafter short for Chinese Law on TCM and TCMP) on 25 December 2016, and the law went into effect on 1 July 2017. Some researchers hold that Drug Administration Law and Chinese Law on TCM and TCMP are both specialised administrative law, where, the latter is more specialised (PharmNet.com.cn 2017). No matter how the law is read, Article 60 of the latter points to a hierarchy between these two, stating that in the case where no provision is provided in the latter, the Law on Medical Practitioners (NPC Standing Committee of the PRC 1999), Drug Administration Law and other relevant laws and administrative regulations shall be applied. Chinese Law on TCM and TCMP contains nine chapters including traditional Chinese medical services (Chapter II), the training of TCM talents (Chapter IV), scientific research of TCM (Chapter V) and TCM inheritance and cultural transmission (Chapter VI). As clearly stated in Article 1 of the law, the law is aimed at inheriting and developing TCM, protecting and facilitating the undertaking of TCM, and protecting people's health. Chapter III, Article 21 on the protection of TCMP is very general, demonstrating that the way to ensure the quality of TCMP is to enact standards and technical specifications on planting, gathering, storing and preliminarily processing of the raw materials. It generally mentions the protection of and research on the wildlife resources possibly used in TCMP, the genuine raw materials of TCMP, the know-how of the production of decoction pieces, and other traditional Chinese medicinal therapies (Song 2014).[16] Therefore, even though the law contains specialised provisions on TCM and TCMP, the provisions mention fundamental issues.

China has enacted many regulations, standards and technical guidelines on TCMP, some of the more important ones include Good Agricultural Practice of Traditional Chinese Crude Drugs (GAP) (SDA of the PRC 2002), Good Manufacturing Practices for Pharmaceutical Products (Ministry of Health 2010; SFDA 2020), Good Supply Practice of Pharmaceutical Products (GSP) (CFDA 2015, Order No. 13), Annex 1 of Provisions for Drug Registration (SFDA 2007; SAMR 2020), Measures for the Administration of Prescription (Ministry of Health 2013, Order No. 53) and Chinese Pharmacopeia (Chinese Pharmacopoeia Commission 2015). These regulations, standards and technical guidelines provide detailed instructions for R&D institutions, manufacturers, providers of raw materials, pharmacies and TCM practitioners to manage TCMP affairs. In addition, the amendment on the Drug Administration Law provides more rules on producing decoction pieces (NPC Standing Committee of the PRC 1984, arts. 24, 39, 44). Besides that, NATCM enacted two provisions. One is the management practice for hospital to purchase,

[16]Some of the TCMPs are proven to only have efficacy when produced from raw material planted in specific location, and this raw material is called genuine raw material.

check, save, cut, prepare decoction pieces (NATCM 2007). And the other is for regulating the packaging of decoction pieces (NATCM 1998). Chinese decoction pieces are treated as TCMP in Chinese medical practice as well as law.

4.3.5 External Environment

Social and regional policy, business, taxation, environmental protection, education, registration system of TCM practitioners, research and innovation, food and farming, and many other factors, compose the external environment of the legal systems functioning on market access of TCMP. Among them, the education and registration system of TCM practitioners are significant for ensuring the safe use of TCMP. The development of TCM education has been pushed in the UK, where the legislation on TCM practitioners has been widely discussed (Cheng and Shen 2010). But they are less developed in the rest of Europe. Comparatively, China has an advanced system of TCM education for registration of TCM practitioners. The two systems ensure TCMP have a sustainable development environment in China.

4.4 The Functioning of EU Pharmaceutical Law Relating to Market Access of TCMP in the EU

4.4.1 Market Access of Registered TCMP in the EU

The EU Committee published a Q&A, and it is a comprehensive guide for applicants to register their medicinal products (HMPC 2014). Three types of registration channels for the medicinal product entering the EU market are provided by EU law. They are called full application, well-established use application and traditional use registration, respectively.

The full application is provided for in Article 8 of Directive 2001/83/EC. Pharmaceutical tests including physic-chemical biological or microbiological tests, pre-clinical tests including toxicological and pharmacological tests and clinical trials are all needed in this registration procedure. An application, which involves a new herbal substance or herbal preparation but does not fulfil the application conditions in Article 10(a) and Article 16(a), must go through the full application channel.

The well-established use application can be applied according to Article 10(a) of Directive 2001/83/EC, in case the applicant can prove that the active substances of a medicinal product have been used within the EU safely and effectively for at least 10 years. The test and clinical trials can be replaced by detailed references in the form of published and appropriate scientific literature.

Traditional use registration for a herbal medicinal product, also called the simplified procedure, is provided by Article 16(a) of Directive 2001/83/EC. Clinical trials can be avoided if the applicant can provide sufficient evidence of the medicinal use of the product throughout a period of at least 30 years, including at least 15 years in the EU. In any case, the competent authorising authority retains the right to consider the product's safety through asking for necessary data as proof.

The Netherlands Medicines Evaluation Board (MEB) has approved SU BioMedicine B.V. for the registration of Diao Xin Xue Kang. Diao Xin Xue Kang is a THMP in the form of capsules for oral use (MEB 2012). It is the first TCMP that went through the legal registration procedure in the EU market (Regulation (EU) No.178/2002 2002).

Four points should be highlighted regarding Diao's registration in the Netherlands. First, the registration went through the simplified application procedure (MEB 2012, p. 3). Second, Diao Xin Xue Kang capsules contain a single substance (MEB 2012, p. 5). Third, Diao Xin Xue Kang was approved with conditions: (1) 'the safety of the product is monitored with a Pharmacovigilance system', and (2) 'results of a genotoxicity test conducted in accordance existing EU guidelines are submitted before the renewal of the registration' (MEB 2012, p. 11). And Fourth, the registration for Diao Xin Xue Kang was granted to SU BioMedicine B.V. Netherlands (MEB 2012, p. 1). In the EU, the applicant can only register their medicinal products through EU companies (Directive 2001/83/EC 2001, art. 8(2)). Such agency system for registration of medicinal product also exists in China.

It is more difficult to gain approval for compound TCMP due to the complex chemical reactions between different ingredients. Providing acceptable and sufficient scientific data for safety concerns is the core for a successful registration application, but it is difficult for many TCMPs to comply with all the requirements of the EU assessment procedure due to the current lack of sufficient data. This is especially because most TCM formulas are compound, which brings more difficulties when using the western scientific method to assess the safety and efficacy of TCMP. The Ph. Eur., which is the most important official collection of data recording safe medicinal products ingredients used in practice, has recorded some similar herbal substances and preparations as those used in Chinese medicinal practice and recorded in the Chinese pharmacopeia. However, they are still very limited resources in comparison with TCM practice (Qu et al. 2014). Furthermore, even when it is possible to test the ingredients and reactions in a compound TCMP, it is not easy to meet the 15 years use assessment in the EU for TCMP. Moreover, the records of using TCMP need a better system for data collection. The current assessment system may have not given enough attention to the long existence of TCM practitioners within the EU.

4.4.2 *Market Access of Non-registered TCMP in the EU*

TCMP can access the EU market after official registration through the competent EU authority or competent authorities of EU Member States. Additionally, TCMP can also access to EU market through Chinese practitioners when the importing situation complies with other legal conditions laid down in EU law. The legal basis relevant to non-registered TCM accessing the EU market is cited in Article 3 (1) and Article 5 (1) of Directive 2001/83/EC.

4.4.2.1 Market Access Forms of Non-registered TCMP

One issue relating to the market access form of TCMP has garnered the attention of EU Member States. Because many TCMP have entered the EU market as nutritional food, novel food and agriculture product and not as medicinal products, some substances and preparations can be used as food, such as dates and ginger, or are parts of plants. The problem is TCM substances and TCM preparations cannot be monitored and registered as medicinal products under EU pharmaceutical law. Therefore, the demand for such TCMP can only be supplied in other forms. However, the situation brings risks to public health when such materials are in medicinal use. Because, first, a drug is different from nutritional food and novel food. So, when substances are used as medicine, they should be well-distinguished from food in many aspects, including the situation of use, the dose of use, and the aim of use. Nutritional food and novel food cannot be advertised for the function of treatment. The EU adopted Regulation (EC) No. 178/2002 of the EP and of the Council on 28 January 2002, laying down the general principles and requirements of food law, establishing the European Food Safety Authority and laying down procedures in matters of food safety. Second, a drug is different from agricultural product, but in practice TCMP is possible to be imported as an agricultural product but in use of preparations or raw materials of TCMP.

EU pharmaceutical law mentions that '[t]his Directive allows non-medicinal herbal products, fulfilling the criteria of food legislation, to be regulated under food legislation in the Community' (Directive 2004/24/EC 2004). So, clarification of 'non-medicinal' use is a priority. In addition, EU law also has pursued a precautionary attitude on medicinal products. It states that:

> In cases of doubt, where, taking into account all its characteristics, a product may fall within the definition of a 'medicinal product' and within the definition of a product covered by other Community legislation the provisions of this Directive shall apply (Directive 2001/83/EC 2001, art. 1 (30) (31) (32)).

However, the problem is that the aim of the use is not easy to be ascertained in the stage of importing. Moreover, TCM substances and preparations cannot be registered as medicinal products, so rules for medicinal products in the EU pharmaceutical law do not adequately apply to them. Regarding this problem, monitoring the use and import of the substances and preparations by practitioners is a good way to distinguish food-used products from drugs, as the aim of the use of TCMP by TCM practitioners is usually obviously for treatment and medicinal use.

4.4.2.2 Market Access Channels of Non-registered TCMP

Chinese medicine practitioners may legally provide non-registered TCMP in the EU. Article 3 (1) of Directive 2001/83/EC states that '[a]ny medicinal product prepared in a pharmacy in accordance with a medical prescription for an individual patient, 'commonly known as the magistral formula', is not covered by the Directive. This clause excludes the application of the Directive 2001/83/EC to TCMP when the product is provided by the prescription of a Chinese practitioner. In addition, Article 3 (2) states that any medicinal product which is prepared in a pharmacy in accordance with the prescriptions of a pharmacopeia and is intended to be supplied directly to the patients in question (commonly known as the officinal formula) is also excluded from registration. Article 3 leaves a space for TCM practitioners to provide TCM substances and preparations to patients in the EU. In practice, TCM practitioners usually store only a certain amount of TCM substances and preparations. They can reference the officinal formulas from either the EU monographs (i.e. Ph. Eur.) or Chinese pharmacopeia.

4.4.2.2.1 General Regulative Status of EU Law on TCM Practitioners

There is no constraint on SR of herbalists in EU-level legislation, and the right to draw up the regulations of health professionals is left to each Member State (McIntyre 2014). Even though EU Member States have regulations on GP, they do not usually use drug substances or preparations to make up drugs for individual patient use. But TCM doctors obey principles of formulation and prescribe customised medicinal products for patients based on their individual syndrome(s). Therefore, generally speaking, the conditions to operate a TCM practice should be specified in the regulations of GP in the EU, but most Member States do not have proper rules for TCM practitioners, or, at most, they provide regulations for acupuncturists (WHO/EDM/TRM/2000 2000).

4.4.2.2.2 Legal Conditions to Fulfil the Exceptional Situation of Non-registered TCMP for Importing

People can find clues for non-registered TCMP in EU pharmaceutical law. Article 5 (1) of Directive 2001/83/EC provides for the legal conditions of importing non-registered TCMP into the EU, it states that:

> A Member State, in accordance with legislation in force and to fulfil special needs, exclude from the provisions of this Directive medicinal products supplied in response to *bona fide* unsolicited order, formulated in accordance with the specifications of an authorised health-care professional and for use by an individual patient under his direct personal responsibility (Directive 2001/83/EC 2001)

Therefore, it is possible for non-registered TCMP to access the EU market if: (1) it is for meeting special need(s) of the patient; (2) it is requested by the patient; (3) it is provided by and under the supervision of an authorised health-care professional; (4) the patient is responsible for his/her individual use of the product. However, two conflicts arise from the practice of TCM when applying this clause. First, many Member States do not regulate Chinese GPs properly, nor do they register Chinese doctors as GPs in the EU at all. So, there is no basis to apply to this clause. Two, it is not clear if the GP can store any non-registered TCMP or prescription TCMP from China. Reading EU pharmaceutical law strictly, the answer goes to the negative. In that case, there is no basis for the existence of TCM in practice at all. Moreover, the information system needs to be further developed for the more efficient collection of data regarding using TCMP from practitioners.

4.4.2.2.3 The Implementation of EU Pharmaceutical Law in EU Member States

Article 3 (1) and Article 5 (1) of Directive 2001/83/EC are the basic rules for EU Member States to follow when they enact their national statutes on traditional medicine. Hereinto, the UK's Medicines Act 1968 can be taken as an example. Its Section 12 (1) and (2) have been deeply discussed and analysed in recent years, with many reports on the reform of these two clauses having been submitted. Before 30 April 2014, Section 12 (1) and (2) left space for non-registered TCMPs to access to the UK market through TCM practitioners. However, after that date, Section 12 (2) can no longer be used to import non-registered TCMP according to EU law. Furthermore, the shortcomings of Section 12 (1) were ever widely discussed and the demand to reform the clause was called for (Aromatherapy Trade Council 2009). The request on reform showed an intention to strengthen the control of TCM in the UK.

In addition, a case in the EU can well explain the intensive trend of EU regulations on importing non-registered medicinal products to EU Member States. A legal adviser from the UK MHRA discussed a legal action taken by the European Commission against Poland for abusing the application of Article 5.1 of Directive 2001/83/EC. The legal action was derived from the decision of the European Commission that Poland was found to have breached an obligation in European medicines law (ECJ 2012).[17] The MHRA adviser noted that the 'use of Article 5.1 of Directive 2001/83/EC for permitting third party supply of manufactured herbal medicines to practitioners following SR would also breach EU law', and 'the

[17] 2001/83/EC, Article 5.1 provides '[a] Member State may, in accordance with legislation in force and to fulfil special needs, exclude from the provisions of this Directive medicinal products supplied in response to a bona fide unsolicited order, formulated in accordance with the specifications of an authorised health-care professional and for use by an individual patient under his direct personal responsibility'.

Commission had advised that the exemptions provided by Article 5.1 could only be used in exceptional circumstances' (McIntyre 2014).

In the case mentioned above, the Court of Justice of the EU strictly ruled that the 'non-approved medicinal products' can only be imported when necessary, 'taking account of the specific needs of patients'. The 'specific needs' would only be considered under individual situations and should meet the individual patient's demand. The court also explained '*bona fide* unsolicited order', and it required that the medicinal product be prescribed by the doctor based on actual examination of the patients and 'purely therapeutic considerations'. Consequently, the court summarised that:

> [T]he derogation provided for in the directive can only concern situations in which the doctor considers that the state of health of his individual patients requires that a medicinal product be administered for which there is no authorised equivalent on the national market or which is unavailable on that market (ECJ 2012, para. 36).

The case states that Article 5.1 provides a chance for the import of the non-registered medicinal products, but the application to the clause is restricted.

The strengthening of the enforcement of EU pharmaceutical law leaves very limited space for Chinese practitioners to import non-registered TCMP, and very rarely has registered TCMP been authorised to enter the EU or met the conditions of registration. In this case, treatment through Chinese practitioner would face a problem of hysteresis. Strictly speaking, according to EU pharmaceutical law, even if Chinese practitioners are still allowed to provide medical service to patients, they cannot easily import TCMPs promptly from China before they complete the examination and give prescription. They might be expected to find a succedaneum in the EU, but the selection of the TCMPs is often adherent to the country of origin. Nevertheless, TCM substances and TCM preparation may still possibly enter the EU market, since they are not strictly regulated by EU pharmaceutical law. But is it good or bad for the patients who really need the drug?

4.4.2.2.4 Other Possibilities to Import Non-registered TCMP

Article 3, Section 3 and 4 of Directive 2001/83/EC mentions two other exceptional situations of the application, including, respectively, '[m]edicinal products intended for research and development trials' and '[i]ntermediate products intended for further processing by an authorized manufacturer'. It is obvious that these two sections are not used for TCMP to gain access the EU market for the normal use of patients. Section 3 provides the possibility for certain TCMP to enter the EU for research purposes in trials. Section 4 would be very rarely used on TCMP.

4.5 Chapter Summary

Based on the above network analysis and comparative study, the chapter conclusion can be drawn as follows.

Firstly, TCMP is covered by EU pharmaceutical law. However, TCM substances and TCM preparations are out of the regulatory scope of EU pharmaceutical law, which brings risks to the safety of public health. Moreover, TCM substances and preparations are imported in practice as of food or other commodities, which does not favour collecting data for medical use or supervising the safe use of drugs.

Secondly, EU pharmaceutical law does not sufficiently reflect the real demand of TCMP in practice, which leads to the chaos of TCMP supervision in the EU market. Therefore, more targeted rules should be enacted instead of blocking the way of TCMP to the market. Supervising the operation of TCM practitioners to monitor the use of TCM substances and preparations is recommended hereinto. Therefore, completion of the information reporting system for TCM practitioners is urged in order to sufficiently record the data of TCMP.

Thirdly, the comparison between Chinese law and EU law shows that both China and the EU request sufficient data for the registration of medicinal products from various pre-clinical trial tests, clinical trials, or exemption of clinical trials in simplified registration procedure with sufficient proof of safety. In addition, official recognised categories recorded by the Chinese pharmacopeia and the Ph. Eur. and the plausible case study on using TCMP also have decisive impact on the approval of market access. There is a big difference on the simplified registration procedure between China and the EU. China highlights the evaluation weight of ancient records, whereas, the EU emphasises the use experience with factors of time and location.

Fourthly, it is understandable that EU pharmaceutical law sets out 15 years used experience within the EU as a condition of market access authorisation, since the clinical effect may be distinguished between different ethnic groups. However, this provision may have created discrimination between EU traditional-use medicinal product and TCMP. If the 15 years used experience in the EU is used for proving plausibility of the safety of TCMP, should the experience of using TCMP in China be counted as evidence of safe use of TCMP on Chinese immigrants in the EU? In addition, herbal medicinal products is just one kind of TCMP. So, EU pharmaceutical law cannot cover the entirety of the practice of TCM and cannot well-regulate some substances and preparations of TCMP.

Fifthly, qualified doctors who can guide the proper use of TCMP are also required if TCMP can be widely accepted in the EU. Current EU legislation has broken the vital relationship between TCM and its product. TCM has developed theories which lead to a different idea of design as compared to Western conventional medicine. The application of TCMP should be well supervised by TCM doctors. Especially in the EU, the use of either OTC or prescription TCMP should be under professional supervision, unless the patient has basic knowledge about TCM. Therefore, SR on TCM practitioners is even more urgently needed.

Finally, along with the recognition of the membership of China in the ICH, China is meeting international pharmaceutical standards on producing chemical medicinal products, and international cooperation in the pharmaceutical industry will be easier. However, internationally, there is a lack of unified standards of TCMP. The exploration of and cooperation in harmonising the herbal pharmacopeia is ongoing. EU law should be prepared to have a more sophisticated legal system for fitting the demand of TCMP in the market along with the break-through of the technical threshold. However, it is sematic that the operation of the existing system has inertia, in the other words, the system readily maintains original standards and retards new techniques.

References

Aromatherapy Trade Council (2009) Reform of Section 12(1) of the Medicines Act 1968 and aromatherapy practice. Industry News of ATC. https://www.a-t-c.org.uk/industry-news/reform-of-section-121-medicines-act-1968-and-aromatherapy-practice/

Blake K et al (2012) The European Network of Centres for pharmacoepidemiology and pharmacovigilance: application to diabetes and vascular disease. Br J Diab Vasc Dis 11 (6):304–307

Cambridge Dictionary (online) Administration. http://dictionary.cambridge.org/dictionary/english/administration

CDE (2017a) Pharmacology and toxicology department. In the centre of drug evaluation of NMPA

CDE (2017b) About US. In the centre of drug evaluation of NMPA

CFDA (2015) Yao Pin Jing Ying Zhi Liang Guan Li Gui Ding (Good supply practice for pharmaceutical products) (revision 2016). Order No. 13

CFDA (2017) Decision on adjusting the administration authorisation procedures on some medicinal product, CFDA Order No. 31

CFDA of the PRC (2010) The announcement about the implementation of the Chinese pharmacopoeia. No. 43

Cheng M, Shen H (2010) Review on the course of Chinese medicine regulation in the UK of the last 10 years. Huanqiu Zhongyiyao (Global Tradit Chin Med) 3(3):210–216

Chinese Medicine Council of Hong Kong (2017) http://www.cmchk.org.hk

Chinese Pharmacopoeia Commission (2015) History of ChP

CHMP (2006) Guideline on quality of herbal medicinal products/traditional herbal medicinal products. EMA/CPMP/QWP/2819/00 Rev. 1

Directive 2001/83/EC (2001) Directive 2001/83/EC of the European Parliament and of the Council of 6 November 2001 on the community code relating to medicinal products for human use. (2001) OJ L 311: 67–128

Directive 2004/24/EC (2004) Directive 2004/24/EC of the European Parliament and of the Council of 31 March 2004 amending, as regards traditional herbal medicinal products Directive 2001/83/EC on the community code relating to medicinal products for human use (2004) OJ L136:85–90

Directive 65/65/EEC (1965) Directive 65/65/EEC of 26 January 1965 on the approximation of provisions laid down by law, regulation or administrative action relating to proprietary medicinal products. OJ 022: 369–373

ECJ (2012) European Commission v. Republic of Poland. C-185/10

EHTPA (n.d.) 'Representing herbal & traditional medicine practitioners across Europe'. www.ehtpa.eu/medicines_legislation/index.html

EMA (2017a) What we do. http://www.ema.europa.eu/ema/index.jsp?curl=pages/about_us/general/general_content_000091.jsp&mid=WC0b01ac0580028a42

EMA (2017b) Committee on herbal medicinal products (HMPC). http://www.ema.europa.eu/ema/index.jsp?curl=pages/about_us/general/general_content_000264.jsp&mid=WC0b01ac0580028e7c
EMA (2017c) HMPC: working parties and other groups. http://www.ema.europa.eu/ema/index.jsp?curl=pages/about_us/general/general_content_000243.jsp&mid=WC0b01ac058002d26c
EMA (2017d) Organisation Chart of EMA. http://www.ema.europa.eu/docs/en_GB/document_library/Other/2009/12/WC500017948.pdf
EMA (2017e) European experts. http://www.ema.europa.eu/ema/index.jsp?curl=pages/about_us/landing/experts.jsp&mid=WC0b01ac058043244a
EU 6655/7/08 REV 7 (2012) Consolidated versions of the Treaty on European Union and the Treaty on Functioning of the European Union and the Charter of fundamental rights of the European Union
EU Department of Health (2004) Regulation of herbal medicine and acupuncture: proposals for statutory regulation
EU HMPC (2005) Template for a community herbal monograph (revision)
EU HMPC (2007) Procedure for the preparation of community monographs for traditional herbal medicinal products (revision 2), EMEA/HMPC/182320/2005 Rev. 2
EU HMPC (2017) Inventory of herbal substances for assessment, EMA/HMPC/494079/2007. http://www.ema.europa.eu/docs/en_GB/document_library/Other/2009/12/WC500017723.pdf
EUR-Lex (2017) European Union (EU) hierarchy of norms. http://eur-lex.europa.eu/summary/glossary/norms_hierarchy.html
Eurofound (2011) Soft law. https://www.eurofound.europa.eu/observatories/eurwork/industrial-relations-dictionary/soft-law
Europa (2017a) EU treaties. https://europa.eu/european-union/law/treaties_en
Europa (2017b) Overview of European council. https://europa.eu/european-union/about-eu/institutions-bodies/european-council_en
Europa (2017c) Overview of European Commission. https://europa.eu/european-union/about-eu/institutions-bodies/european-commission_en
Europa (2017d) Overview of Council of the European Union. https://europa.eu/european-union/about-eu/institutions-bodies/council-eu_en
Europa (2017e) Overview of European Parliament. https://europa.eu/european-union/about-eu/institutions-bodies/european-parliament_en
Europa (2017f) Overview of Court of Justice of the European Union (CJEU). https://europa.eu/european-union/about-eu/institutions-bodies/court-justice_en
Europa (2017g) Transparency and the EU. http://ec.europa.eu/transparencyregister/public/homePage.do?redir=false&locale=en
European Commission (2008) Communication from the commission to the council and the European Parliament concerning the report on the experience acquired as a result of the application of the provisions of Chapter 2a of Directive 2001/83/EC, as amended by Directive 2004/24/EC, on specific provisions applicable to traditional herbal medicinal products. Document 52008DC0584
European Commission (n.d.-a) Medicinal products for human use. https://ec.europa.eu/health/human-use_en
European Commission (n.d.-b) Health policy platform. Available at: https://webgate.ec.europa.eu/hpf/
European Consortium for Political Research (2017) The meaning of politics. https://ecpr.eu/Events/SectionDetails.aspx?SectionID=643&EventID=96
European Directorate for the Quality of Medicines and HealthCase (2017) European pharmacopoeia style guide
Fan T et al (2012) Future development of global regulations of Chinese herbal products. J Ethnopharmacol 140(3):568–586
Gov.cn (2008) Guo Jia Shi Pin Yao Pin Jian Du Guan Li Ju Gai You Wei Sheng Bu Guan Li (The SFDA changes its affliction to be under the Administration of Ministry of Health)

Hameed AA (2012) The legislative hierarchy. Egyptian regulatory reform & development activity. http://www.errada.gov.eg/index_en.php?op=show_feature_details_en&id=13&start=0&type=1

Health & Care Professions Council (2017) Professions. http://www.hcpc-uk.org/aboutregistration/professions/

HMPC (2014) Questions & answers on the EU framework for (Traditional) herbal medicinal products, including those from a 'Non-European' tradition. EMA/HMPC/402684/2013

Hu M et al (2009) Wo Guo Yao Pin Jian Guan Ti Xi Fa Zhan He Gai Ge Li Cheng (Development and reform of the drug administration system in China). Zhong Guo Wei Sheng Jing Ji 28 (8):71–74

ICH (2017a) Membership. http://www.ich.org/about/membership.html

ICH (2017b) History. http://www.ich.org/about/history.html

Li Z (2008) The history, current status and problem of Chinese Health service and governance, taking pharmaceutical governance as an example. In: Regulatory reform review in China: Working Group Meeting. http://www.oecd.org/gov/regulatory-policy/regulatoryreformreviewinchinaworkinggroupmeeting28march2008beijingchina.htm

Mathijsen PSRF (1995) A guide to European Union law. Sweet & Maxwell, London

McIntyre M (2014) The case for the statutory regulation of herbal practitioners

MEB (2012) Diao Xin Xue Kang, capsules for oral use SU BioMedicine B.V., The Netherlands. RVG 102142

MHRA (2016) MHRA and making a success of Brexit. In: GOV.UK. https://www.gov.uk/government/news/medicines-and-healthcare-products-regulatory-agency-statement-on-the-outcome-of-the-eu-referendum

Ministry of Health (2010) Yao Pin Sheng Chan Zhi Liang Guan Li Gui Fan (Good manufacturing practices for pharmaceutical products) (2010 Revision). Order No. 79

Ministry of Health (2013) Measures for the administration of prescription, (dissolved and replaced by NHFPC in 2013) Order No. 53

Ministry of Health of the PRC (2011) Yao Pin Bu Liang Fan Ying Bao Gao He Jian Ce Guan Li Ban Fa (Measures for reporting and monitoring adverse drug reactions), Order of Ministry No. 81

Motaal DA (1998) Overview of the World Trade Organization agreement on technical barriers to trade. In: Globalization and access to drugs. Perspectives on the WTO/TRIPS agreement - health economics and drugs series

NATCM (1998) Zhong Yao Yin Pian Bao Zhuang Guan Li Ban Fa (Regulation on Package of TCM Decoction Pieces). No. 11

NATCM and Ministry of Health (2007) Yi Yuan Zhong Yao Yin Pian Guan Li Gui Ding (Administrative regulation on TCM decoction pieces in hospitals). NATCM Order No. 11

NHFPC (2013) National health and family planning commission stipulate on its affiliated institutions and personnel

NMPA (2018) Gu Dai JIng Dian MIng Fang Zhong Yao Fu Fang Zhi Ji Jian Hua Zhu Ce Shen Pi Guan Li Gui Ding (Simplified procedure for registration of compound Chinese medicinal product deriving from ancient famous and classical formulas), No. 27

NPC (1997) The basic law of the Hong Kong Special Administrative Region of the PRC, Order of the President of the PRC No. 26, Ch. 4, s 4

NPC of the PRC (1982) Xian Fa (Constitution of the PRC) (revision 2018)

NPC Standing Committee of the PRC (1984) Yao Pin Guan Li Fa (The Drug Administration Law of the PRC) (revision 2019). Order of the President of the PRC No. 31

NPC Standing Committee of the PRC (1999) Law of the PRC on medical practitioners. Order of the President of the PRC No. 5

NPC Standing Committee of the PRC (2010) Qin Quan Ze Ren Fa (Tort Liability Law of the PRC). Order of the President No. 21

NPC Standing Committee of the PRC (2017) Zhong Yi Yao Fa (Law of traditional Chinese medicine and medicinal product of the PRC). Order of the President of the PRC No. 59

OECD Global Science Forum (2009) Report on applications of complexity science for public policy: new tools for finding unanticipated consequences and unrealized opportunities
PharmNet.com.cn (2017) Tan 'Yao Pin Guan Li Fa' Yu 'Zhong Yi Yao Fa' De Xian Jie (Discussion on the linking up between Chinese Administrative Law and Chinese Law on TCM and TCMP. http://news.pharmnet.com.cn/news/2017/01/13/462096.html
Qu L et al (2014) Non-European traditional herbal medicines in Europe: a community herbal monograph perspective. J Ethnopharmacol 156:107–114
Regulation (EU) No.178/2002 (2002) Regulation (EU) No.178/2002 of the European Parliament and of the Council of 28 January 2002 laying down the general principles and requirements of food law, establishing the European Food Safety Authority and laying down procedures in matters of food safety. OJ L31: 1–24
SAMR (2020) Yao Pin Zhu Ce Guan Li Ban Fa (Drug registration regulation). Order No. 27 on 22 Jan 2020, enacted on 1 July 2020
SATCM (2017) Main functions of SATCM
SCRATCH (n.d.) 'Pharmacovigilance system and PSMF'. http://www.scratch-pv.com/main-indications/pharmacovigilance-system-and-psmf/?lang=en
SDA of the PRC (2002) Zhong Yao Cai Sheng Chan Zhi Liang Guan Li Gui Fan (Shi Xing) (Good agricultural practice of traditional Chinese medicinal product materials). Order No. 32
SFDA (2007) Yao Pin Zhu Ce Guan Li Ban Fa (Drug registration regulation). Order No. 28, Annex 1
SFDA (2017) Yao Wu Fei Lin Chuang Yan Jiu Zhi Liang Guan Li Gui Fan (Good laboratory practice). Order No. 34
SFDA (2020) Yao Pin Sheng Chan Jian Du Guan Li Ban Fa (Measures of the supervision and administration on pharmaceutical manufacture). Order No.28
Shang Y (2016) Research on the changes of central traditional Chinese medicine management organization after the foundation of China. Med Soc 29(6):28–30. 38
Shenoy P (2016) Multi-regional clinical trials and global drug development. Perspect Clin Res 7 (2):62–67
Song X (2014) Zhong Guo Dao Di Yao Cai De Zhi Shi Chan Quan Bao Hu (The IPR protection on Chinese genuine raw material). Intellectual Property Publishing House Co., Ltd., Beijing
State Council of the PRC (2002) Regulations for the implementation of the drug administration law of the PRC (revision 2019), State Council Order No. 360
State Council of the PRC (2007) Zheng Fu Xin Xi Gong Kai Tiao Li (Regulation on Government Information Disclosure). Order of the State Council No.429. 2019 revision, Order of the State Council 711
State Council of the PRC (2018) The notice of the state council on the setup of institutions, Guo Fa No.6
State Council of the PRC (2019) Decision of the state council on amending certain administrative regulations, State Council Order No. 709
TFEU (2012) Consolidated version of the treaty on the functioning of the European Union. OJ C 326: 13–390
The King's Fund (2009) The King's Fund response to a joint consultation on the Report to Ministers from the DH Steering Group on the Statutory Regulation of Practitioners of Acupuncture, Herbal Medicine, Traditional Chinese medicine and other traditional medicine systems practised in the UK
Tong Ren Xuan (2016) Bei Jing Tong Ren Tang Ke Ji Fa Zhan Ji Tuan Tong Guo Ou Mei GMP Ren Zheng (China Beijing Tong Ren Tang Group Co., has obtained the GMP authentication in the EU and U.S.). In: China quality daily. http://epaper.cqn.com.cn/html/2016-09/08/content_71466.htm?div=-1
UK Department of Health (2003) The herbal medicine regulatory working group by the Prince of Wales's Foundation for integrated health, recommendations on the regulation of herbal practitioners in the UK: report from the Herbal Medicine Regulatory Working Group

UK Department of Health (2011) Statutory regulation of practitioners of acupuncture, herbal medicine, traditional Chinese medicine and other traditional medicine systems practised in the UK—an analysis report on the 2009 consultation
UK House of Lords Select Committee (2000) Select committee on science and technology: sixth report
Wei H (2013) Qian Xue Sen Gou Jian Xi Tong Lun De Ji Ben She Xiang (The basic conception of Tsien Hsue-Shen system construction theory). J Syst Sci 21(1):1–8
Wessel RA (2003) The constitutional relationship between the European Union and the European Community: consequences for the relationship with the member states
WHO/EDM/TRM/2000 (2000) General guidelines for methodologies on research and evaluation of traditional medicine
WTO (1994) Agreement on technical barriers to trade
Xinhua (2016) 66 Chinese herbs listed in European pharmacopoeia
Xinhuanet (2013) Proposal on reformation and transformation of the institutions of state council (Submitted to the 1st meeting of 12th Section of National People's Congress, approved)
Zeng X, Wang L (2009) Legislative law, 3rd edn. China Renmin University Press, Beijing, p 113

Chapter 5
EU Pharmaceutical Law Relating to WTO Rules

The EU is a member of the United Nations (UN), WTO, WHO, and other international organisations. The European Commission ensures the EU is represented internationally in negotiating agreements on international development issues, speaks on behalf of all EU Member States in the area of trade policy and humanitarian aid. Domestic law and regional law are always affected by the global economy and international legislation. On one hand, a country should retain the independence of its legislation, for instance, enacting its own regulations without others' interference; on the other hand, a country may not benefit from protecting its own interests if it impedes on the rights and benefits of other countries, whether those rights or benefits have been secured by international law or not. Anything states do will be mutual, namely, the way state A is behaving today may be repeated by state B in the future. The WTO offers its members a platform to negotiate the proper conditions for opening their market, so to facilitate international trade. However, medicinal products have a unique feature which makes them different from other general products such as clothes and food. Agreements concluded in the WTO, such as TBT and SPS, request the Members of WTO the possibilities to set out proper national rules on market access of medicinal products. Therefore, WTO law is the international law most relevant to the EU regional system on governing the affairs of market access of TCMP.

In addition, as mentioned in Chap. 4, the operation of the existing system has inertia, in other words, the system continues easily with original standards and retards any new techniques. Therefore, the breakthrough to address an internal problem in a system is often found outside of the system, but of course the driving power to solve the problem still lies within the system. Law has area jurisdiction, wherein national or regional law functions mainly within the jurisdictional border. In this sense, it is an application of materialist dialectical theory in society—external cause becomes operative through internal causes (Marx-Engels-Lenin Institute 2017; Hanhijärvi 2015; Mao 1937, 1966). Herein this study, WTO law provides

S. Wang, *Market Access of Traditional Chinese Medicinal Product in the EU under WTO Legal Framework*, Economic and Financial Law & Policy – Shifting Insights & Values 5, https://doi.org/10.1007/978-3-030-52848-5_5

an angle to review EU pharmaceutical law on the issue of market access of TCMP in the EU.

5.1 Background of the Issue of Market Access of TCMP in International Law

TCMP is treated as one kind of CAM in the EU. Taking an international view, CAM has drawn much attention from different international organisations, including the UN, WTO, WHO and so on. Among those governmental organisations, people can find relevant documents specific to herbal medicines in both the WTO and WHO. The WTO is a coordinating authority for adjusting international trade and relevant issues. It provides rules on market access in international trade. It has a complete legislative framework and is involved with many trade affairs. It has established good cooperative relations with many other international organisations and provides a platform for its Members to negotiate trade-related issues and disputes. Similarly, the WHO is the coordinating authority for health. It is responsible for providing leadership on global health matters, shaping the health research agenda, setting norms and standards, articulating evidence-based policy options, providing technical support to countries and monitoring and assessing health trends.

5.1.1 Identifying the Legal Issues Relevant to Market Access of TCMP in WTO Law

The issue of market access is regulated by WTO law in the area of international trade of goods. Even though the WTO aims at encouraging free trade, it is also sometimes used by protectionists against free trade. In the most recent successful negotiation round, the WTO states a goal of facilitating international trade. Indeed, proper protection of domestic trade and interest is necessary, but overprotection will bring unfairness to competitors. In that case, individual producers and consumers will be the direct victims. The conflict between free trade and protectionism against free trade supports the existence of many WTO principles, for instance NT and reasonable exceptions. This forms a dynamic framework for WTO law, and to determine a reasonable exception, states must consider many factors, including scientific, political, economic factors and so on. These factors put different weights on the adoption of exceptional clauses in different situations. Among them, the scientific factor is the first concern when deciding the issue of market access of a medicinal product, and the precautionary principle is applied for bridging the relationship between science and law.

The implementation of WTO law is undertaken through either direct recognition or transformation of national or regional legislation. Therefore, the examination of the legitimacy of national or regional legislation reflects the status of the execution of WTO law. Regarding market access of TCMP in the EU, the book criticizes the appropriateness of EU pharmaceutical law, but also discusses the rationality of adopting such regional legislations.

5.1.2 International Trade Law Principles

5.1.2.1 Principles Relating to the Trade of Goods

International trade law principles include fair competition, non-discrimination, transparency and are based on trade liberalisation. These principles should be considered when talking about TCMP accessing the EU market. The fair competition principle requires that no members or exporters should engage in any unfair trade measures to international trade competition or take any measure which may generate undue distortions. The non-discrimination principle includes general MFN treatment[1] and NT. Hereinto, NT relates to the main question of the study in this book. It essentially means treating foreigners/foreign products and locals equally. A prerequisite to apply NT is to ascertain the similarity of the two comparable products. The transparency principle requires members of the WTO to publish their legislations promptly and sufficiently and ensure easy access of such legislations to foreigners (GATT 1994, art .X).

Furthermore, the precautionary principle in SPS and TBT must be emphasised. SPS concerns food safety, as well as animal and plant health. Members may maintain or introduce measures which result in higher standards if there is scientific justification or as a consequence of consistent risk decisions based on an appropriate risk assessment (SPS 1994, art. 5, para. 7). Although TBT aims at ensuring technical negotiations and standards, as well as regulating testing and certification, it respects that countries have the right to establish protection at levels they consider appropriate. It encourages countries to use international standards where these are appropriate. But TBT does not require countries to change their levels of protection as a result of standardisation (WTO n.d.). The precautionary principle lies within these two Agreements. It provides rational consideration for importing countries to take certain measure(s) in international trade. As defined:

> The 'precautionary principle' is a notion which supports taking protective action before there is complete scientific proof of a risk; that is, action should not be delayed simply because full scientific information is lacking (European Parliamentary Research Service 2015).

[1]WTO GATT 1994, Article I provides: 'any advantage, favour, privilege or immunity granted by any contracting party to any product originating in or destined for any other country shall be accorded immediately and unconditionally to the like product originating in or destined for the territories of all other contracting parties'.

5.1.2.2 Theories Relating to TCMP Related Services

WTO divides international trade into trade in goods, trade in services and trade in intellectual property. Service in business is defined as any activity that involves doing things for customers rather than producing goods, which is relevant to TCM practitioners and regulated by GATS in WTO (Blouin et al. 2006). The use of TCMP is better to be guided by the practitioners of TCM. To a certain extent, the positions of TCM practitioners in the EU reflect the recognition status of TCMP. Commitments of WTO contracting parties reflect the attitude that they would like to open their market to foreign products and services.

Globally, CAM or TM is more generally discussed where TCM is included. GATS divides services into four modes of supply and records the commitments. These include, cross-border supply (Mode 1), movement of customers (Mode 2), commercial presence (Mode 3), and movement of natural persons (Mode 4). Practitioners of CAM could provide their services through any kinds of modes. The authors in International Trade in Health Services and the GATS compared well the commitments of the WTO Members between these four modes (Blouin et al. 2006). Mode 4 was the most restrictive compared to other modes while Mode 2 was the most liberal. Members normally set up limited entries for natural persons, but might feel that it is pointless to try influencing demand patterns once consumers have left the countries concerned. Nevertheless, in the latter case, national rules might exclude health treatment abroad from domestic consumer subsides or a public reimbursement scheme. Mode 1 was often connected to 'e-health', and it encompassed three areas, including 'telemedicine, education and training of health workers and professionals and e-commerce and e-business practices used for health management and health systems, data storage and usage, and using IT in health management for better delivery and increased efficiency' (Blouin et al. 2006, pp. 203, 204). There was a high percentage of nonbinding commitments for Mode 1, especially for hospital services, and some schedules contained footnotes noting that a noncommitment under Mode 1 was because of the unfeasibility of such supplies. Mode 3 (commercial presence) and Mode 4 (presence of natural persons) had drawn the highest share of partial commitments. Most of the limitations scheduled for Mode 4 were horizontal, which apply across all committed sectors and relate to the general barriers of the WTO including quota-type restrictions and mainly setting a ceiling on numbers of foreign employees or denying access to all persons who were not considered to be specialist doctors. Typical NT limitations under Mode 4 related to training and language requirements. Comparing with Mode 4, many commitments for Mode 3 were sector-specific. But Mode 3 also involved economic needs tests, requirements for foreign suppliers to establish a commercial presence and restrictions on foreign equity participation and on permissible types of legal incorporation which have been scheduled as market access limitation (GATS, Article XVI). Such restrictions might be intended to encourage transfers of technology, skills and expertise which were mostly contained in the horizontal section.

Seemingly, many WTO Members have given medical service quite general access to their market through commitments in GATS. In Europe, generally WTO Members do not have national specialised rules for certain CAM, so in some situations the general conditions for registering as a national GP may be used to evaluate the qualification of CAM practitioners while in other situations the operation of CAM practitioners may not follow the rules of medical service at all. The lack of specialised regulations on CAM leads to the chaos of the medical service market. Even though using the same evaluation standard between CAM practitioners and Western GPs complies with the general principle of NT in WTO, it ignores the differences in medical background between these two.

5.1.3 WHO Official Documents Relating to Herbal Medicines

The WHO published Guidelines on Safety Monitoring of Herbal Medicines in Pharmacovigilance Systems in 2004 and Guidelines for Assessing Quality of Herbal Medicines with Reference to Contaminants and Residues in 2007. The former focuses on 'assist[ing] Member States to strengthen national capacity in monitoring the safety of herbal medicines and in analysing the causes of adverse events, and to share safety information at national, regional and global levels'; the latter emphasizes the discussion of standards, quality control, drug contamination and chemistry analysis of herbal medicines.

The WHO sets up the general background for the development of international legislation of CAM. It is written in the WHO Traditional Medicine Strategy 2014–2023 (2013) that CAM may be termed as TM, non-conventional medicine or complementary medicine (CM). Selectively, the WHO Strategy calls CAM as T&CM. It is very difficult to unify the scope of CAM, which is in the similar situation of giving a common name since different states define the scope of CAM differently. For instance, in Europe, people distinguish acupuncture, anthroposophic medicine, Ayurveda, Chiropractic, herbal medicine/phytotherapy, homeopathy, massage, naprapathy, naturopathy, neural therapy, osteopathy and TCM. Among those CAMs, most EU Member States recognise only some of them as legal CAM in their territories (Wiesener et al. 2012, p. 207).

By contrast, TCM is widely used and well recognised legally and practically in China. Although the use of other kinds of CAMs may not be discouraged by Chinese official or people's opinion, practically they are not regulated in a formal and legal way. No matter in the EU or in China, the ambiguous legal position of non-regulated CAMs either stops the trade of such non-regulated CAMs or brings uncertainty for them in accessing the market. In addition, it is very hard to reach just one international standard for all kinds of CAM under the situation that there is no unified recognisable scope of CAM. Subsequently, when talking about a TM strategy, national law should be concerned first, since national legislation on CAM provides basic rules for issues of safety, quality, efficacy, trade and intellectual property rights protection and so on. However international documents and legislation also need to be concerned, especially in case there are already international rules which may affect national laws and be agreed on between nations.

The WHO Strategy is not a compulsory legal document, but all members of WHO contributed to its outcome, and it reflects a common understanding between members and leads to the next level of cooperation on CAM. It calls for improved policy and regulations of its Member States relevant to CAM. It puts expectations on integrating CAM into the Member States' health care system. It also reminds its Member States' to strengthen the safety and quality control of CAM and encourages the development of education and training of T&CM practitioners. Based on these expectations to WHO Member States, the WHO asks for information sharing in order to provide more resources for individual consumers.

The WHO Strategy is based on the informed choice principle and self-health care model. In health care, self-care is any necessary human regulatory function which is under individual control, deliberate and self-initiated (See: Segall and Goldstein 1998). However, lack of adherence to medical advice can make self-care very difficult. Therefore, the basic principle that the WHO strategy pursues must be based on an efficient information exchange platform.

According to the WHO, CAM is found in almost every country in the world and the demand for its services is increasing (WHO 2013). The Strategy also states that CAM of proven quality, safety and efficacy contributes to the goal of ensuring that all people have access to care. Health systems around the world are experiencing increased levels of chronic illness and escalating health care costs. Both patients and health providers are demanding that health care services be revitalised, with a stronger emphasis on individualised person-centred care. CAM involves different issues including safety, efficacy, quality control, innovation, trade and so on. The WHO Strategy assesses all challenges and requires Member States to not only determine their own national situations in relation to CAM but to then develop and enforce policies, regulations and guidelines. It advocates for Member States to organise their activities in three strategic sectors: (1) build the knowledge base that allows CAM to be managed actively; (2) strengthen the quality assurance, safety, proper use of CAM by regulating products, practices and practitioners; (3) promote universal health coverage by integrating CAM services into health service delivery and by ensuring that users are able to make informed choices about self-health care. The WHO Strategy sets out guideline for the development of TCMP internationally as well.

5.1.4 Definition of Medical Services by the United Nations Statistics Division

CAM includes medicinal products and medical services. Legislation on TCMP relates to the former, while the practitioners of TCM relates to the later. The use of TCMP cannot be separated from the practice of TCM, even though the study in this book focuses on the trade of pharmaceutical products.

The United Nations Statistics Division supports the functioning of the United Nations Statistical Commission via compiling and disseminating global statistical information, standardizing statistical methods, classifications and definitions and supporting countries' efforts to strengthen their national statistical systems. Based on the coordination of international statistical programmes and activities, the statistical information is updated regularly according to its data collection and processing. The Division's outcomes provide bases for other nations to develop certain rules. Among its outcomes, Central Product Classification (CPC) provides the classification structure for the harmonized commodity description and coding system. Scrolling down the products' list, health and social services can be found in item 93. Its sub-item 931 is human health services, and it is further divided into hospital services, medical and dental services and other human health services (United Nations Statistics Division 2015). CPC defines general medical services to consist of the prevention, diagnosis and treatment by doctors of physical and/or mental diseases. As noted in item 9312, general medical services are not limited to specified or particular conditions, diseases or anatomical regions. They can be provided by practitioners and also be delivered by outpatient clinics, at home, in firms, in schools, etc. or by phone, Internet or other means. The explanations cover the characteristics of the practitioner of CAM well. Therefore, it is more possible for practitioners' services to be included in medical services. Nevertheless, certain forms of CAM are not treated as non-conventional methods and may be provided in hospital service in some countries, such as traditional Chinese medicine in China.

In addition, GATS references CPC. It gives a detailed explanation of the services activities covered by each listed sector or sub-sector and can be used to avoid any ambiguity as to the scope of the commitment (WTO 2017b).

5.1.5 HS by World Customs Organisation

CPC provides basic definitions for services, while the Harmonised Commodity Description and Coding System (HS) provides definitions for goods (United Nations Statistics Division 2017). HS is 'an internationally standardised nomenclature for the description, classification and coding of goods' (Yu 2008). It was adopted on 14 June 1983 by the World Customs Organisation (WCO) based on the International Convention on the Harmonised System concluded at Brussels. It comprises 5000 commodity groups, and each of them is identified by a six-digit code (WCO 2017). The HS is also one of three integrated components of the EU classification system (European Commission Trade Helpdesk 2017).[2] States which adopt the HS usually

[2]EU Three integrated components are: the HS, the Combined Nomenclature (CN, the EU's eight-digit coding system comprising the HS codes with further EU subdivisions), and the Integrated Tariff (TARIC, information on all trade policy and tariff measures applicable to specific goods in the EU).

add further subdivisions after the basic unified HS sub-headings according to their factual demands. The WTO adopts the HS in trade of goods (WTO 2017a).

5.1.6 Highlighted International IPR Issues Regarding CAM

Public health issues are widely discussed with regard to IPR protection. In light of CAM, IPR issues may focus on pharmaceutical patents and traditional knowledge. The WHO, the World Intellectual Property Organisation (WIPO), the WTO and the UN have put efforts on the protection of medical intellectual property via taking cooperating steps.

Under the WTO legal framework, pharmaceutical patent protection closely relates to Agreement on Trade-Related Aspects of Intellectual Property Rights (TRIPs 1994). The balance lying in the TRIPs agreement is 'between the short-term interests in maximising access and the long-term interests in promoting creativity and innovation' (WTO 2006). For reaching an appropriate balance, TRIPs sets up 'objectives' in Article 7 and recognises that:

> [T]he protection of intellectual property should contribute to the promotion of technological innovation and to the transfer and dissemination of technology, to the mutual advantage of users and producers of technological knowledge and in a manner conducive to social and economic welfare and to a balance of rights and obligations (WTO 2006).

Practical cases have involved various legal aspects, for instance the issue of patentability, the rights of the patent owner to prevent unauthorised persons from using the patented products, compulsory license, many procedural issues, and so on. The CAM product may be affected by any of these issues in practice.

Regarding CAM, IPRs do not only cover patents, but also the protection of well-known trademark, genetic resources—for geo-authentic crude drug—and traditional knowledge. The Convention on Biological Diversity (CBD) is worth mentioning hereinto (UN 1992). It recognises the sovereign rights of States over their natural resources and traditional knowledge. To a certain extent, Article 27.3 of TRIPs combines the idea of protecting generic resources, and it grants Members the right to protect plant varieties either by patents or by an effective *sui generis* system, or by any combination of the two. It is widely accepted that the data of the origin nation from where the generic resources or the relevant traditional knowledge come should be clarified and submitted properly if any patent product includes any such data. The record on such data provides the basis for the protection of the country of origin. However, there is not a unified standard or framework for sharing and protecting such data, yet. In a meaningful and important comment, Ms. Wu Xiaoping (2015) argued that TRIPs and CBD should be implemented in a mutually supportive way. In addition, CAM services or products can be protected under well-known trademark or commercial secret, but the registration for well-known trademark and commercial secret should be built on the legal recognition of such CAM service or product in a society.

The cooperation among international organisations is ongoing on medical technologies and IPR protection, as well as the innovation stimulation. For instance, WHO, WIPO and WTO jointly launched a stepped-up programme of trilateral cooperation on 'Public Health, Intellectual Property and TRIPs at 20: Innovation and Access to Medicines: Learning from the Past, Illuminating the Future' via a symposium on 28 October 2015 at the WTO (WHO 2015). It is believed that more efforts will be continually delivered in the future.

5.2 Export Channels and Status of TCMP in Practice Under the WTO Legal Framework

As aforementioned, TCMP covers all ingredients which are used for the treatment of diseases in different forms including Zhong Cheng Yao, drug preparations or substances, or ingredients composed of herbs, animal origins or minerals. However, EU pharmaceutical law put emphasis on herbal medicinal products when regulating the market access of traditional use medicinal products. Directive 2004/24/EC was published as an amendment of the directive 2001/83/EC for regulating traditional use herbal medicinal products for human use. This part of the book explains the export channels and status of TCMP in practice under the WTO legal framework.

The import channels and status of TCMP have not been well recorded or cleared up in the EU. Thus, an overview of the export channels and status of TCMP from China to the rest of the world will help build an understanding of the trading status of TCMP in the EU. To illustrate the export channels, this book summarises a classification for TCMP from the view of its practical uses and certain legal concerns first. Secondly, this book uses data to state the export status of TCMP from China to the world.

5.2.1 Export Channels

TCMP may access market in the form of medicinal product, nutritious food (health food) or agricultural product. In the EU, the substance of the medicinal product, the medicinal product's preparations, the proprietary product and the generic product are all regulated by EU pharmaceutical law. However, if the TCMP needs to be registered as a traditional medicinal product in the EU, only the approved herbal medicinal product is eligible for approval (Directive 2004/24/EC, art. 1). But in China, TCMP can be accessed by patients in different forms. In Europe, even though *Zhong Cheng Yao* is more possibly approved as traditional use medicinal product, preparations and raw materials can be used by TCM practitioners in practice as well. Therefore, the approved traditional herbal product in EU law is just a part of TCMP, and the raw materials and preparations, which may be produced by animal origins or

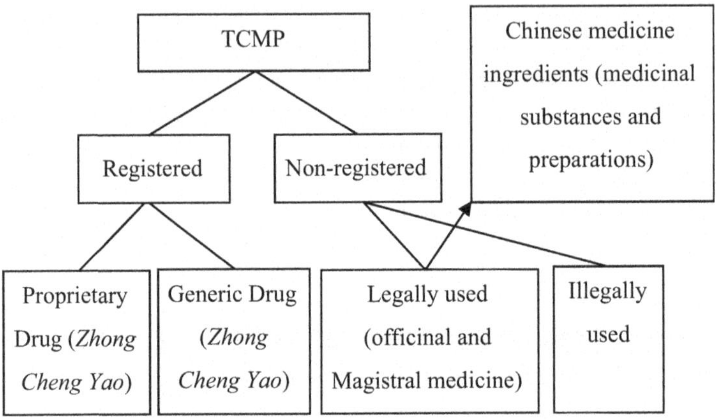

Fig. 5.1 Classification of TCMP based on registration status

minerals, are also available for patients to access in the practice of TCM. Figure 5.1 illustrates the classification of TCMP, and this book has considered the relevant terms used in EU pharmaceutical law for this classification and aims to provide an easier way for European people to understand TCMP.

As stated in Fig. 5.1, generally speaking in law, TCMP can be classified as registered or non-registered. TCMP may be delivered either by pharmacists or practitioners.[3] Registered TCMP and even non-registered TCMP dispensed by registered medicine practitioners are medicines that may be used legally.

Registered medicines can be divided into proprietary medicinal products and generic drugs. A proprietary medicinal product is '[a]ny ready-prepared medicinal product placed on the market under a special name and in a special pack' (Directive 65/65/EEC 1965).[4] It is normally still in the protection period based on patent law if the producer applied for a patent. Therefore, it is also called a patented medicinal product sometimes. However, many Chinese practitioners are not inclined to apply for patents for their formulas and instead they hold the formulas as secrets and use them in practice. Then, under such circumstances, trademark law or other IPR protection provisions can be applied to protect the secrets. By contrast, WHO has noted that '[a] generic drug is a pharmaceutical product, usually intended to be interchangeable with an innovator product, that is manufactured without a licence from the innovator company and marketed after the expiry date of the patent or other exclusive rights' (Alfonso-Cristancho et al. 2015). Both proprietary medicinal products and generic drugs include ethical drugs and OTC drugs. An ethical drug is a

[3]Figure 5.1 has been first published in Saisai Wang, Kim Van der Borght, Xiaoting Song, A Legal Analysis on the Current Trade Status of Traditional Chinese Medicinal Product in the E.U.—from the Perspectives of WTO Law and EU Pharmaceutical Law, AJWH Volume 11 (2), September (2016): 513–535. Amended on 15 January 2020.

[4]This definition was deleted in Directive 2001/83/EC Article 1.1, but the meaning of proprietary medicinal product is maintained in practice.

drug that can be dispensed only with a doctor's prescription, while an OTC drug is a drug that is prepared and packaged for the public's immediate use and has been found 'to be safe and appropriate for use without the supervision of a health care professional such as a physician' (U.S. FDA 2015). In the Chinese market, *Zhong Cheng Yao* can be either a proprietary medicinal product or a generic drug, and it can also be either an ethical or OTC drug. It is formulated and produced based on the principle of compatibility of medicines and is regulated by specialized legislation in Chinese law.

Notably a generic drug is also called copycat drug because it contains the same active ingredients but not necessarily the same excipient substances as the pioneer drug marketed under a brand name. It has a non-proprietary character; namely, the producers of the generic drug do not have the proprietary right to exclude others from producing the drug. In times of economic difficulty, the industry intends to produce many 'generic' medicines because it can quickly go to market. The formula of generic drug has been proven to be effective and acquired approval, in addition, generic drug has passed the protective period according to patent law, so any producer could use it freely.

Non-registered TCMP may be legally used as well. Many herbal medicines might be sold or imported in the form of raw materials or preparations, since Chinese doctors can combine several herbal materials or preparations to cure the disease based on the principles of formulating prescription. Under this circumstance, either the doctors or the practitioners should have a licence to do so. Furthermore, in practice, the raw materials of TCMP can be imported with the HS code of agricultural product or food product. For instance, Ginseng root is classified under a different HS code than the parts of other plants used in medicaments. But in practice it can be used as a component in compound TCMP. Another example is that the Ministry of Health of the PRC published more than eighty types of herbs which can be used in both drugs and foods (Wei Fa Jian Fa [2002] No. 51). Those products have the functions of either foods or drugs. Preparation of TCMP includes a decoction piece and a drug extract. The way of processing the crude drugs is regulated in Chinese Pharmacopoeia (2015) and processing means that to guarantee the safe use of the TCMP, the crude drugs need to be cleaned, cut and to be qualified and prepared into small pieces ready for the decoction, and formula granule are typical decoction pieces which are popularly used in current practice due to its convenient way to be used by the patients (State Council 2003). On the contrary, the extract is the active component(s) extracted from herbs that have a medicinal function. It can be used as the material of *Zhong Cheng Yao* and can be in the form of volatile oil, grease, dry extract, liquid extract, effective ingredients, effective parts and so on. Therefore, both the Chinese decoction piece and the traditional Chinese extract can be included in the preparation of TCMP, but the latter is a more concentrated extract of the active component(s).

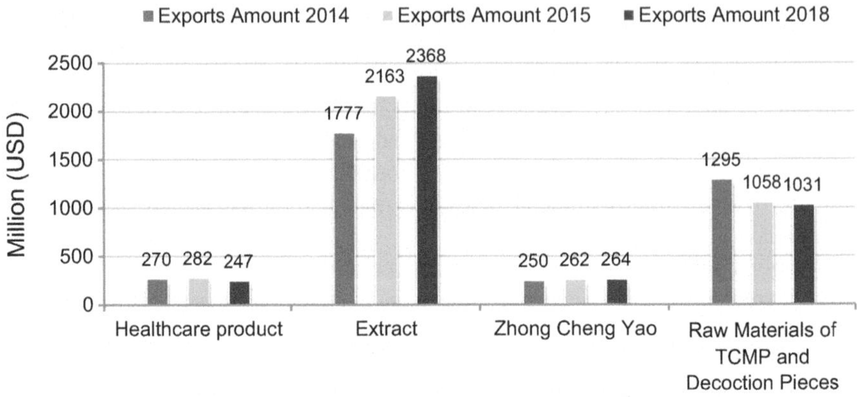

Fig. 5.2 The status of the export of TCM drugs in China in 2014, 2015 and 2018

5.2.2 *Export Status of China*

Figure 5.2 shows the export status of TCMP from China to abroad in 2014, 2015, and 2018.[5] According to it, TCMP is divided into four groups including health care products,[6] drug extracts, *Zhong Cheng Yao* and raw materials of TCMP and decoction pieces. Overall, the export amounts of the healthcare product and *Zhong Cheng Yao* are extremely lower than the extract and raw materials of TCMP and decoction pieces in the three recorded years. However, it is notable that the international market of extract was flourishing, but the export may not be used as TCMP. Healthcare products are not medicinal products, and their imports do not pursue pharmaceutical law. According to Fig. 5.2, the exporting amounts of *Zhong Cheng Yao* were slightly increasing from 2014 to 2018 globally (Liu et al. 2015, 2016, 2019). However, the market of *Zhong Cheng Yao* in the EU was in a disappointing downturn because of the enacting of Directive 2004/24/EC.

In addition, Liu et al. (2015, 2016, 2019) showed that the U.S. became the biggest market of these exporting products in 2018, and Japan was in second. The EU market as a whole was not shown, but Germany became sixth in 2018 comparing with eighth and seventh in 2014 and 2015 respectively. Korea, Malaysia, India and Spain all appeared in top 10.

[5]The figure is produced based on statistical data recorded and published by Liu Y et al. in 2015, 2016 and 2019 on the topic of the export and import of TCMP.

[6]Close to Dietary Supplement regulated by food law of the EU.

5.3 The Most Relevant WTO Agreements

China and the EU are both members of the WTO, so they trade under WTO legal framework. Figure 5.3 lists the WTO agreements most relevant to some healthcare issues. The items which possibly relate to TCM and TCMP have been high-lighted. These items may involve different export forms of TCMP, including *Zhong Cheng Yao*, nutritious food and agricultural products and so on. TCMP access to the market may involve issues in TBT, SPS and general principles in GATT 1994. It is also relevant to service and intellectual property, since it can be provided by the TCM practitioners and has intellectual property rights to be concerned. Figure 5.3 is based on research and analysis in the book International Trade in Health Services and the GATS and also a joint study by the WHO and the WTO Secretariat on WTO agreements and public health (Blouin et al. 2006; WTO/WHO 2002). The authors of the book and the joint study by the WHO and the WTO Secretariat did not concern any specialized issues relevant to TCMP. Therefore, taking into account the various export forms of TCMP, the study highlighted the possibly relevant areas to TCMP, thereby producing Fig. 5.3. The crosses on the table stand for the possibility that the health issue may be triggered in subjects of certain WTO agreements. Hereinafter, the paper discusses the issues highlighted and especially pays attention to the taxation level of the possible TCMP, the standards set up for market access of TCMP, and the IPR protection issues and aims to explore the reasons which may influence the export of TCMP.

WTO Agreement / Health Issue	Agriculture	SPS	TBT	TRIPS	GATS	GATT Art XX(b)
Food Safety		×				×
Access to TCMP	×	×	×	×	×	×
Health Services					×	
Traditional Knowledge				×		

Fig. 5.3 Specific issues of TCM/TCMP and most relevant WTO Agreements

5.3.1 Tariffs Regarding Some TCMP

Does the main obstacle for TCMP accessing EU market exist in GATT? Some important concessions committed to by the EU that possibly relate to TCMP in GATT are shown in Table 5.1.[7] According to HS version 17, the percentage of duty free tariffs applied is 90% on plants, part of plants, seeds and fruit used in medicaments, and medicaments consisting of mixed or unmixed products for therapeutic or prophylactic purposes; the importing ad valorem duties of Ginseng roots is 0. However, the importing ad valorem duty of some extracts, such as liquorice, is very high. Therefore, taking into consideration all forms of TCMP in the Chinese market, customs duty may compose the obstacle for TCMP to a certain extent. But it does not stop the import of TCMP in forms of agricultural products or extracts. However, in the trade of goods, customs duty already committed to is just one of the measures which might form the obstacle. The interim measures and technical barriers may cause obstacles for the medical product.

5.3.2 The WTO Rules Which May Inhibit the International Trade of TCMP

To further explain the issue, the following WTO agreements that may enable members of the WTO to legally stop the international trade relevant to TCMP need to be discussed:

(1) GATT allows measures to restrict the imports and exports of products to protect the health of humans, animals and plants to conserve natural resources (GATT 1994, art. 20);
(2) TBT allows product requirements and procedures to restrict imports and exports of products for the protection of human health or safety, the protection of animal or plant life or health, the protection of the environment, national security interests and the prevention of deceptive practice (TBT 1994, art. 2.2);
(3) SPS allows measures to restrict the imports and exports of products for the protection of life or health (SPS 1994, art. 5);
(4) GATS allows measures to restrict services and service suppliers for the protection of human, animal or plant life of health (GATS 1994, art. 14).

These are the legal bases for WTO members to use measures, and they can legally stop the export of TCMP from one Member to the other. As shown above the

[7]The data is from Tariff Download Facility, WTO (2020). Table 5.1 has been first published in Saisai Wang, Kim Van der Borght, Xiaoting Song, A Legal Analysis on the Current Trade Status of Traditional Chinese Medicinal Product in the E.U.—from the Perspectives of WTO Law and EU Pharmaceutical Law, AJWH Volume 11 (2), September (2016): 513–535. Amended on 15 January 2020.

Table 5.1 Tariffs regarding some selected TCMP committed by the EU in the WTO

	Original nomenclature		Bound data				
Reporter/ Year	HS code level/ HS version	HS code	Average of AV duties	Minimum AV duty	Maximum AV duty	Duty free TL (%)	HS code description
European Union/2018	6/HS 17	1211	0.3	0	3	90.0	Plants and parts of plants (including seeds and fruits), of a kind used primarily in perfumery, in pharmacy or for insecticidal, fungicidal or similar purposes, fresh or dried, whether or not cut, crushed or powdered
European Union/2018	6/HS 17	1211 20	0.0	0	0	100.0	Ginseng roots, fresh or dried, whether or not cut, crushed or powdered
European Union/2018	6/HS 17	1211 90	1.5	0	3	80.0	Plants, parts of plants, incl. seeds and fruits, used primarily in perfumery, in pharmacy or for insecticidal, fungicidal or similar purposes, fresh or dried, whether or not cut, crushed or powdered (excl. ginseng roots, coca leaf, poppy straw and ephedra)
European Union/2018	6/HS 17	1302 12	3.2	3.2	3.2	0.0	Extracts of liquorice (excl. that with a sucrose content by weight of >10% or in the form of confectionery)
European Union/2018	6/HS 17	3002 20	0.0	0	0	100.0	Vaccines for human medicine

Note: *HS* harmonised system, *AV* ad valorem, *TL* taxation level relevant articles of different WTO agreements involve protecting the health of humans, animals and plant, and protecting public interests, environment and national security interests. Noticeably, measures based on those articles may be used if there are possible imports.

This book narrows the research scope further to pharmaceutical products relevant to TCMP in EU law, because the amendment of EU pharmaceutical law in 2004 severely influenced the issue of traditional medicinal products. TBT and SPS form legal bases on which EU members can set up their domestic appropriate standards, which is the implementation of GATT Article 20 and the reason to exempt the application of some general principles of the WTO. Hereinafter, the analysis will focus on NT and the precautionary principle which derive from the exceptional clauses in TBT and SPS in order to discuss the appropriateness of EU rules relevant to TCMP.

In addition, GATS may be involved in the matter of TCM practitioners. Since this book focuses on drugs instead of practitioners, the rules relevant to mainly drugs will be analysed. Furthermore, the low protection level of IPR rights may bring reluctance to export goods as well. This is due to, first, patent rights and traditional knowledge relevant to TCMP cannot be protected sufficiently because of the poor recognition of TCMP, and, second, medical producers cannot answer the suit or claim their rights properly abroad because of the lack of resources and capacity to participate in litigation or non-litigation cases.

5.4 Discussion on the Rationality of EU Rules on Market Access of TCMP

The free trade principle and trade protectionism form a conflict which drives the dynamic mechanism of WTO law in solving many issues, including market access of TCMP. The WTO encourages free trade, which, at the same time, concerns the protection of public health. Similar to the WTO, the EU is concerned with its integrated economic goal while authorising each of its Member States to enact detailed rules based on a common and general goal of protecting public health. Therefore, in the course of applying the precautionary principle, the WTO faced the challenge of finding an appropriate balance between trade liberalisation objectives and protectionism measures. The challenge also creates tension in the EU as it adjusts relations between its Member States.

This book analyses NT and the precautionary principle to assess the rationality of EU legislation. Noticeably, the principles do not only exist in written WTO and EU laws but also in precedents. The precautionary principle has been widely discussed in cases concerning environmental protection and market access of food products but not often seen in cases on market access of medicinal products. Nevertheless, experiences of the use of the precautionary principle provide insight into facing the problem of lack of scientificity in assessing pharmaceutical product's risk.

In addition, the application of NT between TCMP and EU THMP is discussed. The answer to the question—whether EU pharmaceutical rules applicable to TCMP comply with WTO law on the issue of market access—lies in the analysis of the application of both NT and the precautionary principle.

5.4.1 National Treatment in SPS and TBT

The general rules of the WTO which might be relevant to the international trade of pharmaceutical products have been discussed in previous chapters or parts. Hereinto, the focus is given to two specific agreements: the TBT and the SPS. NT has been well-absorbed by these two agreements in specific situations relevant to technical regulations and standards. The TBT and the SPS closely relate to the issue of market access of TCMP. They regard avoiding unnecessary obstacles to trade as a principle for designing technical requirements. To assess the legitimacy of national technical requirements under the WTO framework, two issues should be given attention. First is why NT in the TBT and the SPS should be applied on issue of market access and second is the difference between the application of TBT and SPS.

Firstly, NT is set forth in Article III of the GATT (1994), Article XVII of the GATS, and Article 3 of the TRIPs, and market access of TCMP as discussed hereinto relates mainly to GATT. NT under GATT only applies once a product has entered the market (WTO and WHO 2002). However, market access is highly relevant to the selection of comparable products when making the decision on authorisation. Therefore, correctly ascertaining the same or a similar product to which the same national rule(s) are applied is essential for discussing the application of the principle. In addition, nevertheless, WTO disputes reflect different natures. Arguments in WTO cases relevant to the application of NT often focus on evaluating likeness, nature and quality of the products, tariff classification, their end-uses, and consumers' tastes and habits (See, DS21/R 1991, WT/DS58/AB/R 1998, WT/DS135/AB/R 2001). This book has noticed that the likeness discussion in WTO cases processed between specific products. Referencing the criteria set out in the WTO precedents, this book refines the common characteristics of TCMP to be compared with THMP or Western conventional medicinal product.

Secondly, both TBT and SPS set out the objectives of protecting human health or safety, as well as the environment, through technical regulations and standards (See, SPS 1994, art. 5.7; TBT preamble, para. 6). Therefore, distinguishing between these two is necessary for finding the right WTO rules to apply to the issue of market access of TCMP. For assessing whether SPS or TBT is relevant to any given technical barrier to trade, the purposes of the measures have to be taken into consideration. The joint study made by the WHO and the WTO in 2002 listed four categories for determining application of SPS measures, listed in Table 5.2 (SPS 1994, annex A, art. 1).

Measures covered by the SPS include technical regulations or standards on a claimed purpose of stopping pests and/or diseases carried by food, beverages,

Table 5.2 The definition of an SPS measure at a glance

Measures taken to protect:	From:
Human or animal life	Additives, contaminants, toxins or disease-causing organisms in their food, beverages, feedstuffs
Human life	Plant- or animal-carried diseases (zoonoses)
Animal or plant life	Pests, diseases, or disease-causing organisms
A country	Damage caused by the entry, establishment or spread of pests (including invasive species)

feedstuffs and plants. Where scientific evidence and the appropriateness of measure (s) are emphasised. The SPS might be applied to cases where the imported form of TCMP is novel food, food supplements, agricultural plants or other type(s) of food which may carry pests or diseases.

The TBT aims at ensuring the technical regulations and standards so as not to create unnecessary obstacles to international trade. It recognises that international standards and conformity assessment systems can improve efficiency of production and facilitate the conduct of international trade and desires in order to encourage the development of such international standards and a conformity assessment system (TBT 1994, preamble, paras. 3, 4, 5). The parties to the TBT reached a common recognition that 'no country should be prevented from taking measures necessary to ensure the quality of its exports, or for the protection of human, animal or plant life or health, of the environment', as well as essential security interest, or for 'the prevention of deceptive practices'. Measures should be taken into consideration of appropriateness, subject to the requirement that they are not applied in a manner which would constitute 'a means of arbitrary or unjustifiable discrimination between countries where the same conditions prevail or a disguised restriction on international trade'. In addition, Members shall ensure that technical regulations should not create unnecessary obstacles to international trade. Article 2.2 of the TBT provides that '[f]or this purpose, technical regulations shall not be more trade-restrictive than necessary to fulfil a legitimate objective, taking account of the risks non-fulfilment would create'. Such legitimate objectives include 'national security requirement, the prevention of deceptive practices, protection of human health or safety, animal or plant life or health, or the environment'. It is further explained that '[i]n assessing such risks, relevant elements of consideration are, *inter alia*: available scientific and technical information, related processing technology or intended end-uses of products' (TBT 1994, art. 2.2). In addition, technical regulations should be based on 'product requirements in terms of performance rather than design or descriptive characteristics' (TBT 1994, art. 2.8). Moreover, so long as the Members are satisfied that an assurance of conformity with applicable technical regulations or standards equivalent to their own procedures can be offered, they 'shall ensure whenever possible, that results of conformity assessment procedures in other Members are accepted, even when those procedures differ from their own' (TBT 1994, art. 6.1).

Furthermore, prior consultations are recommended when necessary in order to arrive at a mutually satisfactory understanding regarding these matters.

These technical regulations and standards compose the obstacle for TCMP entering the EU market. To compare the two, the TBT and the SPS both provide legal basis for Member States of the WTO to adopt technical barriers to the trade of TCMP concerning the protection of life and health of their people. However, the scope of the application of TBT is wider. In relevant cases, scientific information might be less relevant in assessing risks than, for example, processing technology and intended end-uses in the course of the application of TBT. In the form of a pharmaceutical product, TBT is more relevant for TCMP. However, in the case of market access of TCMP, there is not much difference when discussing the application of the precautionary principle in risk assessment between the TBT and the SPS.

When comparing the SPS and the TBT, it is clear that the former emphasises that scientific certainty on the necessity of protection is the prerequisite to impose higher standards, which may form an obstacle to international trade, where food products are mainly affected. Necessity of the protection can be proven by factors such as the level of hazard and the certainty of toxicity of the product (SPS 1994, art. 3.3). Scientific justification is also considered in the TBT, but in contrast to the SPS, processing technology or intended end-uses of products are also taken into account in risk assessment as factors that are decisive in determining acceptable measures under the situations provided by the TBT (SPS 1994, art. 2.2). The TBT aims to ensure technical negotiations and standards, as well as testing and certification procedures (TBT 1994, annex 1, art. 1). The SPS and the TBT have crossed concerning sectors on the human health and safety issue, but the SPS focuses more on protecting 'human or animal life or health within the territory of the Member from risks arising from additives, contaminants, toxins or disease-causing organisms in foods, beverages or feedstuffs', as well as from 'diseases carried by animals, plants or products thereof' (SPS 1994, annex A, art. 1). When directly concerning the life and health protection of human beings regarding the products in forms of food, the SPS is more directly relevant, but if the issue of TCMP as the pharmaceutical product drops out of the regulative scope of the SPS, the TBT can be applied. As of the publication of this book no case regarding issues of the standard for TCMP registration has been brought to the Dispute Settlement Body of the WTO, but both the TBT and the SPS have shown the importance of observing the technical rules and standards of EU law in order for TCMP to access EU market.

5.4.2 Explanation of the Precautionary Principle

The precautionary principle, in the case of market access of TCMP in the EU, is hardly seen as relevant to dispute settlement at this moment; instead, relevance lies in the legislation phase. Even though TCMP has been present in the EU for a long time, it is still somewhat alien for the EU because of the monopolistic position of Western conventional medicine. In such cases, the precautionary principle can be applied.

The origin of the precautionary principle can be traced back to the 1970s during the preparation of legislation on air pollution in German law, known as the Vorsorgeprinzip, translated as 'foresight principle' (European Parliamentary Research Service 2015). Since then, it has influenced other national legislations, from environmental protection to other areas (European Parliamentary Research Service 2015, p. 6).[8] Internationally, it appeared in the environmental agreements of the 1980s, starting with the 1985 Vienna Convention for the Protection of the Ozone Layer. 'Precautionary measures' as a concept is mentioned in the preamble. Later on, the 1987 Ministerial Declaration of the Second International Conference on the Protection of the North Sea stated:

> [I]n order to protect the North Sea from possibly damaging effects of the most dangerous substances, a precautionary approach is necessary which may require action to control inputs of such substances even before a causal link has been established by absolutely clear scientific evidence (Ministerial Declarations of the North Sea Conferences 1987, p. 44).

The above concept was expanded in 1990, stating that the contracting governments:

> will continue to apply the precautionary principle, that is to take action to avoid potentially damaging impacts of substances that are persistent, toxic and liable to bioaccumulate even where there is no scientific evidence to prove a causal link between emissions and effect (Ministerial Declarations of the North Sea Conferences 1987, p. 69).

The precautionary principle is widely used in the regulatory area of environmental law. Its form is contained as a guiding principle in Principle 15 of the 1992 Rio Declaration which states:

> In order to protect the environment, the precautionary approach shall be widely applied by States according to their capabilities. Where there are threats of serious or irreversible damage, lack of full scientific certainty shall not be used as a reason for postponing cost-effective measures to prevent environmental degradation.

At the European level, the precautionary principle was added to the Maastricht Treaty in 1992 and is now included in Article 191 of the Treaty on the Functioning of the European Union (TFEU 2012, art. 191, para. 2) among the principles underpinning EU environmental policy.

Obviously, the wording in international legislations are ambiguous and there is a lack of a unified standard and process of implementation. The argument exists, though, in whether the nature of the precautionary principle as a concept is that of a principle or an approach (WT/DS26/AB/R 1998, para. 43, p. 8; WT/DS48/AB/R 1998). In the area of trade law, the application of the precautionary principle is subject to the trade liberalisation rules in the WTO Agreement and, in the European context, the law of the European Community. For instance, Article 28 of the Nice

[8]Germany, France and Sweden have incorporated the precautionary principle into their national legislation. In some EU countries, such as Belgium and the Netherlands, the courts recognise the precautionary principle. The courts in Spain and the UK only make their decisions based on the precautionary principle if the provisions under consideration derive from EU legislation.

Treaty (TEC 2002; TFEU 2012, art. 34) prohibits quantitative restrictions on imports and all measures having equivalent effect. The same sort of prohibition against quantitative restrictions on imports and exports lies in Article XI of GATT (1994). Both systems provide for general exceptions for protecting human, animal or plant life or health, but against arbitrary or unjustifiable discrimination (TFEU 2012, art. 36; GATT 1994, art. XX(b)).[9] Cases regarding the precautionary principle emerged first in cases of environmental protection both in the WTO and in the EU. In written law, the principle is introduced by Article 5.7 of SPS (1994) (WTO 2017c)[10] and Article 174(2) of the Maastricht Treaty of the EU (1997).[11]

In 2000, the EU published a Communication on the precautionary principle as decision-makers were constantly faced with the dilemma of 'balancing the freedom and rights of individuals, industry and organisations with the need to reduce the risk of adverse effects to the environment, human, animal or plant health' (Commission of the European Communities 2000). A structured decision-making process with detailed scientific and other objective information was developed to find the correct balance, so that 'the proportionate, non-discriminatory, transparent and coherent actions can be taken' (Commission of the European Communities 2000). The precautionary principle was designed for situations wherein scientific data do not permit a complete evaluation of the risk. The main aim of clarifying the precautionary principle is to understand how to assess, appraise, manage and communicate risks that science is not yet able to evaluate fully in certain circumstances. The precautionary principle can be applied to market access of EU THMP and TCMP in the EU. However, the EU should not render unwarranted or unproportionate recourse to the principle, as it should not be a disguised form of protectionism. Such considerations of precautionary principle also exist in WTO law. The precautionary principle is applied to market access of pharmaceutical products in the course of the risk assessment and management. The prerequisite of risk management is to assess the safety, efficacy and quality control of TCMP.

---

[9]E.g. TFEU Article 36 which allows measures that are 'justified'; GATT 1994, Article XX (b) allows measures that are 'necessary'.

[10]The wording of 'precautionary principle' does not appear in Article 5.7 of SPS, but the meaning of precautionary principle is expressed and confirmed in the WTO glossary. The full text reads, '[i]n cases where relevant scientific evidence is insufficient, a Member may provisionally adopt sanitary or phytosanitary measures on the basis of available pertinent information, including that from the relevant international organisations as well as from sanitary or phytosanitary measures applied by other Members. In such circumstances, Members shall seek to obtain the additional information necessary for a more objective assessment of risk and review the sanitary or phytosanitary measure accordingly within a reasonable period of time'.

[11]The full text of Article 174(2), first paragraph, reads, '[c]ommunity policy on the environment shall aim at a high level of protection taking into account the diversity of situations in the various regions of the Community. It shall be based on the precautionary principle and on the principles that preventive action should be taken, that environmental damage should as a priority be rectified at source and that the polluter should pay'.

5.4.3 The Application of National Treatment and the Precautionary Principle in WTO Case Law

The use of the precautionary principle has appeared in litigation of both TBT and SPS. If discussing the technical regulations and standards set forth by EU pharmaceutical law, cases relating to international trade of traditional medicinal products are rarely found in practice. The higher standards set forth by the West are the dominant standards. They are widely accepted and are rarely challenged due to the common recognition of the advanced scientific development status of Western conventional medicine.

In the case of traditional medicinal products, the state which owns the knowledge of the product holds more advanced information and techniques on R&D and manufacture. But scientific uncertainty arises when assessing the risk by using the risk assessment mechanism of the West. In such cases, can the rules set forth especially for the guidance of Western medicine be reasonably challenged in law as to market access of traditional medicinal products? The research hereinto chooses three WTO cases to illustrate the application of NT and the precautionary principle in scientific assessment. Two cases are food product-related and one is regarding an industry material, but they all implicate the issue of how to verify the justification of the technical standards in case of scientific uncertainty. For the convenience of reading the case studies, Table 5.3 compares the provisions relevant to the adoption of technical measures based on TBT and SPS.

5.4.3.1 U.S. Shrimp Case

In this case, the U.S. placed an import prohibition on shrimp and shrimp products from non-certified countries (WT/DS58/AB/R 1998). India, Malaysia, Pakistan and Thailand were complainants, and the European Commission also joined as one of the third-party participants. First, the panel found that the U.S. prohibition violated GATT Article XI (prohibition on quantitative restrictions) because 'it did not put forward any defending arguments in this regard'. Second, the AB recognised that the U.S. import ban was related to GATT Article XX(g)—the conservation of exhaustible natural resources, but the ban could not be unjustifiable discrimination because of its intended and actual coercive effect on specific policy decisions made by foreign governments that were Members of the WTO. The ban could also be arbitrary discrimination because of 'the rigidity and inflexibility in its application, and the lack of transparency and procedural fairness in the administration of trade regulations' (WT/DS58/AB/R 1998). Even though the panel and the AB gave a supportive decision of free trade in this case, the EU raised concerns about the environment. The EU stressed that it was bound by the Treaty Establishing the European Community (EEC, 1957) to ensure a harmonious and balanced development of economic activities with respect for the environment. It stressed that the principle of sustainable development as well as the precautionary principle was laid

Table 5.3 Comparison between TBT and SPS on the provisions relevant to the adoption of technical measures

	TBT	SPS
Legal objectives	– Preamble, para. 3: Recognising the important contribution that international standards and conformity assessment systems can make in this regard by improving efficiency of production and facilitating the conduct of international trade; – Preamble, para. 4: Desiring therefore to encourage the development of such international standards and conformity assessment systems. . .	– Preamble, para. 2: Desiring to improve the human health, animal health and phytosanitary situation in all Members. . .
Legal basis for higher technical regulations or standards	– Preamble para. 6: Recognising that no country should be prevented from taking measures necessary to ensure the quality of its exports, or for the protection of human, animal or plant life or health, of the environment; – Art. 2.2: Members shall ensure that technical regulations are not prepared, adopted or applied with a view to or with the effect of creating unnecessary obstacles to international trade. For this purpose, technical regulations shall not be more trade-restrictive than necessary to fulfil a legitimate objective, taking account of the risks non-fulfilment would create. Such legitimate objectives are, *inter alia:* national security requirements; the prevention of deceptive practices; protection of human health or safety, animal or plant life or health, or the environment. In assessing such risks, relevant elements of consideration are, *inter alia:* **available scientific and technical information, related processing technology or intended end-uses of products**.	– Preamble para. 1: Reaffirming that no Member should be prevented from adopting or enforcing measures necessary to protect human, animal or plant life or health, subject to the requirement that these measures are not applied in a manner which would constitute a means of arbitrary or unjustifiable discrimination between Members where the same conditions prevail or a disguised restriction on international trade; – Art. 3.3: Members may introduce or maintain sanitary or phytosanitary measures which result in a higher level of sanitary or phytosanitary protection than would be achieved by measures based on the relevant international standards, guidelines or recommendations, if there is a **scientific justification**, or as a consequence of the level of sanitary or phytosanitary protection; – Art. 5.4: Members should, when determining the appropriate level of sanitary or phytosanitary protection, take into account the objective of minimizing negative trade effects. – Art. 5.7: . . .where urgent problems of safety, health, environmental protection or national security arise or threaten to arise for a Member, that Member may omit such of the steps enumerated in paragraph 6 as it finds necessary, provided that the Member, upon adoption of the procedure, shall: – 5.7.1 notify immediately other Members through the Secretariat of the particular procedure and the products covered, with a brief indication of the objective and the rationale of the procedure, including the nature of the urgent problems;

(continued)

Table 5.3 (continued)

	TBT	SPS
		– 5.7.2 upon request, provide other Members with copies of the rules of the procedure; – 5.7.3 without discrimination, allow other Members to present their comments in writing, discuss these comments upon request, and take these written comments and the results of these discussions into account.
Basic legal request on issuing a technical measure	– Preamble para. 6: . . .they are not applied in a manner which would constitute a means of arbitrary or unjustifiable discrimination between countries where the same conditions prevail or a disguised restriction on international trade; – Art. 2.8: Wherever appropriate, Members shall specify technical regulations based on product requirements in terms of performance rather than design or descriptive characteristics.	– Art. 5.1: Members shall ensure that their sanitary or phytosanitary measures are based on an assessment, as appropriate to the circumstances, of the risks to human, animal or plant life or health, taking into account risk assessment techniques developed by the relevant international organizations. – Art. 5.2: In the assessment of risks, Members shall take into account available scientific evidence; relevant processes and production methods; relevant inspection, sampling and testing methods; prevalence of specific diseases or pests; existence of pest- or disease-free areas; relevant ecological and environmental conditions; and quarantine or other treatment. – Art. 5.3: In assessing the risk to animal or plant life or health and determining the measure to be applied for achieving the appropriate level of sanitary or phytosanitary protection from such risk, Members shall take into account as relevant economic factors: the potential damage in terms of loss of production or sales in the event of the entry, establishment or spread of a pest or disease; the costs of control or eradication in the territory of the importing Member; and the relative cost-effectiveness of alternative approaches to limiting risks. – Art. 5.5: each Member shall avoid arbitrary or unjustifiable distinctions in the levels it considers to be appropriate in different situations, if such distinctions result in discrimination or a disguised restriction on international trade.
	TBT	SPS

down in the first paragraph of the preamble of the WTO Agreement (WT/DS58/AB/R 1998, para. 67). From this case, it can be deduced that protection of the environment, and, possible in other cases, protection of public health, is a common recognition by the WTO. However, decision-making in the WTO is also influenced by other principles, such as non-discrimination, including NT and the MFN treatment. Such principles are reflected by a just administration procedure and equal treatment in the market.

This book notes that first, WTO law principles and procedural rules should always be respected in the course of applying the precautionary principle. Second, risk assessment is the prerequisite to decide scientific certainty and uncertainty. Therefore, the party that is going to take measure(s) against market access should at least provide evidence on damage or possible damage, the hazard that leads to the damage, and the causality between these two, thereby avoiding taking any arbitrary or unjust measures. Third, under a situation of uncertainty, inversion of the burden of proof is one of the core criteria in applying the precautionary principle. However, it may lead to unjust treatment between developed countries and developing countries, or between parties which hold advanced techniques and those with a less advanced position. Since the party holding the advanced technique may claim higher standard (s) within its territory—or internationally—according to a technique framework it sets up by itself preference(s), developing/least developed countries don't have the capacity to pursue the scientific issue due to the limitations of their development level.

5.4.3.2 The Asbestos Case—Properly Defining the Likeness

The argument in this case is relevant to Article III:4 of the GATT 1994, Article XX (b) of the GATT 1994 and Article 2.1 of the TBT (WT/DS135/AB/R 2001).

5.4.3.2.1 Review of the Asbestos Case

Starting from the establishment of the Panel on 25 November 1998 to the adoption of the AB Report on 5 April 2001, this case lasted more than 2 years. The case arose from a ban in a Decree (No. 96-1133, 1996) made by the Respondent, France, represented by the EC, on asbestos and products containing asbestos. Asbestos can be divided into two groups, amphiboles and serpentine with chrysotile belonging to the second. Canada, the Complainant, challenged the ban on chrysotile fibre and products containing it. Canada claimed that the Decree was incompatible with Article I:1 and III:4 of the GATT because the Decree subjected chrysotile fibre and chrysotile-cement products imported from Canada and from any other country to less favourable treatment than like PVA, cellulose and glass fibres and like fibro-cement products of French or foreign origin. Canada also asserted that since the Decree banning asbestos was a technical regulation, Article 2.1 of the TBT Agreement should be applied (WT/DS135/R 2000, p. 106). Therefore, it was important for

Canada to prove the likeness of chrysotile asbestos, on the one hand, and PCG fibres—PVA, cellulose and glass fibres—and/or chrysotile-cement on the other. In examining the 'likeness' of the two sets of products, an approach based on the Report of the Working Party on Border Tax Adjustments (BISD 18S/97 1970) was noted by both the Panel and the AB (WT/DS135/AB/R 2001, p. 32). Under the approach, four general criteria were listed for analysing 'likeness', including (1) the properties, nature and quality of the products, (2) the end-uses of the products, (3) the tastes and habits of consumers, and (4) the tariff classification of the products (BISD 18S/97 1970). Even though the Panel confirmed the likeness, the AB ultimately reversed it. In the appellate procedure, the AB concluded that Canada had failed to satisfy a complainant's burden of proof to demonstrate likeness, specifically that PCG and/or chrysotile-cement are 'like' chrysotile asbestos fibres under Article III:4.

The AB noted that Article III:4 and Article XX(b) were distinct and independent provisions of the GATT 1994, even though both might relate to health risks. The AB explained in its Report:

> Under Article III:4, evidence relating to health risks may be relevant in assessing the competitive relationship in the marketplace between allegedly 'like' products. The same, or similar, evidence serves a different purpose under Article XX(b), namely, that of assessing whether a member has a sufficient basis for 'adopting or enforcing' a WTO-inconsistent measure on the grounds of human health (WT/DS135/AB/R 2001, para. 115, pp. 44–45).

In addition, one of the more impressive arguments from the EC was in response to Canada's claim of likeness between asbestos-containing products and substitute products. The EC argued that the lack of 'similarity' between asbestos-containing products and substitute products was confirmed by the fact that they had different physical and mechanical properties (WT/DS135/R 2000, p. 160). According to precedent, likeness of products can be assessed on a 'case-by-case' basis considering, in particular, end-use of the product, consumers' tastes and habits and the properties, nature and quality of the product (BISD 18S/97 1970).[12] End-use pointed to 'a well-defined and single product' at the end-use stage, where the tariff classifications are also taken into concern. Thereinto, the EC contended that different HS were applicable to asbestos fibres and substitute products/asbestos-containing products.

[12]Working Party Report on Border Tax Adjustments, para. 18 reads, "...the interpretation of the term should be examined on a case-by-case basis. This would allow a fair assessment in each case of the different elements that constitute a 'similar' product. Some criteria were suggested for determining, on a case-by-case basis, whether a product is 'similar': the product's end-uses in a given market, consumers' tastes and habits, which change from country to country, the product's properties, nature and quality." This Report was adopted by the contracting parties in 1970 and referenced by the Appellate Body in case of *Japan—Taxes on Alcoholic Beverages* in 1996.

5.4.3.2.2 Implications for Market Access of TCMP

Taking into account the different forms of market access of TCMP, different HS may apply to different TCMPs. If focusing on the elements of tradition and herbal medicinal products, the properties of TCMP can be compared to EU traditional use medicinal products, and these two are both covered by Directive 2004/24/EC. In such a circumstance, using the risk assessment approach and system of the Western conventional medicinal product for both can be challenged. One the one hand, traditional Chinese herbal medicinal product and EU THMP both have chemical properties and long-standing use records. The precedents of registration of TCMP in the EU have shown the recognition on their comparability in practice. On the other hand, TCMP also has unique characteristics and production process based on theories of formulation covered by a well-developed system of TCM.

5.4.3.3 The Hormones Case—Applying the Precautionary Principle

The precautionary principle has been explicitly discussed with regard to the application of SPS in WTO dispute settlements, namely the U.S. versus the EC (WT/DS26/AB/R 1998, para. 43, p. 18) and Canada versus the EC (WT/DS48/AB/R 1998). The case was initiated by an EC prohibition measure on the market regarding the importation of meat and meat products that were treated with certain hormones. The U.S. requested to establish the Panel on 20 May 1996 and Canada joined on 16 October 1996. The U.S. and Canada are both complainants against the EC, the respondent.

The products at issue were meat and meat products treated with hormones for growth purposes. The Panel circulated its Report on 18 August 1997. It affirmed that the EC maintained sanitary measures which were not based on a risk assessment and, as such, had acted inconsistently with the requirement contained in Article 5.1 of the SPS Agreement. In other words, it affirmed that the EU's distinctions were arbitrary or unjustifiable. On 24 September 1997, the EC notified the dispute settlement body (DSB) of its decision to appeal certain issues of law covered in the Panel Reports and certain legal interpretations developed by the Panel (WT/DS26/AB/R 1998, para. 6, p. 4). The EC claimed that 'the Panel erred in finding that the burden of proof under the SPS agreement rests on the Member imposing a measure' (WT/DS26/AB/R 1998, para. 11, p. 5). The EC submitted that 'WTO panels should adopt a deferential 'reasonableness' standard when reviewing a Member's decision to adopt a particular science policy or a Member's determination that a particular inference from the available data is scientifically plausible' (WT/DS26/AB/R 1998, para. 14, p. 6).

The U.S., as appellee before the AB, claimed that the precautionary principle is an approach—the content of which may vary from context to context—rather than a principle of customary international law (WT/DS26/AB/R 1998, para. 43, p. 18). It noted that Article 5.7 of the SPS Agreement permits the provisional adoption of SPS measures even where the relevant scientific evidence is insufficient. However, it claimed that the EC could not create a risk assessment where there is no relevant scientific evidence at all, nor can a principle create sufficient scientific evidence where there is none (WT/DS26/AB/R 1998, para. 43, p. 18). Nevertheless, Canada considered the precautionary approach or concept as an 'emerging principle of international law' within the meaning of Article 38 (1) (c) of the Statute of the International Court of Justice, and it asserted that Article 5.7 should not override on Article 5.1 and 5.2 (WT/DS26/AB/R 1998, para. 60, p. 24). And therefore, the EC should not focus on the word 'potential' to the exclusion of 'evaluation' by a risk assessment (WT/DS26/AB/R 1998, para. 66, p. 25).

The EC responded on the issue of the precautionary principle regarding the 'sufficient' scientific evidence claimed by the U.S. It argued that the concepts of 'risk' and 'risk assessment' in the SPS Agreement are not a quantitative but a qualitative concept, and the word 'sufficient' also cannot be taken to refer to the quantitative, but rather to the qualitative. It submitted that:

> [T]he real question is not whether the sanitary measure is 'based on' the 'best' science or the 'preponderance' of science or whether there is conflicting science. Rather, the question is only whether the government maintaining a measure has a scientific basis for that measure (WT/DS26/AB/R 1998, para. 81, p. 31).

The above assertion reflected the intention of the EC to distinguish between the legal issue and science.

Finally, AB overturned many of the Panel's views in the Report. The AB rejected the Panel's interpretation of Article 3.1 relating to international standards and rejected the Panel's interpretation of the relationship between SPS Article 3.1, 3.2 and 3.3, concluding that the requirement that SPS measures be 'based on' international standards, guidelines or recommendations under Article 3.1 does not mean that SPS measures must 'conform to' such standards. The AB also reversed the Panel's finding that 'the SPS Agreement allocates the 'evidentiary burden' to the Member imposing an SPS measure' (WT/DS26/AB/R 1998, para. 253, p. 102). The AB upheld the Panel's ultimate conclusion that the EC measure violated Article 5.1 (and thus Article 3.3) because it was not based on a risk assessment, but it reversed the Panel's interpretation and considered Article 5.1 as requiring a rational relationship between the measure at issue and the risk assessment. Even though the AB considered that the EC measure was arbitrary or contained unjustifiable distinctions to a certain extent, it reversed the Panel's finding that the measure resulted in discrimination or a disguised restriction of international trade in violation of Article 5.5. Important to its reasoning was the recognition of genuine anxieties concerning the safety of the hormones and the necessity for harmonising measures for establishing a common internal market for beef. The relevant arguments and the final AB report revolved around technical standards on risk assessment which is a core issue of the precautionary principle.

5.4.4 *Argument on the Appropriateness*

5.4.4.1 The 'Likeness' Between Traditional Chinese Herbal Medicinal Product and Western Traditional Use Herbal Medicinal Product

The EU has traditional use herbal medicinal products—EU THMP. According to a scientific survey done by the EU, 1719 THMP were granted between 2004 and 2016 (EMA/322570/2011 2017, p. 4). From 2009 to 2016, 611 combination products were registered in the EU, compared with 1053 monocomponent products (EMA/322570/2011 2017, p. 4).

There are similarities between traditional Chinese herbal medicinal product and EU THMP. The likeness between traditional Chinese herbal medicinal product and EU THMP can been shown in the following aspects. First, traditional Chinese herbal medicinal product and EU THMP both have chemical properties of herbal medicinal product. Second, they both rely on traditional knowledge. Third, in practice, they both can be produced based on formulas as either monocomponet product or combination products. Fourth, they both have long-standing use records to demonstrate their safety and efficacy.

However, the following concerns weaken the judgment of similarities. First, they have different philosophical and theoretical backgrounds. TCM is based on the philosophy of contradiction and unity in a holistic treating method and has theories of *Yin-Yang* and *Wuxing* for the formulation of TCMP (See, TCM WIKI 2012). By contrast, EU THMP does not base on a developed system as TCM. From a historical perspective, the 'more is better' concept continues to survive today (Schulz et al. 2001, p. 15). Therefore, the current EU registration system relies more on the experience of using such products on the EU market when approving their safety and quality. Secondly, even though both EU THMP and TCMP have a long usage history, they are used differently in different places and work differently on different ethnic groups. Because of the lack of modern scientific data, the use experience of TCMP has not been widely recognised by the EU. Third, as a consequence of the second difference, data and references concerning TCMP, such as the Chinese pharmacopeia which is used to record the safety and efficacy of traditional medicinal products' varieties, are not well accepted by the EU. And lastly, even though China and the EU both have competent authorities to approve the registration of traditional products, the administrative powers have their own territorial jurisdiction.

So then, can these four differences dismiss the similarities between EU THMP and traditional Chinese herbal medicinal product, entirely? Probably not. The first difference—the difference in philosophical and theoretical backgrounds—demonstrates that TCM has more complete theoretical bases, which does not conflict with the 'more is better' concept. Regarding the second difference, difference of use in different places and among different ethnic groups, since the mobility of people from the different areas of the world has existed throughout history, the existence of immigration is the fact. At the least, Asian immigrants belong to the same ethnic group, plus patients have the freedom to choose the treatment method. A precautionary liability can be borne by doctors when they treat EU patients and Asian patients. Third, resulting from the second difference, the data and references produced within the EU and the Chinese territory should be accepted and exchangeable. If these first three differences are not obstacles for the reorganisation of the similarities anymore, the fourth difference relating to territorial jurisdictions of administrative powers may be solved through cooperation or an agreement between China and the EU.

5.4.4.2 Criteria to Define 'Likeness'

There are many criteria to define 'likeness'. Likeness is the prerequisite to consider the further application of NT. Likeness should be evaluated on a case-by-case basis. The nature of the compared products has to be described respectively and after that it is possible to discuss the degrees of likeness. Herein this book, TCMP and EU THMP are treated as two comparable groups of products for a comparison. A few guidelines are given as general criteria to decide the likeness in some WTO cases. As aforementioned, the Report of the Working Party on *Border Tax Adjustments* employed four general criteria in analysing 'likeness', including (i) the properties, nature and quality of the products, (ii) the end-uses of the products, (iii) consumers' tastes and habits, and (iv) the tariff classification of the products (BISD 18S/97 1970). In addition, two other criteria are also mentioned, including the consumer's willingness to substitute one for the other based on perceived functional equivalence (DS29/R 1994) and process and production methods (Hudec 2000).

Comparing traditional Chinese herbal medicinal product and EU THMP in EU pharmaceutical law, criteria (i) can be generally met to determine the likeness of these two. The free choice of medicine from Chinese immigrants in Europe and the consumer's willingness to use TM can both add weight to the similarities between these two.

The above comparisons illustrate that the EU may recognise traditional Chinese herbal medicinal product as one of THMPs. EU THMP is the most comparable product with traditional Chinese herbal medicinal product, even though, the latter is based on a series of TCM systematic theories of diagnosis and formula. Many TCMPs have more than 15 years use recorded in Asia. The territorial limitation to determine the valid data collection of 15 years is understandable but debatable.

Indeed, TCMP is alien to the EU and its scientificity has not been sufficiently proven for a satisfactory illustration and control of its risk. Therefore, finding comparable similar product helps in understanding and evaluating the risks. However, the safety of using TCMP cannot be properly evaluated by contemporary scientific techniques. Relying on current science and technology to prove the safety and function of TCMP would fall in strong contrast with the abundant successful cases of curing patients and the long historical development of TCM in China. The scepticism of the scientificity of TCMP have seriously influenced TCMP to enter the EU market. Practically, TCMP has been given less favourable treatment than EU THMP that is facing the same difficulty of scientific uncertainty. Patients who use

TCM are a minority in the EU, which exasperates the lack of sufficient data to prove its safety and effectiveness in the medical practice of the EU. In such circumstance, a cautious attitude for dealing with such a situation through law is necessary and understandable. However, a way to sustain the development of an alien medicine also needs to be considered in case the merit of TCM is recognised.

5.4.4.3 Argument from the Angle of the Precautionary Principle

The lack of scientific certainty is an often-met problem in dispute settlements relating to the precautionary principle. Therefore, the direction on the development of the precautionary principle provides clues for solving the question on legislation when facing the issue of insufficiency of scientific certainty. The EU has very sophisticated rules on the application of the precautionary principle than the WTO. According to the EU, the criteria to be evaluated in applying precautionary principle include proportionality, non-discrimination, review, examination of the potential benefits, burden of proving injury, etc. (Commission of the European Communities 2000). Therefore, the scientific uncertainty problem of TCMP can be envisaged according to law.

To say the least, before one product enters into an EU Member State, NT is not applicable. Further, members of the WTO have no obligation to set up standards for a product that has never been on their market. The precautionary principle can cast a shadow on the design of the legal system relating to the TUR procedure in the EU. For this reason, plausible evidence and specific risk assessment standards come down to 15 years use within the EU. The rationality of 15 years use within the EU can be challenged by taking into account the precautionary principle for assessing the risk of TCMP.

In practice, when considering market access of TCMP, the EU is generally concerned with the historical development of TCM in the EU and safety, efficacy and quality control. Thus, it is reasonable for the competent authority to conduct the evaluation for authorisation on a case-by-case basis. In this situation, applicants for authorisation bear the responsibility to provide sufficient evidence as required by the risk assessment system. As a consequence of this process, the development of TCM in the EU relies ultimately on the open-mindedness of policymakers who decide whether and how to develop TCM or any CAM at all.

5.5 Chapter Summary

5.5.1 Final Thoughts on Appropriateness of EU Pharmaceutical Law as Applied to TCMP

Even though the WTO aims to encourage free trade, proper protection of public interest and domestic trade is necessary. However, overmuch protection or improper legislation may impair the development of science. It might also create unfair conditions for competitors and individual producers, and in this case consumers, and in the context of this book patients, will be the direct victims. The conflict between free trade and protectionism against free trade supports the reasonable existence of a dynamic WTO mechanism, hereon the issue of market access of TCMP in the EU, NT and reasonable exceptions are focused. To decide a reasonable exception, the states must be concerned with many factors, including scientific, political and economic factors and so on. These factors put different weights on the adoption of the exception clauses in different situations. Among them, the scientific factor is the first concern when deciding issues of market access of the medicinal product. However, before judging the scientific certainty or uncertainty of a factor, it is necessary to conduct a risk assessment. Both the U.S. shrimp case and EC Hormones case have shown the importance of conducting a risk assessment for avoiding arbitrary and unjust measures when considering applying the precautionary principle while the Asbestos case gives clues on clarifying 'likeness' between comparable products. The study in this book doubts the rationality of the EU regulation on 15 years use experience within the EU for application of TUR procedure and holds that the rule is not appropriate.

5.5.2 *Impact on International Trade of TCMP Driven by the Prospect and Development Difficulties of TCM*

The lag of development of TCM has to be concerned when we criticize EU pharmaceutical law on issue of market access of TCMP. To analyse the prospect and development difficulties of TCM in the EU, both the strengths of China and the EU must be considered from a general healthcare perspective. From the EU's perspective, it has advanced tech-knowledge in medical science. The EU also holds a favourable position in IPR legislation and protection; the sign-on to TRIPs reflected the will of Western members of the WTO who originally pushed for IPR to be gradually strengthened and respected in China as well. Nevertheless, protecting TCM patents, secrets and data outside of China is difficult. And if the TCMP is not well-accepted, then traditional knowledge cannot be recognised sufficiently either. Moreover, TCM practitioners also face a difficult situation if TCMP cannot be distributed sufficiently and freely. From China's side, it holds the knowledge of TCMP and can provide education on TCM. In addition, the EU is more attracted to the prospect of economic development, since China has a large market demands in the healthcare area such as in the life insurance market and the medical market. However, the safety and efficacy of TCMP are uncertain in the EU. Therefore, cooperation in the healthcare arena can be developed across sectors based on GATT, GATS and TRIPs under the WTO framework, but the difficulties are obvious.

It must be emphasised that the cooperation in the healthcare arena between China and the EU shall be based on the common goals of public health protection and economic development balance, and the safety concern takes priority over economic development. In addition, the current scientific technique is limited, and legislators also need to consider the development of scientific techniques.

The less developed status of TCM practice and regulation bring difficulties to the trade of TCMP. Referring to the TCM issue, TCM practitioners have existed in the EU for many years, for instance acupuncture has been widely accepted by the European people. Therefore, EU legislators should leave a space for practitioners to develop their practice in the EU. Through proper design and development of a system to regulate TCM practitioners, scientific data relevant to TCMP can be further collected and, subsequently, proper development conditions for TCMP in the EU can be maintained.

Strengthening legislation on EU law on traditional use medicinal products leaves very limited space for TCM practitioners to import non-registered TCMP. On the other hand, very rarely has TCMP been registered in the EU or met the conditions for registration. Therefore, treatment from TCM practitioner would face a problem of hysteresis. Even though Chinese practitioners are still allowed to provide services to patients, procedurally they cannot easily import TCMP promptly from China before they complete the examination to give a prescription. They might be expected to find succedaneum in the EU, but the selection of the TCMP is often very restricted to the country of origin. They can still use the preparations in the prescription, but many other problems still follow. For instance, the EU does not have a specific standard on the quality of TCMP preparation. Therefore, the preparations can be imported, under any HS code, but EU lacks supervision. Consequently, the patient cannot benefit from good formulas. Therefore, the development of both TCM and TCMP actually results in a hardship in the EU.

Are the measures taken by the EU too strict for TCMP to enter the EU market? Should the EU distinguish the patient groups composed of Chinese-orientated and western-orientated patients? If this goal can be reached by clear labelling on the product, should EU insist on the same standards for market access of TCMP and its traditional used herbal medicinal product? This book intends to raise awareness of these questions, rather than lead to conclusive answers.

China and the EU should respect each other's appeals. TCM is a treasure for China. TCMP and its knowledge have been developed and inherited for thousands of years, and the EU can reference advanced administrative and manufactural technologies. The advantages can contribute to the common goal—public health—based on the mutually recognised international legal rules and common principles pursued by the respective legal systems. Economic development can be driven forward, and not backwards, while realising the goal of public health. Regarding the profitable nature of pharmaceutical industries, the policy maker should guide these industries to serve the goals of public health. Law is supposed to convey a compromised opinion between the public and other profitable entities in the pharmaceutical industry. Policy makers balance the power of different stakeholders in the system and are the participants who, importantly are guiding the direction of law, and science provides proof for the policy maker to make the right decision. Moreover, cooperation on scientific research between the EU and China should be enhanced efficiently, and the opinion of pharmaceutical companies should be given adequate attention.

The study in this book recognises that China has more sophisticated SR along with a well-developed TCM practice. Therefore, the study encourages a continually scientific development of TCMP within China before the EU is able to fully accept TCM and TCMP. In a win-win situation, the West shall gain ideas and innovations for medical science, and the outcomes can be used to benefit public health in the EU, which supplements the insufficiency of Western conventional medicine.

In the meantime, the precautionary principle can be applied to face the problem of scientific uncertainty in law. As aforementioned, the precautionary principle is often used in the area of trade in food products and enables the members of the WTO to adopt a more cautious attitude when importing food products with insufficient scientific evidence in order to protect the environment or prove the safety of the product. In the other words, in such circumstances the members of the WTO can adopt trade measures to suspend the import of such a food product. However, herewith the issue of market access of TCMP in international trade, the application of the precautionary principle can thus raise the attention of the EU to rethink and envisage the issue of CAM in the EU.

References

Alfonso-Cristancho R, Andia T, Watanabe JH (2015) Definition and classification of generic drugs across the world. Appl Health Econ Health Policy 13(Suppl 1):5–11

BISD 18S/97 (1970) Working Party Report, Border Tax Adjustments

Blouin C, Drager N, Smith R et al (eds) (2006) International trade in health services and the GATS: current issues and debates. The International Bank for Reconstruction and Development/The World Bank, Washington, pp 88, 93, 94, 203

Commission of the European Communities (2000) Communication from the Commission on the Precautionary Principle. COM (2000) 1 final

Decree No. 96-1133 (1996), France

Directive 2001/83/EC of the European Parliament and of the Council of 6 November 2001 on the Community Code Relating to Medicinal Products for Human Use. (2001) OJ L 311:67–128

Directive 2004/24/EC of the European Parliament and of the Council of 31 March 2004 Amending, as regards Traditional Herbal Medicinal Products Directive 2001/83/EC on the Community Code relating to Medicinal Products for Human Use (2004) OJ L136:85–90

Directive 65/65/EEC (1965) Directive 65/65/EEC of 26 January 1965 on the Approximation of Provisions Laid down by Law, Regulation or Administrative Action Relating to Proprietary Medicinal Products. OJ 022:369–373

DS21/R. WTO Panel (1991) Mexico v. United States, U.S.—Tuna

DS29/R (1994) United States - Restrictions on Imports of Tuna

EMA/322570/2011 (2017) Uptake of the Traditional Use Registration Scheme and Implementation of the Provisions of Directive 2004/24/EC in EU Member States, Rev. 7

European Commission Trade Helpdesk (2017) EU Product Classification System, http://trade.ec.europa.eu/tradehelp/

European Parliamentary Research Service (2015) The Precautionary Principle — Definitions, Applications and Governance

GATS (1994) General Agreement on Trade in Services. In: WTO

GATT (1994) General Agreement on Tariffs and Trade. In: WTO
Hanhijärvi TJ(2015) Dialectical thinking: Zeno, Socrates, Kant, Marx, Algora Algora Publishing, p 151
Health Commission of Jiaozuo city (2019) Ji Shi Shi Pin You Shi Yao Pin De Wu Pin Ming Dan (The List of Substances that Categorised as Food and Drug). http://www.jzswjw.gov.cn/show.asp?id=992
Hudec RE (2000) 'Like Product': the differences in meaning in GATT Articles I and II. In: Cottier T, Mavroidis P (eds) Regulatory barriers and the principle of non-discrimination in world trade law. University of Michigan Press, pp 101–123
Liu Y et al (2015) 2014 Nian Zhong Yao Shang Pin Jin Chu Kou Fen Xi (An analysis on the export and import of traditional Chinese medicinal product 2014). Zhong Guo Xian Dai Zhong Yao (Mod Chin Med) 17(3):257, 258
Liu Y et al (2016) 2015 Nian Zhong Yao Shang Pin Jin Chu Kou Fen Xi (An analysis on the export and import of traditional Chinese medicinal product 2015). Zhong Guo Xian Dai Zhong Yao (Mod Chin Med) 18(2):225, 226
Liu Y et al (2019) 2018 Nian Zhong Yao Lei Shang Pin Jin Chu Kou Xing Shi Fen Xi (An analysis on the export and import trend of traditional Chinese medicinal product 2018). Zhong Guo Xian Dai Zhong Yao (Mod Chin Med) 21(4):419, 420
Mao T (1937) On contradiction. In: Selected works of Mao Tse-tung. Foreign Languages Press, Peking, vol I. In marxists.org (2004) Mao Tse Tung Internet Archive. https://www.marxists.org/reference/archive/mao/selected-works/volume-1/mswv1_17.htm
Mao T (1966) Methods of thinking and methods of work. In: Quotations from Mao Tse Tung, 1st edn. Peking Foreign Languages Press, Peking. In: marxists.org (2000) Mao Tse Tung Internet Archive. https://www.marxists.org/reference/archive/mao/works/red-book/ch22.htm
Marx-Engels-Lenin Institute (2017) Essential texts of Marxism-Leninism. Pravda Media, p 218
Ministerial Declarations of the North Sea Conferences (1984, 1987, 1990) Ministerial Declarations—International Conferences on the Protection of the North Sea. Bremen, Germany, (1984); London, United Kingdom (1987); the Hague, the Netherlands, (1990)
Ministry of Health of the PRC (2002) Fu Jian Yi of Guan Yu Jin Yi Bu Gui Fan Bao Jian Shi Pin Yuan Liao Guan Li De Tong Zhi (Annex 1 of Notice on Further Regulating the Health Food Material Administration). Wei Fa Jian Fa [2002] No. 51
Pharmacopeia of the PRC (2015 Edition) Chinese Pharmacopoeia Commission, Part one
Schulz V et al (2001) Rational phytotherapy a physicians' guide to herbal medicine, 4th edn. Springer-Verlag, Berlin, Heidelberg
SDA of the PRC (2002) Zhong Yao Cai Sheng Chan Zhi Liang Guan Li Gui Fan (Shi Xing) (Good Agricultural Practice of Traditional Chinese Medicinal Product Materials). Order No. 32
Segall A, Goldstein J (1998) Exploring the correlates of self provided health care behaviour. In: Coburn D, D'Arcy A, Torrance GM (eds) Health and Canadian Society: sociological perspectives. University of Toronto Press, pp 279–280. In: Wikipedia. https://en.wikipedia.org/wiki/Self_care#cite_note-hacs-1
SPS (1994) Agreement on the Application of Sanitary and Phytosanitary Measures. In: WTO
State Council of the PRC (2003) Circular on Printing and Issuing the Measures for Administration of the Good Agricultural Practice for Chinese Crude Drugs Inspection (For Trial Implementation) and the Evaluation Standards for GAP for Chinese Crude Drugs Inspection (For Trial Implementation), Guo Shi Yao Jian An [2003] No. 251
TBT (1994) Agreement on Technical Barriers to Trade. In WTO
TCM WIKI (2012) Wuxing. https://tcmwiki.com/wiki/wu-xing
TEC (2002) Treaty Establishing the European Community. Art 28
TFEU (2012) Consolidated Version of the Treaty on the Functioning of the European Union. OJ C 326: 13-390, Art 34
TRIPs (1994) Trade-Related Aspects of Intellectual Property Rights. In WTO
U.S. FDA (2015) Drug Applications for Over-the-Counter (OTC) Drugs. In U.S. Food & Drug Administration. https://www.fda.gov/drugs/developmentapprovalprocess/howdrugsaredevelopedandapproved/approvalapplications/over-the-counterdrugs/default.htm

UN (1992) Convention on Biological Diversity
United Nations Statistics Commission. https://unstats.un.org/unsd/statcom/groups/
United Nations Statistics Division (2015) Central Product Classification (CPC): Version 2.1. ST/ESA/STAT/SER.M/77/Ver.2.1, United Nations, New York
United Nations Statistics Division (2017) Linking CPC to Other Classifications
United Nations Statistics Division. https://unstats.un.org/home/
WCO (1983) HS Convention
WCO (2017) What is the Harmonised System (HS)? http://www.wcoomd.org/en/topics/nomenclature/overview/what-is-the-harmonized-system.aspx
WHO (2004) Guidelines on Safety Monitoring of Herbal Medicines in Pharmacovigilance Systems
WHO (2007) Guidelines for Assessing Quality of Herbal Medicines with Reference to Contaminants and Residues
WHO (2013) WHO Traditional Medicine Strategy: 2014-2023. 7
WHO. http://www.who.int/en/
Wiesener S et al (2012) Legal status and regulation of complementary alternative medicine in Europe. Forsch Komplementmed 19(Suppl 2):29–36
WT/DS135/AB/R. WTO Appellate Body (2001) Canada v. European Communities, EC—Asbestos
WT/DS135/R. WTO Panel (2000) European Communities Measures Affecting Asbestos and Asbestos Containing Product. Report of the Panel, p 106
WT/DS26/AB/R. WTO Appellate Body (1998) United States v. European Communities, EC—Hormones
WT/DS48/AB/R. WTO Appellate Body (1998) Canada v. European Communities, EC—Hormones (Canada)
WT/DS58/AB/R. WTO Appellate Body (1998) India, Malaysia, Pakistan, Thailand v. United States, U.S.—Shrimp
WTO (2006) Pharmaceutical Patents and the TRIPS Agreement
WTO (2015) WIPO and WTO to reflect on lessons of 20 years of TRIPS and Public Health
WTO (2017a) Welcome to the Tariff Download Facility. http://tariffdata.wto.org
WTO (2017b) Guide to Reading the GATS Schedules of Specific Commitments and the List of Article II (MFN) Exemptions
WTO (2017c) WTO Glossary Term: Precautionary Principle. https://www.wto.org/english/thewto_e/glossary_e/precautionary_principle_e.htm
WTO (2020) Tariff Download Facility. http://tariffdata.wto.org/
WTO. http://www.wto.org
WTO (n.d.-b) A summary of the Final Act of the Uruguay Round—Agreement on Technical Barriers to Trade. https://www.wto.org/english/docs_e/legal_e/ursum_e.htm#dAgreement
WTO and WHO (2002) WTO Agreements & Public Health—A Joint Study by the WHO and the WTO Secretariat
Wu X (2015) Protection of Genetic Resources and Traditional Knowledge—Ongoing Work in the WTO. Speech in the Workshop on Law and Policy of Protection of Chinese Traditional Medicines
Yu D (2008) The Harmonized System - Amendments and Their Impact on WTO Members' Schedules. In: WTO, Economic Research and Statistics Division, Staff Working Paper ERSD-2008-02

Chapter 6
Ensuring Safety Efficacy and Quality Control on a Case-by-Case Basis

On one hand, the previous chapter concluded that 'likeness' between traditional Chinese herbal medicinal product and EU THMP is rational, even though the former has its unique process and method of production based on formulation theories of TCM system. So, it is not appropriate to treat TCMP—at least traditional Chinese herbal medicinal product—less favourable in law. On the other hand, the analysis in previous chapters of this book has also shown the scruples with which the EU recognises TCMP. In such case, the precautionary principle may be applied on a case-by-case basis. Thus, this chapter discusses the approach to assess the safety, efficacy and quality control of the applied medicinal product for authorisation in the EU.

6.1 Recalling the Registration Procedure of Pharmaceutical Products in the EU

Hereinafter the registration procedures of medicinal products in the EU are recalled. Since the risk assessment system relates to the types of registration procedures.

There are two registration systems in the EU for the registration of herbal medicinal products. One is the centralised registration system via the EMA (Regulation EC No 726/2004 2004), and the other is the decentralised registration system. However only the decentralised pathway is recommended on the website of EMA for traditional use registration (EMA 2020a).

The EMA is the institution laid down in the Regulation for dealing with the affairs of medicines in the EU. The working tasks of the EMA involve facilitating development and access to medicines, evaluating applications for marketing authorisation, monitoring the safety of medicines across their lifecycle and providing information to healthcare professionals and patients (EMA 2019). It has seven Committees which are in charge of different works of medicine supervision

S. Wang, *Market Access of Traditional Chinese Medicinal Product in the EU under WTO Legal Framework*, Economic and Financial Law & Policy – Shifting Insights & Values 5, https://doi.org/10.1007/978-3-030-52848-5_6

(EMA 2020b). Moreover, the Community issue authorisation for certain medicinal product based on the evaluation and recommendation of EMA, which is called centralised authorisation procedure of medicinal products in the EU.

By contrast, each Member State has its own national competent authority (EMA 2020c). The national authorisation procedure through which medicines pass is the decentralised channel for approval. National competent authorities function widely in the administration of medicine and medicinal products, such as the Medicinal Evaluation Body (MEB) in the Netherlands. Referring to TCMP, they can be registered under the centralised authorisation procedure or national authorisation procedure.

In addition, there are three types of registration channels under EU pharmaceutical law. They are full application, well-established use application and TUR respectively.

The full application is the general authorisation procedure for market access of a medicinal product in the EU. For this application, the applicant must submit results of pharmaceutical tests (including physic-chemical biological or microbiological test), pre-clinical tests (including toxicological and pharmacological test) and clinical trials (Directive 2001/83/EC 2001, art. 8(3)(i)). In addition, some other particulars and documents has to be provided, such as potential environmental risks posed by the medicinal product, manufacturing method needs, and pharmacovigilance system and so on (Directive 2001/83/EC 2001, art. 8).

Well-established use application can apply to well-established use marketing authorisation (WEU MA), the results of pre-clinical test or clinical trials can be replaced by detailed, published references and appropriate scientific literature. Such applications include situations: (1) where the applicant can demonstrate that the medicinal product is a generic of a reference medicinal product which is or has been authorised under the general authorisation rules (Directive 2001/83/EC 2001, art. 6) for not less than eight years in a Member State or in the EU (Directive 2001/83/EC 2001, art. 10); (2) where the active substances of a medicinal product have been in well-established medicinal use within the EU for at least ten years, with recognised efficacy and an acceptable level of safety in terms of the conditions set out in Annex I of Directive 2001/83/EC (Directive 2001/83/EC, art. 10a, 75/318/EEC 1975, Annex).

TUR procedure for herbal medicinal products is also called the simplified procedure. Its establishment shall fulfil criteria including (1) having indications exclusively appropriate to traditional herbal medicinal products which, by virtue of their composition and purpose, being intended and designed for use without the supervision of a medical practitioner for diagnostic purposes or for prescription or monitoring of treatment; (2) exclusively for administration in accordance with a specified strength and posology; (3) in oral form, external and/or inhalation preparation; (4) bibliographical or expert evidence to the effect that the medicinal product in question, or a medicinal use of the product throughout a period of at least 30 years, including at least 15 years in the EU; and (5) sufficient data to demonstrate the traditional use, in particular to prove not to be harmful in the specified conditions of use and the pharmacological effects or efficacy of the medicinal product are plausible in the basis of long-standing use and experience. The application shall be accompanied by particulars and documents provided in Article 8(3)(a) to (h), (j) and (k), the results of the pharmaceutical tests referred to in the pre-clinical tests (including toxicological and pharmacological test), and the summary of the product characteristics except for clinical particulars (Directive 2001/83/EC 2001, art. 16c(a)(i)-(iii)). Therefore, results of pharmaceutical (physico-chemical, biological or microbiological) tests and clinical trials are not compulsory for the application. In case of combinations with vitamins or minerals, the vitamins or minerals shall be ancillary in the herbal medicinal product. In case the individual active ingredients are not sufficiently known, the data shall relate to the individual active ingredients (Directive 2001/83/EC 2001, art. 16c(a)(iv)).

For instance, Diao Xin Xue Kang was the first TCMP approved in EU market. It went through the national authorisation procedure and chose the simplified procedure when the applicant applied for approval. Registration was granted by the Medicines Evaluation Board to SU BioMedicine B.V. from the Netherlands (MEB 2012).

6.2 Risk Assessment and Management of EU Pharmaceutical Products

As aforementioned, there are three types of registration channels for a medicinal product entering the EU market under EU law. They are full application, WEU MA and TUR respectively. Among them, full application is provided in Article 8 of Directive 2001/83/EC. The HMCP published the Guideline on Risk Management Systems (EMEA/CHMP/96268/2005 2005) to guide marketing authorisation Holders (MAHs) and applicants (MAAs) in providing the competent authorities with a description of pharmacovigilance[1] and a risk management system based on EU regulations (Regulation EC No 726/2004 2004, art. 6; Directive 2001/83/EC 2001, art. 8). The risk management system is defined in the Guideline as 'a set of pharmacovigilance activities and interventions designed to identify, characterise, prevent or minimise risks relating to medicinal products, and the assessment of the effectiveness of those interventions'. EU-RMP requires the MAAs to provide information including a safety specification, a pharmacovigilance plan, an evaluation of the need for risk minimisation activities and a risk minimisation plan on demand (EMEA/CHMP/96268/2005 2005).

[1]As explained by the European Commission '[a]ll medicinal products in the EU are subject to a strict testing and assessment of their quality, efficacy and safety before being authorised. Once placed on the market they continue to be monitored so to assure that any aspect which could impact the safety profile of a medicine is detected and assessed and that necessary measures are taken. This monitoring is called pharmacovigilance'.

The Guideline requests a risk management plan (RMP) from the full application product, but the RMP also influences the understanding of risk assessment on THMP. The safe and effective use of medicinal products are two essential elements in an RMP for market access of a medicinal product (Regulation EC No. 726/2004 2004, art. 9). In addition, quality control concerning post-authorisation safety studies, such as good agricultural practice and good manufactural practice control, need to be ensured in pre stage of authorisation (Regulation EC No. 726/2004 2004, art. 23). Therefore, basically, safety, efficacy and quality control comprise three essential elements of the management of the production of pharmaceutical products. In addition, the classification of the medicinal products as well as the conditions or restrictions that should be imposed on the supply or use of medicinal products should be clearly stated (Regulation EC No. 726/2004 2004, art 9; Directive 2001/83/EC 2001, Title VI).

Pharmaceutical tests including physic-chemical biological or microbiological tests, pre-clinical tests including toxicological and pharmacological tests and clinical trials are all needed in full application procedure. The data collected in these tests and clinical trials provide the basis of the risk assessment. An application, which involves a new herbal substance or herbal preparation, but does not satisfy the application conditions in Article 16a, must go through the full application procedure.

The European Commission publishes the Tool of Risk Assessment and Management in a section of its online resource Better Regulation: Guidelines and Toolbox. Therein, hazard is defined as 'any source of potential damage, harm or adverse effects on something' or someone. While risk 'is the chance or probability that a person or thing will be harmed or experience an adverse effect if exposed to a hazard', risk can be identified on the basis of a wide range of evidence, such as past experience, monitoring data, expert opinions, etc. The EU recommends three steps to identify the risk in its tool for risk assessment and management: (1) '[i]dentify and characterise the hazard', (2) '[a]ssess the likelihood of its occurrence', and (3) '[c] haracterise risk' (European Commission 2020).[2] The EU noted that uncertainty is inherent in every stage of risk assessment, and, thus, needs to be carefully evaluated and transparently reported. The significance of risk is determined by risk/tolerability

[2]To provide further detail: '(1) Identify and characterise the hazard, i.e. identify and characterise the inherent properties of the agent/phenomenon in terms of potential negative effects (on population, environment etc.), establish the causal relationship between the hazard and its effect, describe the negative effect and determine its severity (e.g. occurrence of mutations, changes in the cell structure, etc.). Special attention should be paid to induced or secondary hazards (e.g. contaminated river flood). (2) Assess the likelihood of its occurrence, i.e. estimate the likelihood of the hazard (for the population, environment etc.) to occur. (3) Characterise risk, i.e. on the basis of results from previous steps, determine quantitatively (e.g. death, injury, production loss) and if not possible, qualitatively, the level of risk under given assumptions and uncertainties. Although the level of risk can be difficult to express in monetary terms (e.g. in the case of non-market impacts on environment and health), methods exist that can be used to monetise them'.

criteria ranging from scientifically identified tolerable thresholds and controllability to risk-benefit tradeoffs,[3] risk perceptions,[4] or societal values.[5]

A recognisable risk must not be a 'purely hypothetical' risk, nor may it be founded on 'mere suppositions not yet scientifically verified' (ECJ 2003, C-236/01, paras. 36–38). It must be 'adequately backed up by the scientific data available at the time' (ECJ 2002a, b, c, T-13/99). The risk can be potential, it is not necessary to wait 'until the reality and seriousness of those risks become fully apparent' to take an action to avert the risk to public health, as ruled in the judgment of the court of first instance of the European Communities in the Joined Cases T-74/00, T-76/00, T-83/00 to T-85/00, T-132/00, T-137/00 and T-141/00 (ECJ 2002a, b, c, T-74/00 para. 185). All these cases involved medicinal products containing 'amphetamine like' substances and ruled for a withdrawal of marketing authorisations because of the evidential risk to public health (ECJ 2002a, b, c, T-74/00, paras. 15–17).[6] For an appropriate application of the precautionary principle, these cases have shown that firstly, the EU institution must choose the level of protection it considers acceptable in light of scientific evidence as well as social, political or other factors (ECJ 2002a, b, c, T-13/99, paras. 151–153). Secondly, the court has to find out as much as possible about the hazard, the exposure to that hazard, and the kind of risk it poses to human health (ECJ 2002a, b, c, T-13/99, paras. 154–156). The precautionary principle requires the competent authorities to give public health, safety and the environment protection precedence over economic interest and to take appropriate measures in that regard (ECJ 2002a, b, c, T-13/99, paras. 173–184).[7]

Risk criteria can be defined within the existing legal basis or by an existing risk management approach and past experience. Risk management measures include bans or limitations. The risks can be transferred to a third party, for instance by insurance, or mitigated by:

- Reducing the hazard (e.g. through performance standards for products and processes, emissions, etc.);
- Limiting the likelihood (e.g. through preventive, protective and control-related measures, information and education etc.); or
- A combination of both (in cases where both hazard and likelihood can be influenced and multi-hazard situations more generally) (EC 2020).

[3]E.g., *inter alia*, availability of substitutes.

[4]E.g., in case of emerging risks.

[5]E.g., equity or personal freedom considerations.

[6]The applicants in Cases T-74/00, T-76/00 and T-141/00 are holders of marketing authorisations of medicinal products containing amfepramone. The applicants in Cases T-83/00, T-84/00 and T-85/00 hold marketing authorisations for medicinal products containing norpseudoephedrine, clobenzorex and fenproporex respectively. The applicants in Cases T-132/00 and T-137/00 hold marketing authorisations for medicinal products containing phentermine.

[7]See, in particular, order in Case C-180/96 (1996) and C-183/95 (1997) cited in Joined case T-74/00, paras. 173, 184.

6.2.1 Risk Management Impact Factors for Market Access

Risk management in the phase evaluating market access for a pharmaceutical product focuses on the safety and efficacy assessment and quality control of the pharmaceutical product. Safety, efficacy and quality control are three impact factors of risk management for TCMP entering the EU market.

The effectiveness of risk management is widely decided by the employed approaches. For instance, the U.S. FDA approach is designed to 'optimise the benefit-risk balance for regulated medicines throughout the product life cycle' (Lis et al. 2012). It is based on three guiding documents including Pre-marketing Risk Assessment, Good Pharmacovigilance Practices & Pharmacoepidemiologic Assessment, and the Development and Use of Risk Minimisation Action Plans. These three documents form the basis of Risk Evaluation and Mitigation Strategies (REMS) in the U.S.. While, the EU never put any continuing effort into improving the 'spontaneous' reporting scheme, in 2005, legislation (EMEA/CHMP/96268/2005 2005) formalised the introduction of risk management plans. Subsequently the Heads of Medicines Agencies (HMA) reviewed guidelines on risk management systems (2011, 2013), and the European Commission issued a Decision laying down Guidelines for management of the EU rapid alert system (RAPEX) (European Commission 2010). The EMA issued Guidelines on the Formalised Risk Assessment for Ascertaining the Appropriate Good Manufacturing Practice for Excipients of Medicinal Products for Human Use in 2015. As noted in the Report of the International Society for Pharmacoeconomic and Outcomes Research Risk Management Working Group (Lis et al. 2012), both the EU and the U.S. have changed the emphasis of risk management from the reactive collection of safety data—in other words public scrutiny—to a more proactive risk management approach. They concern the identification, monitoring and minimisation of risk to patient safety through the generation of data. The implementation of REMS and RMP both adopted special approaches for pharmacovigilance.

6.2.2 Assessment of the Safety Efficacy and Quality Control of TCMP

The risk management of pharmaceutical products in the EU goes through all the proceedings—from authorisation, manufacture, distribution, marketing and other post-authorisation phases. Many strategies and tools are designed and used for risk control and assessment. Even though the key issue of the study in this book focuses on the pre-authorisation phase, it is notable that the forewarning measures of post-authorisation risk are also required to be submitted by applicants in the first phase. For the registration of a pharmaceutical product, applicants need to prepare the dossier, product name, product information and prescription status; they need to collect efficient data for proving that quality has reached the standard required by law, including GCP inspections and GLP compliance, and they should provide an environmental risk assessment and their pharmacovigilance system (EMA 2020d).[8] Generally they are also required to submit RMP relating to safety concerns or pharmacovigilance activities, but this is not compulsory with an application for traditional-use registration.

6.2.2.1 Safety and Efficacy

Three main regulatory pathways for authorising a herbal medicinal product in the EU are illustrated in a Q&A for Pre-authorisation Guidance as shown in Table 6.1.[9] The first column shows the name and legal basis of the pathways; the second column shows the data collection requirement on safety and efficacy for each pathway; and the third column shows the information of where to apply. TCMP can go through any of these pathways for market access, however it is most possible to trigger the first pathway based on the current development of scientific research of TCMP as well as the nature of tradition.

Ph. Eur. is one of the most important databases for assessing the safety and efficacy of the product in application for market access. The HMPC established Community herbal monographs (i.e. Ph. Eur.) for herbal medicinal products with regard to well-established use and traditional use. The monographs include herbal substances and/or herbal preparations, which the HMPC considers to be legal and scientific requirements that a well-established use must fulfil. Whenever possible, scientific opinions of the HMPC are taken by consensus. If only an absolute majority of the members of the Committee can be reached on a particular case, the divergent opinion of the Committee should be published. Monographs are drafted in the style of a Summary of Product Characteristics (European Commission 2009, Version 2). They reflect 'the scientific opinion of the HMPC concerning efficacy (well-established use), plausibility of efficacy (traditional use) and safety', as noted in the Q&A on the EU Framework for Herbal Medicinal Products (HMPC 2013).

[8]EMA Q&A for Pre-authorisation Guidance 3.4.2 states that '[t]he environmental risk assessment (ERA) concerns the risks to the environment arising from the use, storage, and disposal of the medicinal product. Risks arising from the synthesis or manufacture of the product are under the remits of the national competent authorities'; 3.4.3 states that summary of the pharmacovigilance system should include the following elements: 'proof that the applicant has at its disposal a qualified person responsible for pharmacovigilance; the Member States in which the qualified person resides and carries out his or her tasks; the contact details of the qualified person; a statement signed by the applicant to the effect that the applicant has the necessary means to fulfil the tasks and responsibilities listed in title IX of Directive 2001/83/EC; a reference to the location where the pharmacovigilance-system master file (PSMF) for the medicinal product is kept'. PSMF is not a part of authorisation, but the EU has specific rules and a data collection system to keep the information.

[9]Information in the figure is from EMA (2020a)—Bringing Herbal Medicinal Products to Market within the EU.

Table 6.1 Three main regulatory pathways for bringing a herbal medicinal product to market in EU Member States

Regulatory pathway	Main requirement on safety and efficacy	Where to apply
Traditional use registration (Article 16a (1) of Directive 2001/83/EC)	No clinical tests and trials on safety and efficacy are required as long as sufficient safety data and plausible efficacy are demonstrated Involves assessment of mostly bibliographic safety and efficacy data Must have been used for at least 30 years, including at least 15 years within the EU Are intended to be used without the supervision of a medical practitioner and are not administered by injection	National competent authority of a Member State for national, mutual recognition and decentralised procedures
Well-established use marketing authorisation (Article 10a of Directive 2001/83/EC)	Scientific literature establishing that the active substances of the medicinal products have been in well-established medicinal use within the EU for at least ten years, with recognised efficacy and an acceptable level of safety Involves assessment of mostly bibliographic safety and efficacy data	National competent authority of a Member State for national, mutual recognition and decentralised procedures EMA if centralised procedure applies
Stand-alone or mixed application (Article 8(3) of Directive 2001/83/EC)	Safety and efficacy data from the company's own development or a combination of own studies and bibliographic data	National competent authority of a Member State for national, mutual recognition and decentralised procedures EMA if centralised procedure applies

With the approval of the European Commission, the HMPC sets up 'list entries' of herbal medicinal products based on the Ph. Eur. for traditional use (See, EMA 2020e).[10] The data in the list entries is publicly available and sufficient to document safe use of the included herbal substances/herbal preparations (European Commission 2017a, b). If any herbal substances/herbal preparations are contained in the list entries and the applicant can demonstrate that the proposed product and related claims in the application comply with the information, the applicant does not

[10] As explained on the website of the EMA, "[t]o complement traditional-use monographs on herbal substances, the HMPC gradually develops the European Union list (formerly known as Community list) through 'list entries'. Unlike EU herbal monographs, EU list entries are legally binding on applicants and national competent authorities in the Member States. Draft list entries are developed by the HMPC, but the final list entries are adopted and published by the European Commission."

necessarily have to submit evidence on the safe and traditional use of the medicinal product (Directive 2001/83/EC 2001, art. 16e(1)(c)(d)). However, data demonstrating the quality of the THMP still must be provided in the dossier (See, EMA 2020f).

Nevertheless, adequate and sufficient documentation for traditional use and safety is required in the dossier. If neither a list entry nor a monograph exists, there is still a possibility for registration, and in such cases the decision is made by the authorisation entity (Co-ordination Group for Mutual Recognition and Decentralised Procedures - Human 2013).

For an application of market access of TCMP, firstly, applicants must prove the safety of the medicinal product through a bibliographic review of safety data together with an expert report. Moreover, any Member State's competent authority may request any data when they consider it necessary. Regarding the safety of the substance/preparation or herbal medicinal product, the EMA has drafted a guideline on the standards of the specifications for tests. The guideline is in progress of revision 3. In the guideline, a specification is defined as 'a list of tests, references to analytical and biological procedures, and appropriate acceptance criteria, which are numerical limits, ranges, or other criteria for the tests described'. It contains 'the set of criteria that a herbal substance/preparation or herbal medicinal product should conform to be considered acceptable for its intended use' (CHMP 2018). Specifications are legally binding quality standards that are proposed and justified by the manufacturer and approved by regulatory authorities (CHMP 2018). In addition, results of pharmaceutical tests must be submitted to demonstrate the quality of THMP, including physico-chemical, biological or microbiological tests. THMP in the EU should be designed for use of diagnostic purposes without the supervision of a medical practitioner. So, its indications must be 'exclusively appropriate' (See Public Health 2017, Volume 2A - Procedures for Marketing Authorisation, Chap. 1, p. 22).

Secondly, the Ph. Eur. monographs on herbal substances and herbal preparations are only demonstrated to be suitable for the use indicated. When the standards are available in monographs, it is the perfect situation for the registration of a new product, and these should be used as the primary standards. However, where pharmacopoeial reference standards are not available, non-pharmacopoeial reference standards should be provided. The HMPC publishes a concept paper on non-pharmacopoeial reference standards for herbal substances, herbal preparations and herbal medicinal products/traditional herbal medicinal products. The purpose of the proposed guideline is to identify the criteria for evaluation when using non-pharmacopoeial reference standards and to provide guidance on the documentation for adequately characterising and fitting the product for its intended purpose (See EMA/HMPC/312890/2012 2012).[11]

[11]The concept paper states '[a] non-pharmacopoeial reference standard may be a botanical sample of the herbal substance, a sample of the herbal preparation (e.g. extract or tincture) or a chemically defined substance e.g. a constituent with known therapeutic activity, an active marker or an analytical marker etc. Chemically defined substances are either commercially available or they have to be isolated and purified.'

Thirdly, an adequate safety profile of THMP may be confirmed by its documented history of medicinal use and pre-clinical tests, for instance genotoxicity studies. The EMA published a guideline to describe a general framework and practical approaches on how to assess or to test the potential genotoxicity of herbal substances/preparations and how to interpret the results. The usual procedure for toxicity testing and risk assessment of a mixture is processing in an isolated space and identifying principal constituents individually. This is a recommended option for clearly genotoxic products because this approach provides relevant and reliable information for risk assessment. If the herbal medicinal product contains only one herb, and even in the more perfect situation where there is only one active ingredient in the product, it will be much easier to apply the approach. However, more often a TCMP will be a compound product. The EMA also recognises similar cases in many of its traditional-use herbal medicinal products. The guideline on genotoxicity noted that herbal preparations are complex mixtures with partially unidentified components, and it is quite possible that the compound(s) responsible for genotoxicity may still not be identified at the end of the testing protocol. When this occurs, the EMA introduces an exposure considerations approach as an exception to acceptance in the case of a lack of identified components as put forth in the guideline on genotoxicity. Exposure considerations apply to '[a] risk from administration of a herbal medicinal product might be accepted if its contribution to the overall exposure through food is considered to be small' (HMPC 2008; EMEA/HMPC/107079/2007).[12]

Fourthly, the combinations of herbal substances/herbal preparations bring challenges to the traditional approach(es) of the risk assessment employed on the chemical pharmaceutical product. The HMPC (2006) published a guideline for the clinical assessment of fixed combinations of herbal substances/herbal preparations (HMPC 2006; EMEA/HMPC/166326/05). This guideline aimed to guide applicants on how to structure the clinical documentation of herbal fixed-combination products. It provides advice to assessors for an assessment of the clinical safety and efficacy. The scope of this guideline covers both well-established herbal medicinal products and THMP. For both well-established herbal medicinal products and THMP, the function of each constituent must be clarified, including information on the indication of the combination, the profile of the active substance and its dosage/concentration. The guideline provides evaluation factors for the safety and efficacy of well-established herbal medicinal products. It stresses that '[t]he efficacy and the

[12]According to the HMPC, '[b]ecause many herbal substances and preparations are derived from plants which are also used as food, it is apparent that exposure to various herbal constituents can also occur via diet. It is clear that amounts and ratios of these constituents vary enormously, depending on individual and population dietary preferences. For a proper risk assessment, dietary exposures should be assessed and quantified, as far as possible, and comparative assessment of exposures via diet and herbal substances and preparations consumption should be performed. In many cases it may be advisable to contact dietary health risk assessing bodies for information and/or discussion of risk assessment considerations.' In addition, food product exposure assessment is also noted by European Food Safety Authority (2017), FAO and WHO (2008). It can be conducted in toxicity experiment on food product when necessary.

clinical safety of the fixed combination must be evident from clinical trials or from bibliographic data submitted by the applicant' (HMPC 2006; EMEA/HMPC/166326/05). TUR applies a similar principle, but 'the requirements relating to efficacy will be reduced to the level of plausibility' (HMPC 2006; EMEA/HMPC/166326/05). Therefore, the HMPC requires that the considerations relevant to safety should become more critical in an overall benefit/risk-assessment due to the lack of scientific test on efficacy. Factors to evaluate the clinical efficacy and safety of well-established herbal medicinal products include potential advantages of fixed combinations, potential disadvantages of fixed combinations and justification. The efficacy of the combinations shall be compared with the level of efficacy of each active substance used alone, at the same time taking into consideration of counteracting by one substance of an adverse reaction produced by another one. The guideline should be read in conjunction with the guidance on the assessment of preclinical safety/efficacy together for preparing a completed documentation of assessment on safety and efficacy.

When a TCMP cannot meet the criteria to be considered as well-established or tradition, the data needed are similar to those required for a new product in full application procedure. The difficulties for TCMP to acquire the necessary scientific evidence on safety and efficacy may stem from refining active ingredient(s) and testing the appropriate stability of these active constituents, clarifying toxicity with an interactional mechanism between these active constituents, bearing the high cost of clinical trial in the EU, all in addition to demonstrating the 15 years use requirement in the EU. Moreover, when publication of the formula is required, a patent becomes the only way to effectively protect the intellectual property. However, in the long historical development of TCMP, many formulas are protected as secret, and this has not been adapted to the modern large-scale pharmaceutical industry.

6.2.2.2 Quality Control

Quality control relates to the manufacture, including packaging, batch testing and batch certification, of medicinal products. Quality must be stable and comply with safety and efficacy requirements. The EMA and the EC published guidelines on GMP for the applicant to follow. All sites involved in the production of the finished medicinal product and of the active substance must be described for marketing authorisation, together with a description of each step performed (EMA 2020d; European Commission 2014).[13] Quality control is not the obstacle for market access of TCMP in the EU. Nevertheless, many were concerned about it in practice. A

[13]The sites in the use of following functions should be included: 'active-substance manufacture and packaging; any contract laboratories used for testing the active substance (including ongoing stability monitoring); bulk medicinal-product manufacture; diluent/solvent manufacture (if any); manufacture of any other associated medicinal products (if any); finished-product manufacture and packaging; batch release; any contract manufacturing sites; any contract laboratories used for

Hong Kong study found that 'of 52 clinical case reports of aconite poisoning, the majority were actually related to poor-quality herbs, poor prescribing practices, or dispensing errors' (Elizabeth et al. 2014, p. S47). It explained that '[i]n Europe, adverse events have mainly resulted from contaminated products and a practitioner's incompetence, rather than herbal medicines being inherently risky' (Elizabeth et al. 2014, p. S48). The manufacturing industry must comply with GMP, and the importing country can control quality through spot checks by qualified institutions as even the GMP of exporting countries will be different from those of importing country's. In the past most Chinese institutions put in place to control pharmaceutical products had adopted ISO 17025: 2005, and now China also pursues the international standard—WHO Good Practices for Pharmaceutical Quality Control Laboratories(GPCL) (WHO Essential Medicines and Health Products Information Portal 2010), Problems with quality control should be given attention when assessing risk, however, it may also be controlled with harmonised international standards.

6.3 The Precautionary Principle in EU Legislation

When scientific certainty is not assured, the precautionary principle helps in decision making on market access. The Commission of the European Communities (2000) noted that the precautionary principle is necessary for 'balancing the freedom and rights of individuals, industry and organisations with the need to reduce the risk of adverse effects to the environment, human, animal or plant health,' so that 'the proportionate, non-discriminatory, transparent and coherent actions can be taken'.

6.3.1 Purpose of the Precautionary Principle

The Communication from the Commission on the Precautionary Principle in 2000 (Commission of the European Communities 2000) comprehensively analysed the precautionary principle as having the following fourfold aims:

- outline the Commission's approach in using the precautionary principle,
- establish Commission guidelines for applying it,
- build a common understanding of how to assess, appraise, manage and communicate risks that science is not yet able to evaluate fully, and
- avoid unwarranted recourse to the precautionary principle as a disguised form of protectionism.

testing the finished product; official medicines control laboratory (OMCL) for blood products and vaccines if official batch release is a requirement for the product in question'.

Some important illustrations and rules relevant to application of the precautionary principle are set out in the Summary of the Communication for reaching the above aims. The Communication affirms that even though the precautionary principle had only been prescribed once to protect the environment, it is practically used concerning the 'potentially dangerous effect also on human health'. It notes that the principle authorises the right of the WTO member to establish the level of protection. It also states that the principle should be used to analyse risk by 'a structured approach', including risk assessment, risk management, and risk communication, in case the 'scientific evaluation does not allow the risk to be determined with sufficient certainty'. The Communication stresses that the principle helps the decision-makers manage risk and is different than 'the element of caution that scientists apply in their assessments of scientific data'. In addition, when applying the principle, decision-makers should know the degree of uncertainty, as well as pay attention to concerns of the public and all other interested parties. The result of applying the principle may be a binding legal measure.

6.3.2 Taking Measures or Not Taking Measures

The Communication (Commission of the European Communities 2000) listed criteria for decision making on whether to take or not take any legal measures. Along with the analysis on safety, efficacy and quality control of TCMP in the EU, these criteria can be applied as shown below.

The first criterion is proportionality to the chosen level of protection. This means the measure(s) taken in risk management should adapt to the chosen level of protection based on even incomplete risk assessments due to lack of knowledge. Proportionality should be ascertained on a case-by-case basis by taking into consideration the evidence of safety and efficacy. EU pharmaceutical law set up the TUR procedure for authorisation in Directive 2004/24/EC. Even before the Directive, on which the TUR is based, went into effect, the UK had already produced the Sixth Report for assessing the development of the science and technology of CAM in November 2000 (UK House of Lords Select Committee 2000). However, in the case of TM, scientific uncertainty is obvious in many cases. The TUR procedure was designed based on an understanding of theoretical system of Western conventional medicine, even though it concerned the status of TM. When treating parts of TCMP and EU THMP as similar types of chemical herbal medicinal products, TUR procedure will apply to both. However, if looking at a concern regarding the difference between EU THMP and TCMP, the proportionality needs to be rethought. Even though the EU should be allowed to make the decision on whether it would provide space for TCMP to develop within its territory, it is more proper to collect data of the safe use of TCMP based on ethnicity no matter where TCMP is used. And the developmental history of TCMP and similar theories in China and other Asian areas should also be taken into consideration when assessing risk.

The second criterion is non-discriminatory in its application and requires finding the proper object of reference. In detail, 'comparable situations should not be treated differently', while 'different situations should not be treated in the same way, unless there are objective grounds for doing so' (UK House of Lords Select Committee 2000). Non-discrimination is also a principle of WTO law. It embodies NT and MFN, where the certainty on similarity between the potential importing of goods and the object of reference is the prerequisite to further discussion of the treatment. Herein the study in this book, the similarities between TCMP and EU THMP can be confirmed, but TCMP also has its unique characteristics. As aforementioned, considering the nature of tradition and chemical products, they can be classified into a similar group. However, regarding end users and the philosophy of formulation, they are different. More essentially, they are based on different medicines. In the current stage, however, it is difficult for the EU to distinguish them because of the lack of data and information on TCM and TCMP. However, the difference should not be ignored, and the information system can be better designed in light of the practice.

The third criterion is consistency with similar measures already taken. It requires that in case there are measures which have already been applied to 'equivalent areas in which all scientific data are available', the comparable scope and nature to those already taken should be concerned when making a decision on the application, and existing rules for assessing safety, efficacy and quality control, as aforementioned, need to be taken into account. In the EU, risk assessment methods or criteria differ according to the type of registration first, including stand-alone or mixed application, well-established use marketing authorisation and traditional use registration as illustrated by Table 6.1. The technical regulations and standards set out the detailed evidence that need to be submitted for the risk assessment. When EU law does not treat TCMP as an object with unique characteristics differing from the Western pharmaceutical product, the risk assessment method of Western pharmaceutical product applies. Considering the similarities between Chinese herbal medicinal products and EU THMP, TUR applies to both. However, the differences between them should also be paid attention to and appropriateness of the current TUR procedure to TCMP should be re-evaluated. The detailed risk assessment method significantly influences the result of market access of individual TCMP.

The fourth criterion is that the measures should be based on an examination of the potential costs and benefits of action or lack of action and, such as where appropriate and feasible, an economic cost/benefit analysis. Per this criterion, examining 'costs and benefits entails comparing the overall cost to the Community of action and lack of action'. It also considers the non-economic interest, such as 'the efficacy of possible options and their acceptability to the public'. In the conduct of such an examination, protection of health is given consideration prior to the economic concern. TCM and its products do not take a considerable percentage in the EU health care market at this moment, except that some are putting effort into wider recognition of TCM acupuncture. However, the accessibility of TCMP does relate to the patient's right of autonomy and complies with the trend of patient-oriented medicine.

The fifth criterion subjects the product to review. It requires that new data be periodically reviewed in the light of scientific progress and amended as necessary. GP, TCM practitioners, research institutions, enterprises and NGOs relating to TCM play active roles in pursuing R&D of the product. Strengthening cooperation with such Chinese players is an efficient way to catch up development to the science of TCM.

The sixth criterion is to reverse the burden of proving injury. The competent authority may treat the products as dangerous unless and until scientific evidence demonstrates that they are safe. This criterion imposes a prior approval requirement on products that they deem dangerous and reverses the burden of proving injury so that it lies on the producer, manufacturer or importer in individual cases. In legal practice, the European Court of Human Rights held in a 2009 case: 'even though the applicants had been unable to establish a causal link between exposure to cyanide and asthma, Romania was under an obligation to take adequate precautions to protect the public from potential harm' (European Court of Human Rights 2009).

To sum up, even though the precautionary principle is used on a case-by-case basis in practice, the book adapts it to discuss market access of TCMP as a whole. The precautionary principle can be adopted, when the scientificity in individual case of market access of TCMP is doubted. Thus, pharmaceutical law may provide more equal conditions to both EU THMP and traditional Chinese medicinal product for market access. The basis for applying the principle lies within the framework of WTO law, which makes its adoption reasonable for market access of TCMP in the EU. In addition, certain criteria have been put forth by the EU when considering precaution as an approach for decision making. The case of market access of TCMP in the EU fits employing this approach in situations analysed herein.

6.4 Improving EU Pharmaceutical Law Regarding Market Access of TCMP

Above all, the focus of risk management for market access of TCMP lies heavily in the phase of pre-marketing risk assessment. However, risk assessment and management cover the full cycle of the R&D and manufacturing proceedings of the registered pharmaceutical product. RMP is provided by the EU to manage the risk of pharmaceutical products which apply through the full application procedure. However, TUR of herbal medicinal products follows specific rules. Based on the simplified registration procedure provided by EU pharmaceutical law, namely TUR, risk assessment in phase of clinical trial can be avoided. Article 16c 1(a) of Directive 2001/83/EC, read along with Article 8(3), gives a complete list of the documents that the applicant needs to submit for the marketing authorisation of traditional use herbal medicinal products. Whereas, Article 8(3) provides the documents that the applicant needs to submit for marketing authorisation without regard to different categories of the pharmaceutical product, Article 16c 1(a) lists necessary documents if the application pertains to traditional use herbal medicinal products.

The risk assessment is processed from the results of pharmaceutical testing (physico-chemical, biological or microbiological), pre-clinical tests (toxicological and pharmacological), and clinical trials results. In addition, a risk management plan covering the manufacturing phase, the raw material collection phase as well as addressing environmental protection concerns, etc. needs to be provided to assure good pharmacovigilance practices (GVP) (EMA 2020g). Referring to the specific case of TCMP for the simplified registration procedure, pharmaceutical testing and pre-clinical results are requested. However, the evidence for a long-term safe use history needs to be proven, specifically, 30 years of medicinal use history including 15 years within the Community. In addition, it also can make the application easier if the substance(s) used by the TCMP has/have already been recorded by the Ph. Eur. The potential advantages in the therapeutic situation against the possible disadvantages should be assessed and illustrated, and the adjustment based on TCM principles should be explained, in order to determine whether the product meets the requirements with respect to efficacy or plausible traditional use and with respect to safety in any fixed combination. The tolerability of risk needs to be evaluated even when it is not possible to carry out comprehensive risk assessment due to lack of knowledge, in such cases, proportionate risk management measures can be taken based on the precautionary principle. The criterions of the precautionary principle are clear in the EU, which provides criteria for assessing risks on a case-by-case basis.

Even though, the EU and its Member States have certain rules which apply to TCMP, the law can be improved along with the development of the knowledge of TCMP in practice. Development of this knowledge can be achieved by data collection and international cooperation for construction of a more efficient information system on TCMP, as well as by R&D based on such information system. Currently, there is a good amount of cooperation between the EU and China at the nongovernmental level, such as in academic research and enterprise cooperation. However, further cooperation can be pushed, for instance to collect the data on the use of TCMP in the EU through GP or TCM practitioners and to collect data on the use of TCMP by EU citizens and residents under the supervision of Chinese doctors in China. Therefore, relevant EU institution(s) should set up a system to monitor and pursue the development of TM outside of Europe, so to participate actively in the process of harmonising international regulations on TM.

As for the issue of the market access of TCMP, besides the safety issue, international rules on trade also have an important impact on national and regional regulations. Among them, WTO law provides an important legal basis for market access of international sales of goods, while the WHO provides a platform for discussing standards for the product. Especially, more efforts can be made in establishing a mutually understandable and recognisable list of the Ph. Eur. on specific Chinese herbal medicinal products between the EU and China through using international organisational platforms, such as WHO and WTO. At the academic level, such cooperation has started but focuses more on scientific research. Therefore, policy makers and legislators are called on to expand this cooperation.

EU THMP and traditional Chinese herbal medicinal product have common characteristics, while the latter has its unique characteristics based on TCM. The different philosophies lying between the two must be recognised through a scientific attitude. Setting up a more rational data collection system is necessary. Thereinto, end users of TCMP and ethnicity factors should be given attention. To sum up, the study in this book recommends:

- to identify the suitable target consumers of TCMP in case plausible reference is sufficient;
- to recognise the free-selection choice of the patient;
- to pursue the development of scientific tools for assessing the risk of herbal medicinal products;
- to cooperate with China for collecting data on the use of TCMP;
- to recognise the forms of TCMP in practice, so to set up a comprehensive data collection platform;
- to develop legislation on TCM GP and/or practitioners;
- to develop the educational system of TCM; and
- to strengthen trade relations between the EU and China, which can have a positive influence on cooperation in scientific research as well as the opportunity for trade of TM.

References

CHMP (2018) Guideline on Specifications: Test Procedures and Acceptance Criteria for Herbal Substances, Herbal Preparations and Herbal Medicinal Products3/Traditional Herbal Medicinal Products. EMA/HMPC/162241/2005 Rev. 3

Commission of the European Communities (2000) Communication from the Commission on the Precautionary Principle. COM (2000) 1 final

Co-ordination Group for Mutual Recognition and Decentralised Procedures - Human (2013) Q&A Traditional Herbal Medicinal Products. CMDH/287/2013/Rev.1

Directive 2001/83/EC (2001) Directive 2001/83/EC of the European Parliament and of the Council of 6 November 2001 on the Community Code Relating to Medicinal Products for Human Use. (2001) OJ L 311: 67–128

Directive 2004/24/EC of the European Parliament and of the Council of 31 March 2004 Amending, as regards Traditional Herbal Medicinal Products Directive 2001/83/EC on the Community Code relating to Medicinal Products for Human Use (2004) OJ L136:85–90

Directive 75/318/EEC (1975) Council Directive on 20 May 1975 on the approximation of the laws of Member States relating to analytical, pharmacotoxicological and clinical standards and protocols in respect of the testing of proprietary medicinal products. OJ No L 147/1

ECJ (2002a) Pfizer Animal Health SA v Council of the European Union. T-13/99

ECJ (2002b) Artegodan v. Commison. T-74/00, para 185

ECJ (2002c) Pfizer Animal Health SA v Council of the European Union. T-13/99, paras 151–153

ECJ (2003) Monsanto Agricoltura Italia SpA and Others v. Presidenza del Consiglio dei Ministri and Others. C-236/01

ECJ, C-180/96 (1996) United Kingdom v Commission. ECR I-3903, para 93

ECJ, C-183/95 (1997) Affish. ECR I-4315, para 43
Elizabeth et al (2014) Evaluating the safety of herbal medicines: integrated toxicological approaches. In: Fan T-P et al (eds) The art and science of traditional medicine, the Science/AAAS Custom Publishing Office, Part 3, p S47
EMA (2015) Guidelines on the Formalised Risk Assessment for Ascertaining the Appropriate Good Manufacturing Practice for Excipients of Medicinal Products for Human Use. OJ L C 95: 10–13
EMA (2019) About Us. EMA/338312/2016 Rev.3
EMA (2020a) Bringing Herbal Medicinal Products to Market within the EU. http://www.ema.europa.eu/ema/index.jsp?curl=pages/regulation/general/general_content_000208.jsp&mid=WC0b01ac05800240cf
EMA (2020b) HMPC: Working Parties and Other Groups. http://www.ema.europa.eu/ema/index.jsp?curl=pages/about_us/general/general_content_000243.jsp&mid=WC0b01ac058002d26c
EMA (2020c) National Competent Authorities. http://www.ema.europa.eu/ema/index.jsp?curl=pages/medicines/general/general_content_000155.jsp
EMA (2020d) Pre-authorisation Guidance. http://www.ema.europa.eu/ema/index.jsp?curl=pages/regulation/q_and_a/q_and_a_detail_000167.jsp&mid=WC0b01ac0580b18196#section7
EMA (2020e) European Union Monographs and List Entries. http://www.ema.europa.eu/ema/index.jsp?curl=pages/regulation/general/general_content_001132.jsp&mid=WC0b01ac0580033809
EMA (2020f) Herbal Medicinal Products: Scientific Guidelines—Quality Guidelines. http://www.ema.europa.eu/ema/index.jsp?curl=pages/regulation/general/general_content_000497.jsp&mid=WC0b01ac0580033a9b
EMA (2020g) Good Pharmacovigilance Practices. http://www.ema.europa.eu/ema/index.jsp?curl=pages/regulation/document_listing/document_listing_000345.jsp
EMA/HMPC/312890/2012 (2012) Concept Paper on Non-pharmacopoeial Reference Standards for Herbal Substances, Herbal Preparations and Herbal Medicinal Products/Traditional Herbal Medicinal Products
EMEA/CHMP/96268/2005 (2005) Guideline on Risk Management Systems for Medicinal Products for Human Use
European Commission (2009) A Guideline on Summary of Product Characteristics (SmPC). Version 2
European Commission (2010) Commission Decision, Laying Down Guidelines for the Management of the Community Rapid Information System 'RAPEX' established under Article 12 and of the notification procedure established under Article 11 of Directive 2001/95/EC. C(2009) 9843, OJ L 22: 1–64
European Commission (2014) Good Manufacturing Practice (GMP) Guidelines, https://ec.europa.eu/health/documents/eudralex/vol-4_en
European Commission (2017a) 'Herbal Medicinal Products'. http://ec.europa.eu/health/human-use/herbal-medicines/index_en.htm
European Commission (2017b) Pharmacovigilance. https://ec.europa.eu/health/human-use/pharmacovigilance_en
European Commission (2020) Better Regulation Toolbox Tool #12: Risk Assessment and Management. https://ec.europa.eu/info/better-regulation-toolbox_en
European Court of Human Rights (2009) Tătar v. Romania. No. 67021/01, paras 106, 107. Cited in European Parliamentary Research Service (2015) The Precautionary Principle—Definitions, Applications and Governance
European Food Safety Authority (2017) Margin of Exposure. In: Europa. https://www.efsa.europa.eu/en/topics/topic/margin-exposure
FAO/WHO (2008) Guidelines on Exposure Assessment of Microbiological Hazards in Food. Microbiological Risk Assessment Series No. 7
HMA (2011, 2013) Guideline on Good Pharmacovigilance Practices (GVP) Module V—Risk management systems (Rev 1, 2). EMA/838713/2011

HMPC (2006) Clinical Assessment of Fixed Combinations of Herbal Substances/Herbal Preparations. EMEA/HMPC/166326/05

HMPC (2008) Guideline on the Assessment of Genotoxicity of Herbal Substances/Preparation, EMEA/HMPC/107079/2007

HMPC (2013) Questions & Answers on the EU Framework for (Traditional) Herbal Medicinal Products, Including Those from a 'Non-European' Tradition. EMA/HMPC/402684/2013

Lis Y, Guo JJ et al (2012) A Comparison of US Food and Drug Administration and European Medicines Agency Regulations for Pharmaceutical Risk Management: Report of the International Society for Pharmacoeconomic and Outcomes Research Risk Management Working Group. In: International Society for Pharmacoeconomics (ISPOR). https://www.ispor.org/news/articles/Sept-Oct11/Pharmaceutical-Risk-Management.asp

MEB (2012) Diao Xin Xue Kang, capsules for oral use SU BioMedicine B.V., The Netherlands. RVG 102142

Public Health (2017) Volume 2A - Procedures for Marketing Authorisation. Chapter 1, p 22

Regulation (EC) No 726/2004 (2004) Regulation (EC) No 726/2004 of the European Parliament and of the Council of 31 March 2004 Laying down Community Procedures for the Authorisation and Supervision of Medicinal Products for Human and Veterinary Use and Establishing a European Medicines Agency. OJ L 136: 1–33

UK House of Lords Select Committee (2000) Select Committee on Science and Technology: Sixth Report

WHO Essential Medicines and Health Products Information Portal (2010) WHO Good Practices for Pharmaceutical Quality Control Laboratories. In: WHO Technical Report Series No. 957, annex 1

Chapter 7
TCMP in the EU: Enlightenment

The book notes the difficulty of using Chinese logic to illustrate the concept of TCM and TCMP in the West since Chinese logic is difficult to understand and often criticised as being inconsistent with the modern scientific system established by the West. Indeed, anyone, who intends to insert an exotic idea or cultural practice into a region without understanding and considering the region's customs, then he/she will only confuse people. Therefore, using a Chinese custom to understand TCM and TCMP may mislead Europeans in fully understanding TCM. This does not mean that different cultures and ideas cannot be harmonised or integrated. The exploration and integration of Western medicine and TCM has gone on for a long time in China. Therefore, this book has attempted to insert TCM and TCMP into EU legal system to increase the West's understanding.

7.1 Findings

The book notes the similarities between traditional Chinese herbal medicinal product and EU THMP. They can both subject to TUR. The book also recognises the differences between these two, such as different philosophical foundations and medicine systems they based on respectively, and different production methods. Therefore, equal conditions for market access are reasonable. However, risk assessment should be conducted on a case-by-case basis for ensuring safety, efficacy and quality control in pre-market stage.

There is no explicit ban on TCMP in EU pharmaceutical law, but measures taken to limit market access of TCMP in the EU form an implicit ban in practice, since rarely can TCMP meet the requirement of 15 years used experience in the EU. It is also difficult to go through the full application procedure due to the uncertainty of scientificity discovered in risk assessments by following the philosophy of Western conventional medicine. Even if it is possible to assess the risk, the high cost of a

S. Wang, *Market Access of Traditional Chinese Medicinal Product in the EU under WTO Legal Framework*, Economic and Financial Law & Policy – Shifting Insights & Values 5, https://doi.org/10.1007/978-3-030-52848-5_7

clinical trial may eliminate the opportunity for potential applicants, especially many medium and small size pharmaceutical enterprises, to apply for market access by initiating a full application. Thus, it is understandable why after the enacting of Directive 2004/24/EC, very rarely has the EU approved TCMP to enter the market.

Although the EU has recorded cases of the side effects of TCMP and has noted problems with TCM in practice, the EU is beginning to understand the merits of TCM and recognises the value of potential scientific R&D of TCMP. Lack of scientific certainty is the EU's greatest critique of TCM and TCMP, where scientific certainty is based in the context of Western conventional medicine. The study in this book converts the practical problem into a legal hypothesis: the technical regulation and standards in EU pharmaceutical law form obstacles for TCMP to enter the EU market, and therefore, TCM and TCMP faces a hardship in the EU. Nevertheless, the development of TCM is in line with the legal objectives of EU pharmaceutical law—to protect public health. The current EU pharmaceutical legal framework leads to a bad cycle between trade and the development of science. Trade of TCMP rarely happens in practice, demand for TCM practice further shrinks in the EU, so there is no basis for the development of the science of TCM in the EU. How does the EU solve this dilemma? Exploring a solution external to the legal system is one way to break through the constraints. WTO law provides general principles for analysing the problem of the EU.

The book acknowledges the reality that Western conventional medicine dominates in Europe, and even globally. By contrast, due to scientific uncertainty, CAM is hardly deemed as orthodox, leaving TCM is worse off in the EU. Very rarely has CAM in the EU been fully recognised. Homeopathy is one of the successful exceptions, but many Europeans still doubt its efficacy. EU pharmaceutical law includes a chapter on homeopathy products, but TCM, in contrast, is not treated as a unique self-contained system. Traditional Chinese herbal medicinal product is regulated together with EU THMP by EU pharmaceutical law in the current legal framework. Some researchers have thought about the possibility of establishing a separate system to regulate TCM, but the West lack knowledge of TCM in general and, more specifically, finds scientific proof of its safety and efficacy to be lacking. The PRC has set up a complete system to protect TCM and TCMP and is always working to improve the monitoring system for TCMP's registration process and quality control. However, the natures of TCM and Western conventional medicine differ substantially, and treating two different types of medicine the same can hinder the development of one of them. While there has been some thought about using heritage knowledge to protect TCM, the United Nations Educational, Scientific and Cultural Organisation (UNESCO n.d.) has stated the meaning of heritage knowledge. TCM knowledge recorded by renowned ancient TCM books can be protected as intangible cultural heritage of humanity. As a whole TCM develops with the development of science.

Comparing the studies between the West and China, the book notes that for most Europeans, TCM is not an orthodox medicine due to the lack of scientific basis, and at most TCM might be treated as an alternative medicine based on empirical traditions. But for many Chinese people, TCM is well accepted and trusted and has been well-integrated with Western conventional medicine in China. The different understandings of TCM between the EU and China makes the recognition and development of TCMP in the EU difficult. Western medical scientists are engaging in finding each active ingredient in singular or compound formulas of TCMP. They try to prove each component's safety and efficacy as well as the formulas as a whole by using the developed scientific approaches. Indeed, they are taking a responsible attitude to evaluate new medicines. The safety of TCMP should be proven through channels other than empiricism. In theory, botanicals should be well-characterised and TCMP should be produced to the same level of quality standards of Western conventional medicinal products. However, many herbs containing multiple compounds cannot be identified by employing the current approaches used to assess Western conventional medicinal products. Chemical fingerprinting is in its early stages and is lacking for virtually all herbs. New techniques for assessing the risk of TCMP should be developed. Compared to allopathic idea, holistic view and dialectical contradiction theory back of the philosophy of TCM should be recognised when analysing TCM and its therapies. Plenty formulas have been recorded by renown ancient Chinese books, which provide a basis for scientific research. Therefore, cooperation on finding better tools for assessing the safety and efficacy of TCMP should be fostered. And to that end, the relationship between S&T and law should be clarified and law should reflect the development of science.

7.2 The Relation Between Science, Economy, Politics and Law

The current legal framework has formed a system in which science is in the dominant position of driving the direction of pharmaceutical law, and economic concerns function subordinately. The study in this book affirms the order set by law and supports that protecting public health is in line with the natural demand of people and forms an objective goal of law.

Legislation, including WTO law and EU pharmaceutical law, has highlighted both the protection of public health and economic development as legal objectives. However, the realisation of these objectives is not at an ideal status. Even though the law puts forth the goal of protecting public health in a position prior to economic development, policy makers have been nagged by the latter too much in practice. In such a situation, remaining clearly focused on the former is extremely important. Realising the legal objective of protecting public health relies on an administrative system that is affected by politics and law but primarily restricted by science. Therefore, the impact of scientific uncertainty on decision making must be envisaged.

The intention in designing a democratic system is, of course, good; it aims at balancing and hearing voices of different groups. Hereinto, different groups reflect various demands because of the natural and social resources being controlled.

However, the design of a democratic system cannot accommodate many of the essential limitations of human nature, such as the lack of the capacity for understanding the world and egoism, so it is not able to fully reach the goal of fairness and equality in many situations. Therefore, even though people recognised and designed the beautiful goals of fairness and equality in law, it is difficult to entirely reach those goals. The world exists either in a periodically and comparatively stable status or in chaos. If an inappropriate goal is pursued by people, a society may flourish in the short term, but a more serious hazard may also soon arise. The order of protecting public health first and developing the economy second cannot be overturned in regulating market access of a pharmaceutical product.

The governance of a group of people within a territory should be given deference, and therefore, the sovereignty of the state should be respected. The limited availability of natural resources should be kept in mind, as any intention to exploit natural resources without this consideration would only worsen the development of the world as a whole. As such, what should be the intention of a deal between a developed country and a less developed country in international trade? Ideally, it is twofold, encompassing the improvement of living conditions for less developed countries and processed products produced in line with the standards of the developed country concerning the protection of the environment and human rights.

Therefore, it is significant to develop international organisations for protecting environmental and human rights. Self-restriction in the exploration of natural resources, no matter within a sovereignty or globally should be encouraged. Further, the sovereignty of the state must be respected within a good international legal framework.

Marx's theory put idealisation of communism on the extreme enrichment of material in a society. Communism is a direction that a society with extremely enriched material would go. However, before that stage, when people try to personally enrich from the materials but ignore other individuals interests, or when a state tries to enrich the material nationally but ignores other states' interests, or when a region tries to enrich the material regionally but ignore the world's interest as a whole. . .the natural rule of law punishes them, resulting in pollution, slaughter, war, and violence as evidenced by, for instance, environmental degradation, endangered natural resources and natural and social disasters. Therefore, politics must have the goal of restricting the egoism of people, and this goal sits in law. It is not proper to let the goal of economic development drive the design of law, since wealth is not a direct demand of people. The negotiation of international law should focus on and always return to the purposes of forming good standards and persisting sustainable development of the world.

Regarding the relationship between S&T and trade, market access of TCMP in the EU is a cross sector issue between EU pharmaceutical law and WTO law. The level of development of the science has an effect on legislation in the form of technical regulations or soft law including standards and guidelines. However, the function of law is distinguishable from S&T. Technical regulations and soft law can describe and transform the rules of S&T into the needed readable legal language when they are certain, whereas, the precautionary principle works on the situation of scientific uncertainty.

7.3 Final Remark

This book initiated from an investigation of the practical issue—the hardship that TCMP faces in the EU. The problem raised criticism of the appropriateness of EU pharmaceutical law on the issue of market access of TCMP. Therefore, the study in the book set up as a central question whether EU pharmaceutical law complies with the WTO rule on the issue of the market access of TCMP in the EU. By answering this question, the book aimed to disclose deep-seated problems in EU pharmaceutical law on regulating TM, while it also paid attention to the law's rational parts for registration of medicinal products.

To conclude, traditional Chinese herbal medicinal product and EU THMP are similar product, even though it is not proper to treat these two as exactly the same. Both the similarities and differences between these two should be recognised on a case by case basis. For recommendations, two channels for developing TCMP can be encouraged. The first is to well regulate TCM and foster the development of TCM in the EU. The second is to pay attention to the merit of TCMP for protection of human health, all data and records on the safe use of TCMP should be taken into consideration for authorisation. When the knowledge and data of TCM and TCMP are collected sufficiently, it is recommendable and considerable that the EU to treat TCM as an independent medicine in the EU.

Reference

United Nations Educational, Scientific and Cultural Organisation (n.d.) What is meant by 'Cultural Heritage'. http://www.unesco.org/new/en/culture/themes/illicit-trafficking-of-cultural-property/unesco-database-of-national-cultural-heritage-laws/frequently-asked-questions/definition-of-the-cultural-heritage/

Index

S. Wang, *Market Access of Traditional Chinese Medicinal Product in the EU under WTO Legal Framework*, Economic and Financial Law & Policy – Shifting Insights & Values 5, https://doi.org/10.1007/978-3-030-52848-5

The manufacturer's authorised representative in the EU is Springer Nature Customer Service Centre GmbH, Europaplatz 3, 69115 Heidelberg, Germany. If you have any concerns regarding our products, please contact ProductSafety@springernature.com

Printed and bound by CPI Group (UK) Ltd, Croydon, CR0 4YY
30/09/2026
02225492-0013